IRISH POETRY FROM MOORE TO YEATS

IRISH POETRY
FROM
MOORE TO YEATS

Robert Welch

Irish Literary Studies 5

COLIN SMYTHE
Gerrards Cross 1980

Copyright © 1980 Colin Smythe Ltd.

First published in 1980 by Colin Smythe Limited
Gerrards Cross, Buckinghamshire

British Library Cataloguing in Publication Data

Welch, Robert
  Irish poetry from Moore to Yeats – (Irish literary
  studies: 5   ISSN 0140–895X).
  1. English poetry – Irish authors – History and
  criticism
  I. Title.   II. Series
  821′.009   PR8769

ISBN 0–901072–93–1

FOR MY MOTHER AND FATHER

Contents

Acknowledgements

I would like to express my deep gratitude to Professor Seán Lucy of University College, Cork, who first awakened my interest in nineteenth century Irish literature; and to Professor A. N. Jeffares of the University of Stirling, who directed my doctorate research work on nineteenth century translation of Gaelic verse at the University of Leeds. Without their guidance and encouragement, their sanity and learning, this book would never have been written. Professor Jeffares has read the manuscript in various drafts, and has made numerous suggestions. I thank him for his patience and his generosity in giving so freely of his time. These men are in no way to be held responsible for any inaccuracies of thought or expression that remain. They are all my own.

I would like to thank my publisher, Colin Smythe, for his tactful forbearance with a book that went through many transformations. I am grateful to Professor B. G. MacCarthy of Cork, who advised me on some crucial points about J. J. Callanan, and whose 1946 essays in *Studies* remain the best introduction to that poet; to Mr R. L. Thomson of the University of Leeds, who advised me about Gaelic matters; to Mr Pádraig Ó Maidín, Cork County Librarian, who drew my attention to and supplied some rare material; to Mr Finbarr O'Leary of Cork, who loaned me his copy of Callanan's poems; to Dr Éamonn Norton of Wakefield, who checked out some bibliographical material, and to M. Jacques Chuto of Paris, for his comments about Mangan.

I would like to thank Mrs Jeanne Jeffares, for her serene and practical wisdom over the years. My thanks go too to Tom Murphy and Seán Courtney of Cork, and Dr John Pitcher of Leeds, whose talk and friendship kept me going during critical times.

I am grateful to the librarian and staff of the University of Leeds; University College, Cork; the Royal Irish Academy; the National Library of Scotland; Leeds City Library; and the British

Library. I would like to thank the School of English at Leeds for letting me have research bursaries from time to time, which enabled me to travel to London and work in the British Library.

Though they do not appear in the list of works cited – because they are not referred to in the text – I would like to acknowledge the debt anyone working on Yeats must owe to the writings of Harold Bloom, Denis Donoghue, Richard Ellmann, T. R. Henn, and Thomas R. Whitaker.

Lastly, I would thank my wife, Angela, who has been so patient with this book and with its author, particularly since she has had to type its various versions.

Introduction

The nineteenth century in Ireland saw the slow, sometimes painful emergence of an Irish literature in English. There had been Irish writers in the English language in the eighteenth century, even in the seventeenth, but these writers, Nahum Tate, Swift, Farquhar, for example, wrote for a predominantly English audience with predominantly English values and assumptions. Not that the audience for Irish literature changed drastically in the nineteenth century. Most Irish writers still had their eyes on London as the market to which they wished to gain entry. This was true of Sydney Owenson (Lady Morgan), Gerald Griffin, and Thomas Moore for example. In 1799 the young Moore left his life in Dublin, a life fractured by the violence and intrigue of the rebellion of 1798, to find a patron for his translations of Anacreon, translations he had been working on in Marsh's library near St Patrick's Cathedral while his friends and acquaintances, among them Edward Hudson and Thomas Addis Emmet, were arrested and interrogated.

But while Moore left a Dublin which had become too complex, too fragile, for a young man who wanted to make his way in the literary world with as much social approbation as he could gather, nevertheless he did not desert the memory of his dead friends. His *Melodies* are probably his continued tribute to, or perhaps even his exorcism of, their memory. They seem to haunt the languid musical syntax, and help to give it its perpetual note of melancholy.

Here we have one of the main accents of nineteenth century Irish writing in English: there is a continual remembering of the dead, a keeping faith with their memory. The dead can be the recent dead, the martyrs for Ireland's cause within living memory, as in Moore, or they can be the more remote dead of the legendary past: Oisin, Caoilte, Fionn, Cuchulainn. It often happened, in fact, that the recent dead, the political martyrs, and

11

what they stood for, became interinvolved with the recalling of the figures of legend, so that the recent past is dramatized by contact with legend, the legendary figures made more immediate by reference to issues still fresh in the memory. Much of nineteenth century literature is what Yeats would later call, with reference to the 'Noh theatre of Japan, a 'dreaming back', a re-calling of the past into the present, a re-invigoration of tensions buried though far from dead.

Nineteenth century Irish writing takes its cue from Macpherson's Ossianic fragments of the late eighteenth century. These fragments, falsified and distorted as they were, gave a salient quality to nineteenth century Irish writing, a quality of imaginative freedom. The excitement of Macpherson's 'measured prose' does not come across to us now, but it certainly did to late eighteenth century readers. The excitement derived from Macpherson's crude sense that he was in touch with unlimited reserves of native Celtic emotion. The rediscovery of the native past was a source of imaginative power and freedom. This is certainly something we find in the Irish writers of the nineteenth century, especially in the poets, and it was a lesson they learnt from Macpherson. For them the Gaelic past was associated with authentic imaginative power and energy. Almost immediately, of course, this became translated into political terms, the idea took form that Irish literature should somehow assist in the great work of achieving some sort of political independence for Ireland.

Writers had different views about how literature could help Ireland. Moore, for example, hoped that his *Melodies* would make English men of power sympathetic to Ireland's state. Lady Morgan hoped her writings would make Englishmen understand their Irish brothers more clearly. Ferguson thought that a re-invigoration of Celtic manliness would contribute to Ireland's progress and make her a full and significant member of Britain's Victorian empire. Mangan thought differently. He saw his Irish poems as having a direct relationship with the overt political writings of Charles Gavan Duffy, Thomas Davis, the founders of the *Nation,* and especially with the more extreme propagandizing of John Mitchel.

In fact, the rise of Irish poetry in English in the nineteenth century is completely interrelated with the rise of modern Irish nationalism, the kind of separatist nationalism which owes more to the American Revolution than to the French. It is almost always a damaging relationship, in that the poet, because of his nationalist convictions, is inclined to fall into the kind of emotional simplicity which turns poetry into rhetoric. While contemporary English Romantic and Victorian poetry was exploring the dark side of the self, the blankness of life, the lack of vitality and inspiration, the problem of evil, and trying to square these negatives with the positive side of imagination, that side which likes to sing its praise of life, the Irish poets were inclined to blame England for everything that went wrong, even with themselves. Instead of Blake's Urizen, we tend to have the 'iron Saxon', or worse (as in the verse of the Cork poet, J. J. Callanan), his Irish representative, the flint-hearted Protestant. In Callanan's 'The Recluse of Inchydoney' we can actually see this simplification taking place. Callanan's emotional honesty brings him up against the problem of self. Why is he unhappy? Why does he feel separate in his heart from the lovely mountains and lakes of West Cork? Callanan does not have enough imaginative flexibility to sustain the inquiry and he gives up, retreating into the emotional simplicity of blaming the English for his lack of energy, and eventually the established church, the Church of Ireland. The established Church consumes natural vitality, the natural vitality of the Gael. When Yeats later wrote (in *A Vision*) of the need for 'simplification through intensity' this was not what he had in mind. This is more like intensity through simplification. We also find a similar externalization of guilt in Mangan, especially in 'A Vision of Connacht in the Thirteenth Century'.

But why this lack of imaginative flexibility in nineteenth century Irish poetry? Why these easy simplicities? For one thing the Catholic Irish had just come out from under a cruel system of penal laws, where they were severely handicapped merely for being Catholics. For another, life for many Catholics continued to be very hard, despite the relaxation of the penal laws and Catholic emancipation in 1829. Many of them lived on tiny farms, paying exorbitant rents to landlords who were mostly Protestant, and were, therefore, in the Irish Catholic mind, associated with England and authority. Not all landlords cruelly and consciously exploited their tenants, but many of them, through absenteeism, and by allowing their Irish affairs to be handled by unscrupulous agents, did make life hard for the penurious tenantry. As a result the economic facts of life in Ireland were such that imaginative flexibility was something of a luxury. For writers concerned about the state of the country it was all too easy to locate evil in the harsh system of oppression rather than trying to think of it as something inherent in human nature.

This externalization of evil was facilitated by the Great Famine of the 'forties where it seemed to many Irish people that there was a malicious and cruel element in Whig policies towards Ireland. After the Famine nothing could be the same again. It now became all too easy for political agitation to add violence to misery by fomenting hatred of England and of English rule in Ireland; to take so little account of the English themselves as people that it did not really matter if one blew a few of them to pieces. Now, to the ever-increasing host of the Irish dead were added the miserable casualties of Famine, dead wives and children, a dog eating the face of a loved daughter.

This kind of imagery was used by political extremists to create a mood of turbulence, of violence, about the recent past. The pressure of events became so overwhelming after the 'forties that for a long time the art of poetry seemed to be a submerged art. Aubrey De Vere answered the emotional complexity of his time with a system, a system he took over from Catholic dogma, the religion to which he, an Anglo-Irish Protestant, was converted. Allingham's answer was yet another system, one taken over from Ruskin and Morris, a system of liberal idealism, of which Laurence Bloomfield is a living, and indeed moving embodiment. Yeats's answer, not just to the Ireland of his time, but to the increasing complexity of civilization itself, was eventually to be another system, but one with fidelity to the flexibility of the imagination, one which took account of the shifting interrelationships between the individual mind and the racial memory, between the living and the dead. In 'The Wanderings of Oisin' we see a preliminary examination of that interrelationship, an examination that shows great flexibility and freedom. Yeats draws upon the old sources of power and energy, the legends, but they in no way delimit him. They free him into himself. And while the poem keeps faith with the dead of Ireland, he retains a grip on his identity. He is no unthinking medium for the insatiable rage of ancient passions.

Another reason why nineteenth century Irish poetry lacks flexibility, why it tends towards the simplicities of rhetoric rather than towards the self-scrutiny of emotional responsibility, is the simple fact that Irish poetry in English had no tradition it could call its own. There was, alluring but overmastering, the great richness of contemporary English poetry from Wordsworth right up to Browning. But that poetry rested on foundations older than Chaucer, and its entire structure was foreign to the native Irish genius as that was beginning to be thought of in the late eighteenth century and the early part of the nineteenth. Swift and Goldsmith were Irish but they belonged to an older and much different Ireland. Their national feeling, while it was real, was not the intense, self-conscious, Romantic nationalism of the nineteenth century, such as we find in Moore, Callanan and Mangan. For better or for worse Irish poetry would have to be intensely and recognisably Irish before it could be anything else. In such an atmosphere the larger scope of a Swift, a Goldsmith or a Burke was inappropriate.

Macpherson's mishandling of Ossianic lore opened up a possible direction. There was a native Irish poetic tradition, as old as anything in England, older in fact. The trouble was that that tradition was buried in a language inaccessible to those very people wishing to establish an Irish literary tradition in English. At the beginning of the nineteenth century Gaelic poets (such as they were) probably could not have cared less about a new Irish poetry in English. It is amusing to think what Brian Merriman, author of *Cúirt an Mheáin Oíche,* would have made of Thomas Moore. Writers writing in Irish have no problem about whether they are Irish or not, whereas some of the Irish poets writing in English did. In a very real sense they had neither language nor tradition, just the memory of one, and scraps of the other. They were starting from scratch. Small wonder then that there is little imaginative flexibility in Irish poetry of the nineteenth century. It does not have the confidence of an established tradition behind it. That might not have mattered so much if there had been a poet, earlier in the century, capable of making a tradition of what scraps there were, as Dante made a tradition in his time. But it was not until the close of the century that a poet with that kind of vision and force emerged. That poet was W. B. Yeats.

Before him, in most Irish poetry of the nineteenth century, there is a hesitancy, a lack of directness, an inability to speak out, that may have a great deal to do with linguistic uncertainty.

Not that Irish poets did not know English properly; the question is more than just one of linguistic competence. What these writers lacked was a sense of the deeper resonances of English words, the reverberations of mood and meaning, of emotional association, that such words as 'ale', 'father', 'home', 'Christ' have on an Englishman's lips. As Stephen Dedalus realises in *A Portrait of the Artist as a Young Man* these words will never be quite the same for him as they are for the English Dean of Studies at Newman's University. At the end of the nineteenth century, and the beginning of the twentieth, Irish writers (such as Hyde, Synge, Yeats and Lady Gregory) adopted the radical stratagem of making English recognisably Irish by fashioning it according to Gaelic and/or Anglo-Irish speech rhythms. English would have to be recognisably Irish before it could be naturalized.

The present book is an examination of these difficulties as they arise in the work of seven of the century's leading Irish poets. Other issues are dealt with as they arise in the chapters devoted to the individual writers. This is not a literary history; there are inevitably many poets who are not discussed, even briefly. Miss Balfour is missing, for example, as are Edward Walsh (apart from a couple of mentions), George Darley and Denis Florence McCarthy. But a choice had to be made, and the present seven were chosen firstly because they are probably the best the century had to offer, secondly because they illustrate the central concerns of the Irish poetry of the period. A tradition can be discerned, and though often it is a tradition of rhetorical simplification, of a too easy slide into hatred, or into the comforts of dogmatic belief, nevertheless it has its moments of poignant intensity, of clarity and energy, especially when in touch with the native tradition. Nineteenth century Irish culture should not be hastily dismissed. Out of its passion and complexity, its misguided and often dangerous intensities, come many of the preoccupations of twentieth century Irish consciousness.

1

Thomas Moore: An Elegiac Silence

I

A notorious fabrication lies behind much nineteenth century Anglo-Irish poetry, Macpherson's *Ossian,* which had its genesis in a holiday conversation between John Home and William Collins at Moffat, in Scotland, in 1759. Ten years earlier William Collins had dedicated to Home the 'Ode on the Popular Superstitions of the Highlands Considered as Subject for Verse'. In it, Collins had urged him to make Scotland a subject for verse, saying that a Celtic theme and atmosphere would bring greater imaginative freedom and a brooding power. In the years that passed Home had done nothing in this way so that when he met the young Macpherson at Moffat, who began to tell him of a great native Scottish epic, shattered by time, but recoverable in the Gaelic speaking Highlands, he was excited. Home listened to what Macpherson told him, and read his Gaelic 'fragments' with rapt enthusiasm and drew them to the attention of others. Almost immediately a subscription was got up to enable Macpherson to travel throughout the Highlands gathering the shards of the lost Ossianic magnificence.

The story of the success of *Fingal* and *Temora,* and the subsequent virulence of the debate about whether they were the genuine article or not is one of the more well-rehearsed oddities of literary history. One probable reason for the extraordinary success of this now unreadably turgid prose was that Macpherson's atmospheric ramblings went some way towards satisfying

17

the long-cherished eighteenth century desire for a vernacular epic, with the added virtue that this was so vernacular that what the reader got was a mere translation of some wonderfully barbaric original. So, at the end of the age of Augustan restraint, Macpherson's inept syntax became a virtue, in that in the minds of its readers it was a metaphor for Celtic wildness and irrationality. As often happens, what they were actually reading was less important than what they imagined themselves to be reading. Macpherson's fabrication could not fail; it satisfied a classical desire for vernacular epic through an excess of sensibility, thus combining the diametric opposites of late Augustan culture.

The cult of sensibility continued to increase, Macpherson's Ossianic writings contributing in no small way to the heady emotionalism and vague grandeur it delighted in. So that, when Sydney Owenson (later Lady Morgan) appeared on the scene, looking rather like the female harper in Elisabeth Harvey's frantically gestured painting 'Malvina Mourning Oscar' (1806), singing 'Éamonn an Chnoic' to her own accompaniment, respectable audiences were ready to be fascinated. Later, Moore was also to fascinate respectable society, actually reducing his auditors to tears on occasion, by singing his songs of Erin's woes in a slow, free recitative, underlining his words with long dark chords and trickling cadences on the piano. Each phrase and syllable was dwelt upon, ransacked for the maximum emotional impact.[1]

II

Apart from contributing to the cult of sensibility which led to Moore's form of lyric emotionalism Macpherson had other effects. He both enraged and stimulated contemporary Irish scholarship. He appropriated to Scotland (and in doing so became an international success) the entire Ossianic tradition, maintaining that the Irish versions of the story were mere absurdities, debasements of the pure Caledonian strain. The fact was that the Ossianic tradition was entirely Irish, the lives and actions of Fionn and the Fianna being inextricably linked with Irish landscape and topography. Their open air life was a celebration of the freedom of an old Gaelic world. Macpherson's concoctions ignored all this, playing lachrymose ducks and drakes with the facts and atmosphere of whatever Gaelic originals he knew, much to the fury of the Irish literati, who would have liked a Macpherson themselves.

Luckily they did not find one. Furthermore, it was some time before Irish scholarship could muster up enough knowledge and certainty to refute Macpherson's claims for sure. If there were any native speakers of Irish capable of authoritatively asserting Ireland's prior claims to Ossian (which is doubtful), such speakers would not normally be among the readers of contemporary English writing. As it happened, the first to substantiate Irish claims to Ossianic sovereignty was Charlotte Brooke, daughter of Henry Brooke, a sentimental novelist, who in 1789 (twenty years after the meeting at Moffat) published her *Reliques of Ancient Irish Poetry*. The *Reliques* was an anthology of translations *and* originals, so here at last a literary public wary of Celtic fabrications could have no reason to doubt.[2]

Coincident with this interest in native Irish poetry was a growing enthusiasm for the native music. In 1792 Edward Bunting had been employed at the Belfast Harp Festival to take down the airs from the playing of the old harpers there. After this he made the collection and publication of Irish music his life's work, tramping Connacht and Leinster gathering the old airs. In 1796 his first volume appeared: the *General Collection of Ancient Irish Music*. By this time Thomas Moore was a student at Trinity College Dublin.

When Bunting's collection appeared Moore and his friend Edward Hudson delighted in the Irish airs; they seemed spirited, unique. Hudson played the airs on the flute and Moore accompanied him on the piano. But this was not just simply the enthusiastic sensibility of the late eighteenth century suburban drawing room. The music also had for them vibrant political overtones. The emotional longings the Gaelic airs inspired became nationalist and republican ones. Of course, the context out of which Bunting's collection emerged was itself one fraught with all sorts of political tensions. At the Belfast Harp festival of 1792 Wolfe Tone himself had been present, not listening to the music, but busy outside, organising protest marches. Furthermore, Bunting himself was fed, housed and clothed by the McCracken family of Belfast, a family which gave a martyr, Henry Joy McCracken, to the '98 rebellion.

So, in the atmosphere of the time, the airs of Bunting's collection became intertwined with republican political sympathies. Robert Emmet himself, after hearing Moore play 'Let Erin Remember the Day' out of Bunting, jumped up and said, rather melodramatically, 'Oh that I were at the head of twenty thousand men, marching to that air'.[3]

To the terror of his mother Moore became friendly with certain men who were on the periphery of the United Irishmen, contributing a couple of pieces to *The Press,* their Dublin organ. After the second of these Emmet took Moore for a stroll in the countryside, advising him to keep his connections with the United Irishmen on a casual level. Moore took him at his word, retiring to the dim recesses of Marsh's library to work on his translations of Anacreon while the political storm was gathering without. During the rising itself he appears to have been ill, or convalescing, and in any case, in 1799 he went to London with the *Anacreon,* seeking a publisher and a patron.

The *Anacreon* translations are curious poems to be written during this intense and packed time, a time which was to form the basis for much of his later work, and, most notably, for the first numbers of the *Irish Melodies.* This period, up to and including the '98 rebellion, shaped his political thought and sympathies for the rest of his life. And yet the *Anacreon* is all poise and artifice, is completely nerveless, and consciously celebrates the rejection of weighty themes. The cup the young voluptuary wishes to drink from should be graven with brilliant and graceful reliefs, not with

> the barbarous rites
> In which religious zeal delights.[4]

The translations (although the word 'translation' is something of a misnomer, as Moore makes his own of the Greek) celebrate the momentary, the rosy gleam of transient pleasure. The verse achieves a kind of static, non-progressive grace. A poetry which approaches the condition of music, it expends a good deal of metrical dexterity in order to get nowhere and say nothing. It is a movement away from the actual, certainly from what was quotidian reality on the Dublin streets. It may well be that in these poems we find a deliberate cultivation of an imaginative alternative to the actual, but an alternative that is clung to, not one that sets up a dialogue between the imaginary and the real, the kind of dialogue that can, in fact, if he is able for it, be the making of a writer. The Prince of Wales enjoyed the poems, however, and agreed to have the book dedicated to him.

III

When Moore came to work on the *Irish Melodies,* he was preoccupied with what he saw as the close interrelationship between Irish music (at that time, chiefly those airs collected in Bunting's volume) and the national identity. In his letter to Sir John Stevenson (who was to be his musical collaborator for most of the *Melodies*) Moore says that he will devote as much energy as he can to the project because it is so 'truly national'.[5] 'In Ireland at least', he says, music and politics are deeply intertwined, as 'appears too plainly in the tone of sorrow and depression that characterises most of our early songs'. In an introduction to the *Melodies* he wrote for the collected edition of his works Moore again took up this interrelationship; clearly the connection he made between a nation's mood and atmospheric identity and its airs was fundamental to the way he thought. In this late introduction Moore says that during the oppressive legislation of the penal code Irish music was made to share the fate of its people. It was exiled, banned, shut out from civilised life. Bunting's collection, however, seemed to draw together, and to some extent be an emblem of, the national and revolutionary forces stirring in the Ireland of the 1790s. He writes:

> The national spirit and hope then wakened in Ireland, by the rapid spread of the democratic principle throughout Europe, could not but insure a most cordial reception for such a work.[6]

Moore thought of the words he put to the *Irish Melodies* as giving articulation to that national spirit, as rendering verbally the sentiment the music evoked. In so doing the words and music together would be a presentation of the essential goodness of long-suffering Éire.

When, in 1789, Charlotte Brooke made her metrical versions of Gaelic poems, she expressed the hope that those versions of hers would help towards a fuller, more tolerant relationship between Ireland and England; she wished them to be 'sweet ambassadresses of cordial union'[7] between the two countries. By the beginning of the nineteenth century, however, Moore could not be so idealistic; the best he could hope for was that Ireland's music, and the words he would give it, would make England more compassionate towards Ireland, would relax Fionnuala's curse that kept her in a sub-human state amid cold and bitter waters, by showing forth her pitiful inarticulate despair. In the last stanza of 'Oh! Blame not the Bard' he gives a poeticized description of the bard's function, where through a re-employment of one of the oldest sleights of hand in Irish poetry, indirection, he speaks of what he considers his own function to be. It is a curious statement, a compound of sentiment, pleading, sweetness, sedition, and despair:

> But though glory be gone, and though hope fade away,
>   Thy name loved Erin! shall live in his songs;
> Not even in the hour when his heart is most gay
>   Will he lose the remembrance of thee and thy wrongs!
>
> The stranger shall hear thy lament on his plains;
>   The sigh of thy harp shall be sent o'er the deep,
> Till thy masters themselves, as they rivet thy chains,
>   Shall pause at the song of their captive, and weep.[8]

This is poetry with something of a design upon the reader. It wishes to be effective, to gain concern for Ireland's state, by affecting the sentiments of its auditors and readers. The 'stranger', while he did not hear Moore's laments on his plains, nevertheless heard them in his drawing room. It was part of Moore's contract with the Power brothers, publishers of the *Melodies,* that he should pay fairly frequent visits to London during the season to sing his airs there and in that way publicise them. The *Melodies* were a commercial venture, which was also a 'truly national' one.

Moore, then, thought of his words to the *Melodies* as verbalising the 'general sentiment which the melody appeared . . . to express', at times even going so far as to make re-adjustments in the airs themselves as he found them in Bunting in order that

they might more completely 'express' to the Regency period
what Moore regarded as their essential qualities, which he related
to the essence of Ireland herself. Had he not done so, had he
not re-arranged them, and put appropriate words to them, these
airs would still, Moore said in 1840, be lying in Bunting's volumes,
'with all their authentic dross about them'.[9]

We have since then come to value that 'authentic dross', those
spiky embellishments in Irish music which are very different in
effect from the flurry of grace notes we associate with the
Romantic cadenza. However, it is too easy to be smug about
Moore's shortcomings and the limitations of the musical taste
of the day. Clearly Moore was moved by what he found in
Bunting, associating it with the national identity. More than that,
he felt that music was in some way (which he never fully
explained), involved with the primary imaginative stimulus.
'Music', he wrote, 'is the only art for which, in my opinion, I
was born with a real natural love; poetry, such as it is, having
sprung out of my deep feeling for music'. It was 'the source of
my poetic talent, since it was merely the effort to translate into
words the different feelings and passions which melody seemed to
me to express'.[10] Music is the expression of the national identity,
poetry the attempt to translate music's unutterable verities into
words. It is a dangerous poetic, the first of many dangerous
poetics of the nineteenth century in Ireland, because it is beaten
from the start. Poetry, words, cannot express the evocations of
melody. Words have a double life, one as sound the other as
meaning. Any writing that attempts to concentrate on one aspect
of that life at the expense of the other is courting danger. On
the one hand there is the Scylla of sweet, deceitful concords; on
the other the Charybdis of barren fact or idea. Poetry operates
in the interconnection of the two. A poetry that tries to capture
the moods and atmospheres of a melody is doomed to failure; it
cannot metamorphose itself into some other kind of thing. What
will tend to happen is that the poetry will become soft, passive,
sentimental, revelling in dreamy images, attempting to blur as
much as possible the inherent vitality of words, their connexions
with the actual, with reason, with each other – all this in order
to increase the melodic suggestiveness, the affective potential, of
the verse.

Despite the dangers attendant on the kind of idea Moore
loosely entertains about poetry, the *Melodies* themselves consti-

tute an interesting achievement, both in themselves and as a starting point for an Anglo-Irish poetry now fully conscious (one might say *self*-conscious) of its Irishness.

IV

There are two points to be dealt with before considering the *Melodies* themselves; firstly, can they be thought of not just as songs, but as poems in their own right; secondly, to what sort of audience did Moore address them? It has often been maintained, most forcibly by L. A. G. Strong, that it is an injustice to the *Melodies* to subject them to any sort of rigorous analysis as verbal constructs.[11] Strong maintains that they are songs, not poems, and that being such constitute a genre of writing different to the Romantic lyric, a genre which has its own conventions and which has to be approached bearing those conventions in mind, that, for example, a greater degree of emotionalism is permitted in song than in verse, that a higher rhetorical pitch is allowable because of the public rather than private nature of the form, and so on. This view has merit, of course, but it limits the discussion of the *Melodies* in the context of nineteenth century Anglo-Irish poetry. Much can be revealed about the sort of sensibility Moore typifies and about the sorts of difficulties Irish writing in English had to face up to in the nineteenth century by looking closely at what the words do (or do not do) on the page. Furthermore, we have Moore's own testimony that though his verses for the Melodies are to be sung rather than read, and that he can 'answer for their sound with somewhat more confidence than for their sense', yet he does say, in a preface to the third number of the *Melodies* (1810), that 'it would be affectation to deny that I have given much attention to the task'. He hopes that the words he has found will not be unworthy of the 'taste', 'energy' and 'sweetness' of the original airs.[12]

In the same place (the preface to the third number) Moore gives us some idea of the audience he had in mind, of the kind of people, apart from the general public, upon whom he wished the songs to have a real effect. There had been criticisms of the first two numbers, that they had mischievously abused the old airs by inflicting 'dangerous politics' upon them. Moore answers these attacks by saying that his songs are not for indiscriminate public consumption; like many an Irishman after the '98 rebellion he felt he had to deprecate 'any appeal to the passions of an ignorant and angry multitude'. Rather, his work was to circulate in a higher level of society, and the *Melodies* were to be found, he says, on 'the pianofortes of the rich and educated', those 'whose nerves may be now and then alarmed with advantage'. Advantage, needless to say, to Ireland.

These are lyrics then, where according to Moore's own disclaimer, the sound can be vouched for with more confidence than the sense. And yet, the sense is not so hopelessly wrapped in sweet concords as to decontaminate it, politically. From one point of view the lyrics are beautiful patterns of intricate interwoven sound, verbalisations of music's unutterable verities. From another point of view, though, the poems are political statements with designs upon a vaguely defined, but possibly powerful readership. In other words, Moore wants it both ways; he wants the songs to be political and yet he does not. Here there is an uneasy alliance, an ambiguity of intention, an uncertainty about the medium itself and what it is supposed to be doing that underlies many of the tensions, ambiguities, and stylistic difficulties of the *Melodies* themselves and much subsequent Anglo-Irish poetry.

V

Those men of '98 that Moore admired during his college days in Dublin – among them Thomas Addis Emmet, his brother Robert and Lord Edward Fitzgerald – came to haunt his imagination when he began work on the *Melodies,* his 'truly national' design. He wanted to give articulation to Ireland's spirit as it breathed through her music, but this became interwoven with the memory of his dead friends, men whose lives and deaths had been heroic and simple. As Moore himself said 'it was in those times, and among the events then stirring, that the feeling which afterwards found a voice in my country's music, was born and nurtured!'[13] As time went on, the emotional recollection of these early days began inevitably to blur; the ghosts of the two Emmets and his other acquaintances were either laid to rest or just simply covered up by the passage of life itself. When this happened, when the shades of these dead men no longer haunt the *Melodies*, they tend to become less good. In the early numbers, however, their presence is palpable, if somewhat vague. Their gestures are made heroic through retrospection; they are at a distance so their actions (about which Moore was so silent at the time) can be sentimentalized. They can be associated with other heroes and martyrs of Irish history and by this magical process their lives and actions can be transmuted out of the everyday into the timelessness of emotional mythology. They join the potent dead of Ireland: Brien Boru, Patrick Sarsfield and so on.

In the 'War Song' for example, the second poem in the first number of the Melodies, the remote medieval past of Brien Boru and the recent past of the '98 rebellion are drawn together. Recent events recall ancestral memories, and the ancestral memories give the recent events a touch of mythic significance. Moore's syntax, alluring and suggestive, is the perfect medium for joining the two pasts and for the emotional conjuring of a mood for the present. The two pasts mingle with a present that may flame up into violent intensity. The song toys with this exciting possibility:

> Remember the glories of Brien the brave,
>   Though the days of the hero are o'er;
> Though lost to Mononia, and cold in the grave,
>   He returns to Kinkora no more!
> That star of the field, which so often hath poured
>   Its beam on the battle, is set;
> But enough of its glory remains on each sword
>   To light us to victory yet.[14]

Though verse of this sort (and there is much of it in Irish writing past and present) tends towards a static non-progressive grace, a kind of musical suspension of the proper activity of the intelligence, nevertheless a metaphor persists, and the metaphor is one of light, a light that stays, a 'star of the field'. The glory has not faded entirely, and it may shine out again now, in the present.

The light imagery is taken up again in the last stanza, which is based on an episode from Sylvester O'Halloran's *History of Ireland*. According to this, the Dál gCais, Brien Boru's own clan, having fought and defeated the Danes at Clontarf, have to fight Fitzpatrick of Ossory on the way back across Ireland to Clare. The wounded men from Clontarf, seven or eight hundred of them, insist on fighting, asking to be tied to stakes stuck in the ground and placed among the sound men in the front of the battle. In the 'War Song' itself, the light that saw those legendary martyrs fall still shines, blessing the armour of the men who are supposed to be chanting the very words that commemorate the brave Dalgassians. Distinctions between past and present dissolve in the fluid medium of the poem: the remembrance of the hopeless but brave sacrifice of Brien Boru's men, their betrayal by fellow-Irishmen, fits in well with Moore's romanticised recollection of Lord Edward Fitzgerald and Robert Emmet. Their stand, like the stand of the Dál gCais, was hopeless and heroic; they too were betrayed by fellow-Irishmen, whether it be an actual betrayal, or a betrayal of the spirit. There may well be, in the 'War Song' and other of the *Melodies,* a touch of the plangency of self-reproach on the part of Moore. Thus do history, friendship and personal remorse often come together in the *Melodies*:

> Forget not our wounded companions who stood
>   In the day of distress by our side;
> While the moss of the valley grew red with their blood,
>   They stirred not but conquered and died!
> The sun that now blesses our arms with his light,
>   Saw them fall upon Ossory's plain! –
> Oh! let him not blush, when he leaves us to-night,
>   To find that they fell there in vain!

The sun ('he' in the last two lines) is the source of light, identified with liberty, and is seen to be the constant that links remote past, recent past and present. That sun, however, will leave the chanters of the song that night, to go into darkness again. Its light, the light of freedom, will no longer be visible, so all that is left for the singers is the heroic stand in the manner of the Dál gCais, despite the hope of victory the first stanza holds forth. So the thought of the poem is not consecutive. Initially the poem maintains that enough glory is left to light the warriors of the present to a new victory, but in the second stanza that light is doomed to darkness. This contradiction is not surprising considering the emotional irresolution underlying the piece. On the

one hand it is a political document inciting to heroism in the
present; on the other it is a piece of aural excitement, owing
much of its power to vague allusions to a dim past. It remains
transfixed by the beauty of its own verbal movements, trapped
by its own evocative music. What need is there of exact meaning,
of reference to the actual, when words can create such elegant
harmonies? It is enough to gesture towards some undefined
heroism that happened once, and may happen again. But even
if it does happen, the sun, symbol of liberty, will return to
darkness, as ever. So the heroism is doomed before it can begin.
This kind of poetry does not really engage with the issue it
ostensibly presents. Rather does it create and elaborate a mood
of melancholy dwelling on past glory. In the creation of such a
mood ordinary thought sequences may easily get mislaid, the
poem or song may unwittingly contradict itself.

This is certainly the mood created in 'Oh! Breathe not His
Name', based, Moore himself has told us, on Robert Emmet's
injunction from the dock that his epitaph should not be written
until Ireland takes her place, a free nation, among the nations
of the earth.[15] Moore's song tries to do the impossible. It is a
poem about Emmet's burial, and, being a construction of words,
thereby undertakes to say something. Yet it also wishes to obey
his command, seeing that Ireland has not yet been freed, and
keep faithful silence. Moore would write and yet not write his
dead friend's epitaph, again wanting to have it both ways. Silence
becomes a virtue, something to be praised. Grief remains dumb,
constrained, under strict instructions from the dead. Word-music,
evocation is all. The song is a lyrical epiphany, a framing of grief
in beautiful static concords, that are static in the sense that the
words do not go inwards: they explore themselves, the medium,
and by so doing, the subject itself:

> Oh! breathe not his name, let it sleep in the shade,
> Where cold and unhonoured his relics are laid:
> Sad, silent, and dark be the tears that we shed,
> As the night-dew falls on the grass o'er his head!
>
> But the night-dew that falls, though in silence it weeps,
> Shall brighten with verdure the grave where he sleeps;
> And the tear that we shed, though in secret it rolls,
> Shall long keep his memory green in our souls.

Just as the night-dew, weeping in silence on Emmet's grave, shall brighten the green of his grave, so the tears of the mourners, sinking down into their souls (by implication they are graves too, their life a death-in-life) will keep his memory green. The implication of this rather silly image sequence is that the souls, kept green by tears, will put forth fresh shoots, but this 'uprising' remains very much an implication; the word-pattern draws our attention to little else but the mood and its soft rhythm.

Throughout the *Melodies* the verse is drawn to the necessity and inevitability of silence, darkness, death. The harp, that once 'shed' the soul of music (and thus, for Moore, of Ireland) through Tara's halls now hangs mute on the walls:

> The harp that once through Tara's halls
> The soul of music shed,
> Now hangs as mute on Tara's walls
> As if that soul were fled.

The soul is not actually 'fled', it is only 'as if' it were. It is still there, haunting the sweep of the gloomy syntax like Emmet's ghost haunts his elegy. The song continues with images of sleep:

> So sleeps the pride of former days,
> So glory's thrill is o'er,
> And hearts that once beat high for praise
> Now feel that pulse no more!

The 'pride of former days', the days of Tara's glory and the days when Emmet and Hudson listened to Moore playing Bunting's airs on the piano in a Dublin suburb are all gone. They are buried in silence, in a kind of suspended animation, just as the harp lies mute on the wall. That pride, which is a pride in national identity, Moore again associates with music. He uses rhythm to suggest what it was once like to experience that identity, placing and emphasising the word 'thrill' with its slender consonants in a sharp yet quiet relief against the broad, open vowels of the rest of the line. Unquestionably Moore is a master of evocative plangent suggestion.

In the second stanza of the poem Moore imagines the harp making one last sound in an environ of silence and death. The

bright and glittering audience responds no more to its swelling
tones:

> No more to chiefs and ladies bright
>   The harp of Tara swells;
> The chord alone, that breaks at night
>   Its tale of ruin tells.
> Thus Freedom now so seldom wakes,
>   The only sound she gives
> Is when some heart indignant breaks
>   To show that still she lives!

The context of that twangling, dissonant chord, when the strings
break, is silence, a desolation all the more complete because of
the colour and vitality that once surrounded it. In the same way
the desire for 'Freedom' when it rises in a man's heart suffers
similar isolation. It too is a dissonant twangling in a desert bereft
of human feeling. The heart breaks indignantly, just as the strings
do, because it lacks a context, a context, it can only be, where
action is possible. But action is not possible, so the heart that
would hope for freedom must keep silence, and keep faith, under
similar injunctions as the mourners are in 'Oh! Breathe not His
Name'. Its 'tale of ruin' is mere frustrated jangling in the night
air. And yet, ironically, there is no dissonance in the piece itself:
a poem which has for theme a broken ancient music is itself
poised and exquisite, each syllable structured to the smooth
iambic flow. The mood of melancholy weariness, of silent,
repressed grief, predominates over the idea in the fourth line that
the soul of this music is *not* dead, and by the time the poem
closes this hope has been snowed under by the force of the
impeccably rhythmic lament for a time and feeling lost beyond
all recovery. The faint hope that briefly makes a shy entrance is
overwhelmed by the sweep of the word-music that bemoans its
passing. Once again the poem concludes with silence, darkness,
death – easier, more effortless themes to deal with than those that
would have arisen had Moore explored the tensions between
nationalist hopes and sentimental lament for a Gaelic world.
Instead, masterful proficiency takes over, dissolving the encounter
with a living language (which a poem *should* be) in melancholy
evocation of a past that never existed. The encounter with a
living language, with the implications of the words used, is

inevitably an encounter with the present state of the self. This may lead to difficulties, but language remains human, in contact with its deepest sources of strength, and in the long run it retains its health. Moore left the psyche unexplored. His rhythms suggest a mood rather than subtly delineating the contour of an inner state of being, as Wordsworth's do in *The Prelude* completed in 1805. Moore's words wash over his unease about Irish nationalism, about the dead men of '98.

The first number of the *Melodies* set the tone and manner of the remainder: an idealised and distant Gaelic world, faint hints that the glory associated with that world might once again re-activate itself (Tory reviewers felt Moore's verse to be bordering on sedition), and a magnificent diction and rhythmic power that tended to overwhelm all else. Not infrequently, the coy 'Anacreontic' note intruded, bringing to the *Melodies* an adolescent attitudinising. It could be said, perhaps, that the intoxications of lamenting words in the *Melodies* are a natural extension into an Irish context of the doctrine of Anacreontic indulgence, set forth in the *Odes* of 1800. In 'The Legacy' in the second number of the *Melodies* (1808) we have a curious mixture of a Regency version of ancient Ireland – bardic harps, ancient halls and so on – and an equally Regency version of the Greece of the voluptuary – foaming cups, the balmy drop of the red grape and such like.

More characteristic however, are 'Let Erin Remember the Days of Old', and 'The Song of Fionnuala', both also from the second number. In 'Let Erin Remember' we have the familiar evocation of Gaelic Ireland before the days of the 'proud invader', her pristine green unsullied and untouched, not just an emerald in a stranger's crown. In the second stanza, however, Moore attempts to construct an image series which will convey how Gaelic Ireland impinges upon the present. It is a curious and characteristicaly ornamental piece of work. He takes up an old idea, from Giraldus Cambrensis, that fishermen in clear weather can see the beautiful turrets of a submerged city in the depths of Lough Neagh. This is Gaelic Ireland to the early nineteenth century, beautiful, distant, shimmering, asphyxiated:

> On Lough Neagh's bank as the fisherman strays,
>   When the clear, cold eve's declining,
> He sees the round towers of other days

In the wave beneath him shining!
Thus shall memory often, in dreams sublime,
    Catch a glimpse of the days that are over;
Thus, sighing, look through the waves of time
    For the long-faded glories they cover! [16]

Water, of course, like time, is a refractory medium, subtly
distorting the images perceived through it. Here Gaelic Ireland
is, if anything, more remote from the present than it is in 'War
Song' or 'The Harp that Once'. It is marooned in the waters of
time, and water is a silent medium. Only occasionally, at evening,
can the fisherman get a glimpse of its otherworldly beauty. It is a
buried, submerged glory.

In 'The Song of Fionnuala' he makes use of another old tale,
which he found in 'some manuscript translations begun under the
direction of that enlightened friend of Ireland, the late Countess
of Moira'. The version of the story Moore came upon there was
somewhat different to the standard version generally received
now. According to it, Fionnuala the daughter of Lir was transformed by some supernatural power into a swan, and condemned
to wander Ireland's lakes and rivers until the coming of
Christianity. Moore makes no mention of Fionnuala's brother
and sister who feature so strongly in standard versions, nor of
the old father and wicked stepmother. He is not really interested
in narrative at all (unlike Coleridge, he had no desire to imitate
the ballad form); instead he is interested in the lyrical intense
moment, and in Fionnuala's sub-human state as image of Ireland.
She is the beautiful creature cursed to a seeming eternity of
dumb grief, waiting for the day-star that will warm an Ireland
surrounded by freezing water. This, incidentally, was James
Joyce's favourite song, an appropriate favourite for the author
of 'The Dead':

Silent, oh Moyle! be the roar of thy water,
    Break not, ye breezes your chain of repose,
While murmuring mournfully, Lir's lonely daughter
    Tells to the night-star her tale of woes.

It is night again, the star is remote, the swan is desolate, alone,
as is the harp in the first number. And then follow two questions:

When shall the swan, her death-note singing,
Sleep with wings in darkness furled?
When will Heaven its sweet bell ringing,
Call my spirit from this stormy world?

The only release will be death. When Christianity's bell does come to Ireland, releasing Fionnuala from her curse, she will be so old that she will die straightaway. There is no earthly release from her curse. In the next stanza there is a direct correspondence between Fionnuala's sub-human state and 'Erin's darkness'.

Sadly, oh Moyle, to thy winter wave weeping,
Fate bids me languish long ages away;
Yet still in her darkness doth Erin lie sleeping,
Still doth the pure light its dawning delay!

Presumably, it is still Fionnuala who is singing here, but in the first stanza she refers to herself in the third person, as 'Lir's lonely daughter', whereas here the personal pronoun is introduced, giving a greater immediacy to the grief. To some extent it also introduces an element of confusion as it is conceivable that it is Moore who is the singer and that the personal pronoun refers to him. Here Moore is exploiting a confusion in order to bring in an air of contemporary reference. The 'pure light' is not just the light of Christianity brought by Patrick to pagan Ireland but it is also the light that filled Robert Emmet's head, the same light that blessed the armour of the chanters of the 'War Song'; it is the light of liberty, of Grattan, Fox, Sheridan, Lord Edward Fitzgerald and Edward Hudson. As always, this transfer works by implication, and the implication dies in the sad unanswered questions that conclude the poem. Once again, there is the dying fall; the questions vibrate in the all-encompassing silence and darkness:

When will that day-star, mildly springing,
Warm our isle with peace and love?
When will Heaven, its sweet bell ringing,
Call my spirit to the fields above?

The last couplet turns back to the original story, dropping all the contemporary associations gathered by the increased immediacy of the personal pronouns. It is Heaven that solves all, perhaps because if the day-star of liberty were really to rise, it would not 'mildly' spring but would rise in turbulence and violence. Moore had been in Dublin in '98, and by 1808 it was quite clear that Burke had some of the truth at least about the French Revolution.

Despite the inbuilt reserve of these poems Tory reviewers were shocked by their politics, feeling that Moore had turned from the sly erotic innuendo of *The Poems of Thomas Little Esquire* (1801) to treason and sedition. Clearly, even if modern readers do not pay a great deal of attention to the words Moore wrote readers in the Regency certainly did. The *Melodies* did not just estrange; they also had a sympathetic audience among the more liberal-minded of the Whigs, those in the tradition he honoured above all himself, that of Sheridan and Fox.[17]

Of the third number of the *Melodies,* issued in 1810, the *Hibernia Magazine* said it contained more politics than harmony.[18] The third piece in it, 'Oh! Blame Not the Bard', is an imagined apology from one of those 'wandering bards' castigated by Spenser in his *View of the Present State of Ireland.* Their poems were, Spenser thought,

> sprinkled with some pretty flowers of their own natural devise, which gave good grace and comeliness unto them, the which it is great pity to see so abused to the gracing of wickedness and vice, which would with good usage serve to beautify and adorn virtue.[19]

Moore quotes the above passage (incorrectly) in a footnote to 'Oh! Blame Not the Bard' and indeed allows it a certain truth. The song is intended as an apology uttered by one of these Elizabethan bardic poets for debasing imagination by using it to grace 'wickedness and vice' when its proper use is 'to beautify and adorn virtue'. Here Moore is not just thinking of the inflammatory and seditious verse of the bardic poets of Elizabeth's reign castigated by Spenser; he is also thinking of his own semi-erotic productions, the *Anacreon* and the 'Little' poems. Perhaps those poems too used the imagination to grace 'wickedness and vice'. So 'Oh! Blame Not the Bard' is, to a certain extent, an *apologia.* It begins by apologising for the

pleasurable indulgence verse allows, and the easy relationship
there exists between 'pleasure' and 'Fame':

> He was born for much more, and in happier hours
> His soul might have burned with a holier flame.[20]

But then the apology becomes one which certainly would not
have pleased Spenser. It becomes an apology for not being
patriotic enough. Admittedly, it is all in the subjunctive mood,
the 'might' in the last line quoted above setting the tone. Nevertheless, if we look closely at the diffused series of images spun
out over the four lines that follow, it becomes quite apparent
that the poetry that could have been written, had the time been
right, would have been such as would spill out spontaneously
from a patriotic heart, overflowing with zeal. Romanticism and
nationalism combine in the subjunctive mood:

> The string, that now languishes loose o'er the lyre,
>   Might have bent a proud bow to the warrior's dart,
> And the lip, which now breathes but the song of desire,
>   Might have poured the full tide of a patriot's heart.

In the notes to this poem Moore indulges in a piece of curious
and fantastic etymology: referring to the conjecture of one
Wormius, he says that the word Ireland is derived from *Yr,* 'the
runic for a *bow,* in the use of which weapon the Irish were once
very expert'. The above lines, if we look closely at them, make
interesting use of this piece of quasi-information. The string that
now lies slackly on a lyre that indulgently sings of pleasure and
passing things might 'have bent the proud bow' of Ireland ('Yr'),
tensing it for offensive action. In other words, if the string of
poetry, verse, music (they are almost interchangeable in Moore)
were to become an intrinsic part of the nation's life it would
tense it, making it lethal, dangerous, effective. This is a curious
apology from the imaginary Elizabethan castigated by Spenser.

The conditional quality of the stanza, the 'mights', diffuse the
impact, making the meaning more remote, and the syntax has to
be closely examined to find out what is going on. The vagueness,
the hesitancy, was probably part deliberate, part congenital.

Stanza two laments the passing of Ireland's hopes: her sons
cannot hope to succeed unless they betray their inheritance. The

torch that would light them to place and prestige must be picked from the funeral pyre of Ireland's dying hopes. So who then, stanza three goes on to ask, can blame the bard if he tries to forget, if he uses 'dream' as an opiate to escape from the stress and failure of national disgrace?

> Then blame not the bard, if in pleasure's soft dream
> He should try to forget what he never can heal.

If hope were a real possibility then what a change there would be; the myrtle, now entwined in the poet's crown as he reclines in the neo-classical bowers of fancy and ornament would act as camouflage for his sword:

> Oh! give but a hope – let a vista but gleam
>   Through the gloom of his country, and mark how he'll feel!
> That instant his heart at her shrine would lay down
>   Every passion it nursed, every bliss it adored;
> While the myrtle, now idly entwined with his crown,
>   Like the wreath of Harmodius, should cover his sword.

But there is not much chance of that sort of hope presenting itself; all that can be done is to dally with pleasure's dream, make harmless music, wait, and bear witness. There is one further objective, however, the sentimental one. In the third stanza Moore says that the name of Erin will live in the bard's songs, and that these songs will be heard on the stranger's 'plains'. Although the songs will not be able to effect a change of heart in the auditors, they at least will make them pause and listen. If the string cannot tense the bow of nationhood and make it lethal, then its sweet lament will make the stranger weep:

> Thy masters themselves, as they rivet thy chains,
> Shall pause at the song of their captive, and weep.

If 'Oh! Blame Not the Bard' goes some of the way at least towards being both an *apologia* and a statement of artistic credo, then another poem in the third number entitled 'On Music' gives a good deal of insight into Moore's conception of his art, and also throws some light on Moore's conception of his medium. 'On Music' is an important piece in the context of the *Melodies,* when we remind ourselves that music for Moore was an expression of the national identity, and was also indissolubly linked with the fundamental imaginative processes.

Music, as Moore understands it in 'On Music', is an art of memory, of evocation of the past in a present that has become faded. Music is an equivalent to and a celebration of the death of intensity:

> Like the gale that sighs along
>   Beds of oriental flowers,
> Is the grateful breath of song,
>   That once was heard in happier hours.
> Filled with balm the gale sighs on,
>   Though the flowers have sunk in death;
> So, when Pleasure's dream is gone,
>   Its memory lives in Music's breath.[21]

The perfume that wafts from a flower we tend to think of as being in some way associated with the deepest life of the flower, its essence. Here the 'song' is the breath of 'oriental flowers', 'oriental' because Moore wishes to make the whole experience as remote as possible, as distant from the living eye as the turrets under Lough Neagh. But these flowers, though their perfume lingers on, are dead. Music then is a disembodied remembrance of something that once lived, but is now no more. It is an art of memory, an art of death, a ghostly art. It is so powerful in its disembodied sweetness that language is awkward and intractable by comparison:

> Music! oh! how faint, how weak,
>   Language fades before thy spell!
> Why should feeling ever speak,
>   When thou canst breathe her soul so well?
> Friendship's balmy words may feign,
>   Love's are even more false than they;
> Oh! 'tis only Music's strain
>   Can sweetly soothe, and not betray!

Language, words, betray, because they lead one into denotation. One has to say things, to struggle with meaning, to be careful, too, of giving offence. Music creates no such problem, it denotes nothing, it simply is. A note is not something that can be argued about. But this poem also attempts to suggest, in a medium which it denies, that there are feelings lying too deep for words and that these, through inappropriate words, may be betrayed. Silence therefore, is the best answer; failing that, music, which is a disembodied medium, free of denotation and all its betrayals; and failing that, song, where words and rhythm can be brought to a fineness of movement and elegance suggestive of music itself, and ultimately of silence. To sum up, here is a poem on the impossibility of writing about anything of real significance. An evocation of music's power, it is also a confession of failure in the chosen medium. It is a curiously honest poem, and forthright in its own roundabout way.

'The Origin of the Harp' which concludes the third number is a slight and pretty poem, but it is interesting for a number of reasons. Moore himself tells us he was inspired to write the poem by the memory of a charcoal drawing of the 'fancied origin of the Irish harp' Edward Hudson had done on the grim wall of his cell in Kilmainham jail, when Moore went to see him in '98. Hudson was 'immured for four or five months' for his part in the United Irish conspiracy and was then deported to America.[22]

The poem for once is a narrative, albeit brief. It tells the story of a 'sea-siren of old who sung under the sea'. At evening, however, she would often come up out of her underwater silence to meet the mortal youth she loved, on the 'green' shore. He leaves her and she becomes stricken with grief. Heaven takes pity on her and (strange evidence of pity) transforms her into a harp, her hair forming the golden strings, her white arm becoming the strut:

Still her bosom rose fair – still her cheek smiled the same –
While her sea-beauties gracefully form'd the light frame;
And her hair, as, let loose, o'er her white arm it fell,
Was changed to bright chords uttering melody's spell.[23]

Some form of deity to begin with, she is transformed through the intervention of a compassionate Heaven into a sub-human state, a musical instrument, the shape of which freezes her in her grief-stricken attitude, her golden hair falling over a white arm. She is now released from the agony of her sorrow, released from consciousness of loss into a dumb frozen permanence. Though

inarticulate now she does produce music, 'uttering melody's spell'. The images imply a desire to escape from the denotative impurities of words to the colder, more beautiful, more expressive, less human medium of pure sound. The poem is about the origin of the *Irish* harp; it implies strongly that only music can express the otherwise inexpressible sorrow of being Irish. In other words, the third number of the *Melodies* concludes with a poem the implications of which call doubt on the validity of the medium, and thus the enterprise itself. Moore's objective, we remember, was to translate the Irish identity which Irish music seemed to him to express, into words that would be worthy of its 'energy' and 'tenderness'. In these two poems, 'On Music' and 'The Origin of the Harp', he comes face to face with the difficult fact that there can be no such translation between different media. Music has its purity, words their eccentricities of meaning and sound: one may not become the other. The problem was that Moore's technical mastery and wonderful aural gift made him think at times that the impossible could be effected.

VII

The fourth number (1811) continues to luxuriate in the evocation of moods, in sentiment, gesture, and in beautiful sound patterns. In 'She is far from the Land', his poem about Sarah Curran, Robert Emmet's young love, he again celebrates a grief that cannot speak its name. Sarah Curran is envisaged as singing 'the wild song of her native plains', which Emmet had loved to hear, but while she sings this out, to the delight of her foreign audience, she is holding back an unutterable sorrow.

From the third and fourth numbers onwards, the political content of the *Melodies* becomes increasingly muted. Although from time to time touches of political passion do inflame them, Moore's political energies went increasingly into his Whig satires, the *Melodies* becoming more and more mere pleasant concatenations of sound, with a faintly Hibernian feel. From now on he seems to have lost interest in the enterprise, and in his prefaces frequently hints that they are coming to an end. However, public demand and financial pressure insisted he keep them going.

At this point Moore's imagination seems to move in two
directions: one is towards satire, and he eventually became
'keeper of the Whig conscience' to adapt Howard Brogan's
phrase.[24] He was respected and feared as a satirist from *The
Twopenny Post-bag,* issued in 1813, the year of the fifth number
of the *Melodies,* and onwards. Moore afterwards liked to pretend
that his satires were harmless squibs, but they were often in fact
bitter and powerful denunciations of hypocrisy and cant in
Government, the Prince Regent, who had assumed the Regency
in 1811, being a favourite target.[25] He is frequently vituperative,
and often concentrates his scorn on physical blemishes, in a way
that is faintly reminiscent of Pope. Whence this forthrightness,
we might ask, bearing in mind the deliberate veiling of the more
intense political feelings in the early *Melodies*? Probably it
seemed to Moore that bitter, frequently personal attack from
the standpoint of liberal reformist Whiggery was one thing, but
that the direct expression of nationalist, revolutionary sentiment
was another. Ireland, of course, does receive Moore's attention
in his explicitly satirical writings, verse and prose. His *Memoirs of
Captain Rock* (1824), a subtle and vigorous denunciation of
English policy in Ireland, supposedly the memoirs of a Whiteboy,
lent force to the cause of Catholic Emancipation. But, the 'Irish
question' was now seen in the larger context of liberal reform.
To some extent the ghosts of Emmet and of Fitzgerald had been
laid, the clear light of his satirical intelligence (a light, one might
say, borrowed from the eighteenth century he and Byron so
loved) allowing little intrusion of adolescent idealism. Maturing
politically, he had drawn away from the revolutionary inclinations of his young manhood, so the need to mask those
inclinations with elegantly patterned music became less. Also, he
was now speaking with the confidence of a considerable body of
political opinion behind him. He became a favourite at Holland
House, and was a friend of Lord John Russell. His social connections had always been good, but now (in the first years of
the second decade) he was becoming the semi-official Whig
laureate.

The other direction Moore's imaginative powers took could
be regarded as the obverse of the satirical: they moved towards
the fanciful, the ornamental, the fantastically precious, typified
for us now by that extraordinary production, *Lallah Rookh*
(1817). This has strong political overtones, bearing on the Irish

situation, 'Iran' being a proto-Joycean nomenclature for 'Erin', but the impression the poem leaves on us is one of elaborate, vaguely Islamic interiors (a fashion of the times, as Maria Edgeworth's *The Absentee* reveals) and richly aromatic exteriors. Moore knew very little of the East, but it was a useful setting for the more pleasurable sorts of imaginative indulgence. The fancy could run free among the shifting veils of the harem and the softly waving palms of the oasis.

This kind of fantastical decorativeness is an extension of the taste for sheer verbal pattern to be found in the *Melodies*. The delight in the remote past we find celebrated there translates into the geographical remoteness of *Lallah Rookh;* the Grecian attitudinising of some of the *Melodies* becomes a sensuous delight in exotic descriptive detail. The politics become even more muted, the ubiquitous Robert Emmet turning up as Hafed, leader of the Ghebers, who are in revolt against Al Hassan, the Muslim tyrant. Lallah Rookh is Sarah Curran.[26]

However, the *Melodies* continued to appear. After the fifth number (1813) there were actually five more collections, the last one, the tenth, appearing in 1834.

The fifth number contains the famous 'At the Mid Hour of Night', which has been highly praised, is frequently anthologised, and is regarded as a precursor of what Thomas MacDonagh in 1916 in his *Literature in Ireland* called the 'Irish Mode'. This 'Irish Mode', which, it is said, gives Irish verse a distinctive voice and movement in English consists basically of two elements: a) a long line with a strong anapaestic beat, and b) a wavering movement counterpointing the fundamental anapaestic rhythm, complicating it, enriching it, giving the metric of the poem a loose, angular, somewhat reckless quality.[27]

Irish nineteenth century poetry gave a certain freedom to English metrical usage. Also, Moore may be regarded as the prime example of this prosodic freedom, and he came upon this through fortunate circumstance, not genius. By fashioning English words to the Irish airs he found in Bunting, his English rhythm discovered a new resource, a flexibility, stimulating after the long reign of the heroic couplet. The Romantics had, of course, initiated a revolution in metric, but Moore's contribution was no mean one. This new rhythmical freedom was not all beneficial: the reckless, flowing, long-lined anapaestic rhythm offers a sometimes all too tempting opportunity for word-spinning.

'At the Mid Hour of Night', for all its rhythmical complexity is word-spinning, felicitous twaddle. A tissue of atmospheric gesturings, the poem engages with nothing. It hardly has a theme at all, other than that someone once loved someone, who may now be listening, and may be answering. The reader will be familiar with the conditional quality of Moore's imagination, but the engagement with theme here (and therefore with the language) is much less intense, even than, say, 'The Song of Fionnuala'. Nothing happens, the poem is all surface, the words in no way open up their own buried levels, their strata:

> At the mid hour of night, when stars are weeping I fly
> To the lone vale we loved when life was warm in thine eye;
>   And I think that if spirits can steal from the regions of air
>   To revisit past scenes of delight, thou wilt come to me there,
> And tell me our love is remembered, even in the sky!
>
> Then I sing the wild song it once was rapture to hear,
> When our voices, commingling, breathed like one on the ear;
>   And as Echo far off through the vale my sad orison rolls,
>   I think, oh, my love! 'tis thy voice from the kingdom of
>   souls,
> Faintly answering still the notes that once were so dear.[28]

Theme, location, personalities, are all submerged, rendered silent in the opaque medium of the rhythm. This is entrancing as a model for poetry, in that it is wonderfully eloquent and beautifully worked, but it is a bad model in that it obscures, and indeed becomes a substitute for, the encounter with self and language.

At the end of the sixth number (1815), which was to have been the last, he bids farewell to his harp, employing the well-worn image of the harp of Aeolus:

> I was *but* as the wind, passing heedlessly over,
>   And all the wild sweetness I waked was thy own.[29]

Although a conventional image, the Aeolian harp acquires a somewhat more pointed overtone in the context of the *Irish Melodies*. Here, at the planned end of the series, Moore does a poetic vanishing act, disavowing the self entirely. He was the wind that stirred the strings, having no personality, no self. Such a degree of 'negative capability' is humanly impossible, but the fiction of it here, at this point, shows us again that Moore's *Melodies* are a poetry of non-encounter, of flight from the self, and finally of irresponsibility towards the medium, at a time when that kind of irresponsibility was lethal to the future health of Irish poetry.

Moore's influence and prestige were immense; when the tenth and finally last number appeared, it contained a denunciation of O'Connell and his politics, entitled 'The Dreams of those Days'. The poem was received in Ireland and England as if it were a political statement, whereas what strikes the reader now is how loose and generalised the piece is, and unless we knew of the context already, we would never guess from it that it was about O'Connell. O'Connell himself is said to have wept when he read the poem, so potent a force was Moore's displeasure and disapproval. He thought O'Connell had deserted the liberal principles of the eighteenth century to become the 'mighty Unit of a Legion of Ciphers' in his appeal to the vulgar emotions of the mob. He was shocked that 'the liberator' knew little and cared less about the great men of '98, the 'ultimi Romanorum' of Ireland as Moore called them.[30] By the 'thirties he had become an institution, the national poet of Ireland and guardian of the liberal conscience, a castigator of everything in public life he considered less than plain dealing. In 1832 he was asked to become M.P. for Limerick, but refused, fearing that his independence and freedom of conscience might be compromised.[31] Thinking of this we come to understand how Byron felt that Moore was one of the foremost and most honourable men of the age, and why in 1819 he trusted him with his memoirs when Moore visited La Mira where Byron was staying with the Countess Guiccioli.

VIII

Moore brought into Irish verse a freedom and flexibility of movement which sprang out of his attempt to fit English words to Irish airs. The words, and the sweeping rhythms they compose have a fluidity and musicality missing from much eighteenth century English verse. However, from the point of view of Anglo-Irish poetic tradition, which was in bad need of an Irish voice in English at this time, the *Melodies* offered too much technical proficiency, too little verbal seriousness. In other words Moore showed nineteenth century Irish poetry a great deal about the exterior effects of rhythm, but very little about taking those rhythms into the psyche. Generalised moods are created in the long, expansive rhythms, but states of feeling are not delineated. We are given no sense of what the words felt like inside Moore's head. Moore built, right over the real deposits, a Celtic-looking fabrication, with dark turrets, winding stairways and gloomy interiors, where white-skinned maidens played on harps with golden strings. He built a shaky romantic edifice when what was needed was excavation. The excavators, the poetic archaeologists, were to come later, and they mostly came from the North, from Ulster, men such as Ferguson and Allingham. Moore's elaboration of aural effect at the expense of sense contributed to the markedly rhetorical and sentimental quality of a great deal of nineteenth century Irish poetry.

Moore's was an impressionistic version of ancient Ireland, based on loose bits of information gathered here and there and presented in a language dripping with sensibility. He belongs to the tradition of Macpherson. He differs, though, in that his images of Gaelic Ireland are sometimes designed to carry contemporary political overtones, whereas the fascination of Macpherson's imaginings lay in the fact that his reckless barbarism was entirely irrelevant. Macpherson was the ultimate in emotional aesthetics. There was a good deal of emotional aestheticism in Moore too, but he does give the contemporary situation some weight, if only obliquely. Moore's emblems, the harp, the shamrock, the round tower, became the insignia of nineteenth century nationalism, trite emblems of political energy.

There is a fundamental uncertainty about the *Melodies*, an uncertainty deriving from two impulses, which in Moore were contradictory. The first impulse was towards the creation of lovely verbal patterns, suggestive of the moods the Irish airs evoked; the second was towards the writing of political songs, that would stir up political feeling through remembrance of the past. Moore did not achieve a synthesis of the two impulses; they separate in his later work, into ornamentation on the one hand and satire on the other. What he did achieve was a rich opaque musical medium that allowed a tense if often unsatisfactory interaction between the two; a medium full of hesitation, implication and images of inarticulacy, of grief struck dumb, of the faithful keeping of silence. Despite this jumble of themes and images, the atmosphere of the *Melodies*, conveyed through the fluid word-music, was very strong, creating in Irish poetry a tendency towards rhetorical ornament, obliqueness, and beneath the obliqueness, sentimental sedition.

2

J. J. Callanan: A Provincial Romantic

I

Moore was the most significant Irish poet throughout the Romantic period, from 1800 up to and well into the Victorian era. But there is a sense in which Moore cannot be thought of as a Romantic at all. No doubt his sweet tones of Celtic lament contributed to that movement; he was admired by Shelley and was Byron's friend and biographer, yet, if we think of Romantic poetry as involving the articulation of an individual vision of things, a plunging into the deepest levels of the psyche, and an awareness of the secret forces of nature, then Moore can hardly qualify as a Romantic. He belonged in spirit, rather, to the world of neo-classic sentimentalism, which continued to thrive alongside the Romantic movement, practically obscuring it to the popular view. Intellectually he paid homage to the clear light of Augustan reason, as did his friend Byron. But Byron's temperament was massive and restless in its great discontented energy. His work is all personality, whereas if we look for personality in Moore's work we are at a loss where to find it. J. J. Callanan's work, on the other hand, is full of personality and anguished temperament, after the manner of Byron, his model. Callanan also has Byron's responsiveness to landscape, a quasi-mystical sense of its power, especially in its wilder aspects, whereas Moore had very little sense of nature's power, taking a semi-Augustan delight in it at times, for its proportion, order and grandeur. The wilder scenes of nature, however, such as those he saw on a visit to the Niagara

46

Falls, made him think of God; and when he first went to Bermuda he allowed his fancy to people its luxuriant tropical growth with nymphs bearing classical names inhabiting 'grots' and groves. For Callanan the landscape of West Cork was a place of refuge, and far from associating its scenery with classical scenes and episodes (as some of his acquaintances liked to do) he revelled in its raw power, its energy, its irregularity.[1] It was for him what Albania was for Childe Harold, the difference being that Callanan's Albania was no more than twenty or thirty miles west of his native city. Life was simpler there, more intense, less complicated, less wasteful than it had become for him in Cork.

To turn from Moore to Callanan is to turn from someone with a world-wide reputation to someone who led an obscure provincial life, whose only venture into the British literary world was a handful of translations from the Irish in *Blackwood's Magazine* in 1823, placed for him there by another, infinitely more successful Corkman, William Maginn. Moore, on the other hand, was the fêted author of *Lallah Rookh,* spokesman for the radicals, champion of the Catholic cause. It was the sort of reputation of which provincial writers dream, and Callanan was not above dreaming about it, though conscious always (too conscious in fact) of his own shortcomings as a poet. Cork was a place admirably suited to literary or artistic pipe-dreams. Indeed, there is much about Callanan that is quintessentially provincial, in that he epitomises the kind of literary aspiration which involves on the one hand a desire to break free from all the nets a native place casts about the spirit, and on the other a reluctance to stray too far from local roots.

His body of work was small – two long poems, a handful of short lyrics, some of them surprisingly good; eight or nine brilliant translations from the Irish – and yet in some ways he is a much more interesting writer than Moore, certainly a much more spectacular failure. He failed to find a fruitful line of creative development that would express his nervous energy, but he went on searching. He did not, could not, rest content with mellifluousness, as Moore often did. For Callanan poetry was a more intense business than framing words to express the sentiments melody rouses; for him it was an attempt to find articulation for the complexities of personality. He was, in a word, a Romantic.

II

In the early nineteenth century Cork was a prosperous city. The French wars had made it rich and, as Crofton Croker said, the fitting out and the supplying of all vessels trading with America 'created an extensive consumption for its staple commodities'.[2] After 1815, however, the city, along with other mercantile centres in Britain and Ireland, suffered some decline in trade and wealth, yet it managed to do quite well in the export of butter, salted beef and pork until the late 1830s.[3] This meant that the better-off Cork citizenry could afford the time and leisure for cultural pursuits, all the more enthusiastic for being amateur. Magazines, journals and miscellanies appeared in which part-time literati enjoyed seeing themselves in print; people drew and painted in the new and spacious villas along the Douglas Road and in Tivoli; the Apollo Society allowed Cork thespians the opportunity to take to the boards; and in the summer months excursions were got up to view the spectacular scenery lying on all sides of Cork. There must have been a good deal of excited talk about current literary fashions, about styles of drawing in vogue in London. Henry Bennett, a successful lawyer who became sheriff of Cork in 1814, took time off from his professional duties to write 'The Steamboat', a jocular account of a pleasure trip from Cork to Cove along the Lee, which is full of topical detail and light local satire. He used the *ottavo rima,* the metre *Don Juan* had made fashionable. Richard Alfred Millikin, on the other hand, wrote pastiches of folk songs, and 'De Groves of De Pool' is about the return of the Cork militia to their relatives in Blackpool (the 'hoop-coilers', 'tanners' and 'glue-boilers') after the French wars. It makes fun of the flat Cork dialect:

> De naggins of sweet Tommy Walker
> We lifted according to rule,
> And wetted our necks wid de native
> Dat is brewed in de groves of de Pool.[4]

Here Millikin is enjoying himself at the expense of the lower orders, but it does betoken interest in their patois. There were other Corkmen of the time who took the speech of the urban lower classes more seriously. Bishop Murphy, the Catholic bishop of Cork, learnt Irish to better his understanding of his flock. Among the tanneries and cooperages of Blackpool the flat nasal English was not the only language spoken; the Irish of the surrounding countryside would also be heard there. Irish impinged on the life of Cork city as it did at the same time on the life of Belfast.[5] Still at Carrignavar there was a school of weakened Gaelic verse, the latter-day inheritors of the bardic tradition. So, in an afternoon's walk from a city suburb it would be possible to go to see a Gaelic poet and hear his slackened verse celebrating in hopeless, futile energy, the return of the Stuart. But it would not have been necessary to go so far, perhaps; between 1816 and 1820 Bishop Murphy had employed Micheál Óg Ó Longáin as a teacher of Irish and a transcriber of Gaelic manuscripts, and Ó Longáin was the most accomplished of the Carrignavar poets.

We can be fairly sure that not many of the denizens of the South Mall or the Grand Parade made such visits to Carrignavar, or that they knew of the existence of a school of Gaelic verse at such close quarters. Even if they did, not many of them would be interested. Those of them with cultural pretensions would prefer the more obviously civilised activities of the Apollo Society, and who can blame them? Cork was not, nor had it ever been, a Gaelic city. What is surprising though, was that there was some interest, and it is this interest, minimal though it was, that was the background to Callanan's enthusiasm for the songs, stories and life of West Cork.

Bishop John Murphy was not the only one to get Irish scribes to work for him; John Windele, scholar-antiquary, folk-lorist, part-time literary man, and friend to Callanan also employed them and corresponded with Robert McAdam, a Belfast businessman with similar interests. Windele was a remarkable man: he had a 'megalithic library' in his house on Blair's Hill in Cork, and Ogham stones were his dominant passion. He and a number of others, among them Richard Rolt Brash, a Cork architect, and the Rev. Matthew Horgan, parish priest of Blarney, tramped the wild Cork countryside, looking for megalithic monuments in their natural setting, attempting to supply explanations for their gaunt, mysterious grandeur. They eventually became convinced that the Ogham stones were covered with Orphic fragments of great potency and learning. Windele was so impressed that he had one erected over his grave.

Windele had an interest in Irish, a natural interest for an antiquarian intent on deciphering Oghamic mysteries. But that interest was not entirely antiquarian; it embraced the living language and the people who spoke it. Whatever the ardour of his convictions with regard to Ogham stones his antiquarian enthusiasm did not cut him off from the country people who guided him and his friends to the ancient sites, and, as his manuscripts in the Royal Irish Academy show, he took an interest in their customs and beliefs.[6] For most antiquarians of the time, the country people were mere incidentals, there being no lively or living contact between the ancient monuments in the landscape and the patterns of their lives. But for Windele archaeology tended to shade off into folklore, and this was a tendency he shared with Crofton Croker, another Corkman, who, like Callanan, wrote for Windele when he edited *Bolster's Magazine*. They were all – Windele, Croker, and Callanan – members of, or visitors to, 'The Hermitage', where a Cork literary and artistic set called 'The Anchorites' would meet. In 'The Hermitage' Callanan was known as 'The Recluse', Windele as 'Dr Mc Slatt'.[7] Windele became Callanan's unofficial literary executor, and his manuscript entitled *The Literary Remains of Jeremiah J. Callanan,* is our main source for Callanan's life and work.[8]

It would be difficult to decide who was the leading spirit among these three men, Croker, Windele and Callanan, who shared an interest not only in folk lore but in the country people from whom they collected it.[9] Croker, who published his *Researches in the South of Ireland* (1824) was the most successful. Like Croker, Callanan wandered around West Cork. He too wished to be an observer of local custom and habit, but in going into West Cork among the country people he was also seeking to assuage his inner turmoil and restlessness, by losing himself in the harsh outline of the mountains, or in the angular beauty of a Gaelic love song.

III

Looking over the course of Callanan's life there is a recurring pattern of restlessness, followed by inaction. In some sense he felt trapped by Cork, by his background, and more seriously by guilt

over mislaid opportunities and unfulfilled responsibilities. He
seems to have felt some guilt over leaving Maynooth, where he
had gone to study for the priesthood. This may explain the fact
that throughout his poetry there is a yearning for and admiration
of the single uncomplicated act, where mind and heart are keyed
to one intense purpose. For this reason he was drawn to military
life. At one point he enlisted, and found himself on the Isle of
Wight, immediately regretting his decision. He bought himself
out and was back in Cork in a fortnight. If a life of Byronic
action could not be his, then perhaps a retreat to the countryside
would be more feasible. The countryside he was naturally drawn
to was that of West Cork; there, in prospect, after his grim
experiences at Maynooth (paralleling those of Fr Peadar Ó
Laoghaire, as recorded in his autobiography, *Mo Scéal Féin*) he
would find a clearer air, a more expansive freedom, a local
version of the dream of a fuller life that had caused him to
enlist in the army. Furthermore, West Cork was a place with
family connections; he had relatives there, and the Callanans
had been well-known doctors in the area. For a time (1820-1822)
he was a tutor in Millstreet, a small, nondescript village in
northwest Cork. There his Irish improved and he began to collect
folk song and poetry, inspired perhaps by Crofton Croker's visit
in 1821 when he had been collecting for his *Researches*. Callanan
appears to have had some vague plans in his mind at this time
for a collection of what he called *Munster Melodies,* no doubt
thinking of Moore's *Irish Melodies.* But his would have a more
regional flavour, and would have much closer contact with the
original Irish poems. Clearly he thought of himself as a more
authentic Moore, though he did have the conventional respect
for the established writer. He also seems to have wished to beat
Croker at his own game. Later, in 1826, while he was at Bantry,
Croker (who had praised Callanan's *Blackwood* versions in his
Researches in the South of Ireland) wrote to his fellow-Corkman,
to persuade him to contribute to a collection which was to be
called *The Minstrelsy of the South of Ireland.* Callanan refused,
because he felt he had to devote all his energy to his own collection of *Munster Melodies.*[10]

Despite the good face he puts on his activities for Croker's
benefit, only nine pieces survive by him which are either translations or poems inspired by Irish originals. It is not clear how he
spent his time 'in the field', as a modern folk-lorist would say;

he was probably something between a J. M. Synge, fascinated by the energy of the life he found in West Cork, and a Lady Morgan, all too ready to exaggerate and sentimentalize. Not much can be gathered from a letter he wrote to his friend Windele from Bandon in January 1827 save that he was engaged in some kind of collection, and that he was envious of Croker's cornering of the Cork folk lore market:

> I have made a great harvest in the Irish way. If I'm not before Croker in one way, I think I shall be in another. I'm living here á là J.O.L. Priests and Doctors, Police Officers and Bourgeois are feeding me; – I must get visiting cards at last – *Go vóire Dia oruing;* but I'll fly to the mountains.[11]

What happened to the great harvest? Was there a great harvest at all? Those who knew Callanan personally or by repute tell us that he had a prodigious memory, and it is claimed that what he actually committed to writing was a fraction of what he had collected and composed.[12] If this is true, then Callanan would appear to have imbibed more than just the spirit of the folk songs and stories he collected, but something of the practice – loose, careless and casual as it is – of the oral tradition itself. It was a tradition entirely suited to his imaginative waywardness and lack of discipline. No doubt its fluid disregard for the niceties of consistent structure appealed to him. In the simple direct emotions of folk song he found the purposeful intensity he lacked in life (strange transformation of the Byronic impulse!). In their odd, exotic, sometimes absurd image sequences he found a kind of corroboration for his own shifting imaginative processes, an 'objective correlative' for his own imaginative flux and uncertainty.

But nothing came of the *Munster Melodies*. In January 1827 he and Alicia Fisher, a Cork Methodist with whom he was in love with a mixture of romantic passion and Catholic scrupulousness, drifted apart.[13] His health, never strong, grew worse, and when a job was offered as tutor with a Mr Hickey, a Cork businessman living in Lisbon, he accepted. After a typical and somewhat ridiculous Cork farewell (where he was put on board ship blind drunk at Cove, only to turn up, some hours later, at 'The Hermitage' in Cork where his friends were lamenting his departure), he left the city for the last time.

The notes and jottings he made while in Lisbon show that Callanan's mind was all the time on Ireland, and on West Cork in particular. He was homesick and discontented in the sun. For him Lisbon was a barren place. In his notebooks he sketched outlines for poems and prose tales on Irish themes, which, he hoped, would raise Irish literature in the opinion of the world. But they remained sketches. He died of a throat infection in September 1829. Towards the end he appears to have received some relief from the pressures and anxieties of his mind through contemplation of the Blessed Virgin.

IV

Callanan's body of work is small. Despite its smallness, however, it has an interest in inverse proportion to its size. Callanan, in his feeble, encumbered way was trying to be a modern poet, a poet of the 1820s, in a language the traditions of which were not native, which belonged in fact to a people whom Callanan regarded as conquerors.

For an Irish poet of the nineteenth century wishing to be recognisably Irish in his work, the inescapable fact that he had to write in English created an obvious problem. The same problem beset Synge at the end of the century and the beginning of the present one, and his solution was to convert English into a special Irish form, the notorious 'Synge-song' as Joyce called it. This achieved remarkable effects, in its own way, but such a solution to the problem of making literature Irish and not English could not (had he even thought of it) have presented itself to Callanan. Callanan's solution was to make his writing unmistakeably Irish in theme; this was the solution of most subsequent nationalist writers of the century. It led to the institutionalisation of those drastic icons of sentimentality, the wolfhound, the round tower, the Saggarth Aroon ('the dear little priest'), and to the associated debasement of the currencies of feeling. In notes to a projected poem, to be called 'The Outlaw of Caom-ané', Callanan writes of the native tradition in Irish literature. He also feels that the writer should go to lengths to maintain the differences between that tradition and the English one:

The peculiar manners of the Irish chiefs at that time should be

preserved in the persons, and the peculiarity of scenery kept
in view – lakes, naked rocks, heather, mountains, wooded hills,
bays, promontories, old castles, ruin and desolation – characters
daring, desperate, rude, high-minded. Can these be all treated
in a manner different from English writers? [14]

This is a plea for cultural separatism, a literary version of Repeal,
long before that movement began. But it is to Callanan's credit
that he avoided the worst kinds of nationalist excess, in his
writing at least, whatever he did in life. One reason for this was
his choice of Byron as a model rather than Moore, which showed
a certain amount of Romantic adventurousness, despite the
constraints of his provincial Catholic background. Moore was all
the rage, and surely the choice for an aspiring writer to model
himself on; he had created a market for plangent Irish strains,
and the title of Callanan's proposed collection (*Munster Melodies*)
shows that that had not gone unnoticed. But he was too safe.
Byron offered range, emotion, temperament; just the thing an
irresolute provincial, enmeshed in his background, would like to
think about. But where Byron chose all Europe as his province,
Callanan made West Cork his world. To read his poems with an
ordnance survey map on the table alongside is to realise that he
knew the topography of the country intimately, both coast and
inland from Bandon through the Cork and Kerry mountains to
Kenmare and beyond. In having this wild, rugged, and beautiful
country as his poetic terrain, there was no question of his verse
not being Irish in one respect at least. This was his country of the
mind, and he felt it to be his duty to give expression to its vivid
life, a life that seemed to him the opposite of the careworn and
flat dreariness life in Cork had become for him. So when he came
to write what is in effect an attempt at an Irish 'Childe Harold'
(he used the same stanza as Byron did) he called it, 'The Recluse
of Inchydoney'. Inchydoney is an island peninsula about two
miles south of Clonakilty in West Cork, countryside full of
inexpressible longings for him.

The Recluse of the title has fled from the city to West Cork
and the poem opens with a sense of relief at leaving the city
behind:

> Once more I'm free – the city's din is gone,
> And with it wasted days and weary nights. [15]

Here he will find, he says, nature, simplicity, freedom and inspiration: the pastoral dream. It is an intense dream, not a languorous one, and is involved with the deepest processes of Callanan's personality, his wishes for himself, his recognition of the misery of his real state. The dream of Inchydoney is to embody all that Callanan would wish to become; it is a kind of proto-Yeatsian dream of re-making the lacklustre self.

The recluse is filled with self-disgust and self-reproach at having dissipated his talents in the city among drinkers and other wasters. He has a Byronic hatred for those with whom, against his better judgement, he had wasted his time. Now, here, in the countryside, there is enough of space and time to be free, to allow nature's forces to work through him, to stir the 'Spirit of Song' in him. 'False ones' may have led him away from poetry and 'nature', but here the 'wild lyre' will be his only friend, he will have 'no heritage but song'. A natural simplicity, a freedom from internal strife, will be his, in surroundings like these.

If the poem went no further than this, it would, of course, be entirely unremarkable, differing very little from a hundred other such nineteenth century fantasies. But the flow of the poem is interrupted by the introduction of a strange, unnamed figure, whom the recluse can just see from the land as this mysterious figure walks the deck of a ship anchored in the bay. All others on board are asleep:

> tho' undefined and dark
> His bearing speaks him one of birth and pride,
> Now he leans over the vessel's landward side,
> This way his eye is turn'd – hush did I hear
> A voice as if some loved one just had died?
> 'Tis from yon ship that wail comes on mine ear,
> And now o'er ocean's sleep it comes distinct and clear.

Unlikely as it seems, the figure leaning over the landward side of the ship breaks into mournful song, which the recluse over-hears. This is imitative of Childe Harold's sad but heroic farewell to England in the first canto, but it is not entirely ridiculous to ask what Callanan intends by the introduction of this song. It breaks the flow of the poem, which up to that is all subjective reflection; now another voice is introduced, singing. Whose is this voice?

On Cleada's hill the moon is bright,
Dark Avondu still rolls in light,
All changeless is that mountain's head
That river still seeks ocean's bed,
The calm blue waters of Loch Lene
Still kiss their own sweet isles of green,
But where's the heart as firm and true
As hill, or lake, or Avondu?

The recluse, who hears this music over the water, is a version
of Callanan, but the lone singing figure is another, different
version. This latter version is caught on the point of an imagined
exile, bidding his farewell to West Cork and Kerry, countryside
he knows intimately. The song dilates on an almost Tennysonian
moment of intensity before action, a time of suspended life, full
of anticipation. The recluse on shore has been, up to now,
entertaining a dream of natural simplicity, where hill, rock and
river will free his creative powers to their own vital energy,
opening up his life to new possibilities. But the figure on board
the ship is leaving these very scenes; he is only too aware of the
gap there is between the simple beauty and changelessness of
nature and the shiftlessness of the human heart:

Where's the heart as firm and true
As hill, or lake, or Avondu?

He is deliberately going into physical exile from this beauty
because he is an exile from it already in his heart. The rest and
quiet of nature is for him unattainable, giving his description of
it a sharp clear plangency:

O Avondu I wish I were
As once upon that mountain bare,
Where the young waters laugh and shine
On the wild breast of Meenganine,
I wish I were by Cleada's hill,
Or by Glenluachra's rushy rill,
But no! I never more shall view
Those scenes I loved by Avondu.

Knowing that such scenes, though beautiful, need not necessarily
transform the human heart, it is better to be away from them

altogether, in exile, than to bear the torture of being an exile *among* them, cut off by 'the heritage of sin and clay' from vital contact with them.

The lay of the exile, then, unsettles our easy identification with the recluse's meditations, just as it unsettles those meditations themselves. Here is an ex-recluse, someone who was just like the man on shore, but who has found that the peace and freedom of nature does not always transform the heart. It is an amazingly bold stroke, to introduce the antithesis of the emotional movement of the opening of the poem in such a way. But Callanan has no idea what to do with it. The poem flounders after this, and he knows it, but he fumbles on desperately, hoping that something will come to knit it together. It does not. And Callanan has not the poetic energy and verbal resource to hold opposing structural and emotional tensions in creative suspension as Yeats was later to do. The poem becomes more and more disorganised, veering further and further away from the opposition at its core, that between the pastoral dream of the recluse, and the realization, expressed in the strong, firm lines of the exile's song, that the dream is just that, with no power to inform reality. And, as with all structures that desert their centre, anarchy takes hold. The verse becomes feeble and Callanan becomes conscious of its feebleness. Tormentingly, Byron comes to mind, with his indefatigable energy. It is almost as if the massive torrent of his energy has left some reservoir of poetry exhausted:

> Too short he dwelt among us and too long,
> Where is the bard of earth will now aspire
> To soar so high upon the wing of song?
> Who shall inherit now his soul of fire?
> His spirit's dazzling light? – vain man retire
> Mid the wild heath of Albyn's loneliest glen,
> Leave to the winds that now forsaken lyre,
> Until some angel–bard come down again
> And wake once more those strains, too high, too sweet for men.

Until such time as another unearthly visitation like Byron's takes place lesser poets must be content with lower flight. Emulation of one whose power seemed to involve him with the processes of nature itself, in that vision which the recluse wishes for, is impossible:

> The sun still sets along Morea's hill,
> The moon still rises o'er Cithaeron's height;
> But where is he, the bard whose matchless skill
> Gave fresher beauty to their march of light?

By contrast with this 'matchless skill' Callanan's own verse is hopelessly inadequate, and he begins to accept his own failure; in bidding farewell to Byron he admits his own feebleness:

> Bard of my childhood's love, farewell to thee;
> I little deemed that e'er my feeble lay
> Should wait thy doom.

If he had greater poetic talents, he goes on to say, he would more fittingly lament Byron's death, but others will come, more talented men, whose lays will be as 'immortal as the theme' itself. But when these come they will be tributes, Callanan says, from 'free-born men', men not born in slavery and subjection to 'the Saxon yoke', as he was. The logic is beginning to be horrifyingly familiar. His sense of failure, his inadequacy as writer and as man (in him as in Byron writer and man are indistinguishable) have their origin in the misfortunes of Irish history. The perennial Irish blur is beginning to form. Responsibility for one's own nature is being shelved; one becomes instead a victim of the dark forces of historical process, and that means in the Irish context, persecution. Here Callanan's private distress is transformed into political or rather racial rancour; through the simplifications of abstract hate the foreigner, the Saxon, becomes the reason for personal unhappiness. Clearly, one's emotional state cannot be dissociated from political history, but to make the latter the reason for the former is a dangerous and habit-forming simplification. In the present context it helps Callanan to avoid the delicate and necessary rigours of self-scrutiny. Since Ireland 'stooped beneath the Saxon yoke', her harp that once would call to freedom, giving expression to the deepest energies of the Irish people,

> forgot the strains that once it woke
> And like the Banshee's cry of death alone hath spoke.

The rhetoric of lament, the wail of sorrow takes the time-worn predictable path and gives itself over to the rhetoric of violence. In a desperate attempt to give his verse some kind of energy, despite the inevitable enfeeblements of historical process, he whips it up to the only intensity he can manage, a white froth of anti-Protestant (which is also anti-Saxon) hatred:

> Famine hath plough'd his journeys on thy cheek,
> Despair hath made her dwelling in thine eye,
> The lordly Churchman rides unheeding by.
> He fastens on the sweat that dries thy brain,
> The very dogs that in his kennel lie
> Hold revels to thy fare! but don't complain,
> He has the cure of souls – the law doth so ordain.

This of course is powerful stuff, and in its own vicious way well written, but 'The Recluse of Inchydoney' did not begin as a satire against the Established Church to help the cause of Catholic Emancipation, nor indeed does it end as such. This flash of violence at least allows Callanan the excitement of a moment of intensity, but it remains a momentary thing. After this the poem meanders along on its eccentric path picking up other themes and ideas, then laying them aside. It forecasts the coming of a revolution employing conventional Romantic apocryphal imagery; a Shelleyan wind is imagined sweeping through caverns, bursting them, making the hills 'quake'. As well as being turbulent Romantic convention all this looks back to the excited prophesies of Gaelic Jacobite poetry, the kind of oracular forecast we find in 'Róisín Dubh'. Mangan was later to respond to this strain, his nervous temperament finding release in similar images of violence in 'Dark Rosaleen'. The Irish, Callanan says, will 'break their long dark silence' and they will then possess the tempestuous energy of violent natural forces, the sort of energy from which the recluse and his alter ego, the exile, are cut off.

Callanan concludes the poem with a couple of stanzas about his own private misery, about how his mind is like some place where

> in its cold dark chamber all unseen
> The water trickles through the lonely grot,
> And weeps itself to stone.

Presumably this stone will turn to lava too, when the natural
eruptions of revolution come.

> The far Seven-Heads thro' mists of purple smile,
> The lark ascends from Inchydoney's height,
> 'Tis morning – sweet one of my native Isle,
> Wild voice of Desmond hush – go rest thee for awhile.

Here, in the last line, he addresses himself as the 'wild voice
of Desmond', almost as if he has achieved what the recluse wished
for at the opening, union with the natural simplicity, grandeur
and energy of the landscape of West Cork, his poetry being the
articulation of that energy. Needless to say, the assertion the
image contains is rhetorical. Despite the earlier metaphor he
could never be stone and be that stone's voice. Nor indeed could
Byron, or anyone. His frustration, his lack of energy, his fragmentary intensity, do not allow him the necessary consistencies
of metaphor for a satisfactory fictive shape to be achieved. But
the poem is an interesting failure, for its introduction of opposing
tensions in the dim personae of the recluse and the exile, and for
its attempt at making a unity between private discontent and
public concerns. Because the poem is unable to sustain a grip
on an imaginative centre it dissolves into a series of fragmented
sensations, topical references, and the frustrated contemplation
of imagined apocalypse. It shows the failure of the imagination
to reconcile the opposing tensions into which Callanan's sincerity
led him. The recluse is Callanan, the exile is also Callanan, but
instead of finding some way of drawing these opposites into active
alert engagement (the kind of confrontation that Yeats's masterful energy made him capable of, a hundred years later) the poem
splits down the middle, victim to its own honesty. Callanan papers
over the fissure with rhetoric and maudlin self-pity, but a real
structure where theme and counter-theme could work themselves
out is beyond him.

V

Water and its movement were powerful symbols for Callanan.
In 'The Recluse of Inchydoney' the recluse stands on a strand,

looking out to sea, listening to the exile's song floating over the still water. It is not surprising that Callanan was drawn to water: Cork city is built on it and the river Lee (Spenser described its 'divided flood' in the great river cantoes of *The Faerie Queene*) spreads out when it meets the city into a complicated network of waterways making many of the streets quays.

The Lee has its origin in Gougane Barra in West Cork, and the dark still lake, set among steep cliffs, was another powerful symbol for Callanan. From there the Lee comes, following its winding way until it breaks up when it reaches Cork, making it something of a delta city. For Callanan Gougane Barra became associated with pure, authentic (meaning Gaelic) life, the city with the disintegration and pollution of that life. There the true fount was to be found, the unpolluted source of inspiration. It was all the more appropriate for being difficult of access, even forbidding. West Cork was a place where traces of the ancient Gaelic life still lingered; for Callanan Gougane Barra was a reservoir and fortress of that life, an Irish nationalist version of Wordsworth's Windermere or Coleridge's pleasure dome and caves of ice.

Not only was the lake associated with the source of his imaginative energy; he also thought of it as a natural fortress for the dispossessed Gaelic bards of the seventeenth and eighteenth centuries, a place for them to hide from the ravaging of the Saxon invader. He felt himself to be their latter-day spokesman, the inheritor of their pride and their secret places.

'Gougane Barra', Callanan's poem on the lake and its surroundings, expresses his wish to shed his Cork background (a place of futility and inaction for him, linked in his mind with English presence in Ireland) and to go over to the other side, the side of the Gaelic bards of Gougane Barra:

> There is a green island in lone Gougane Barra,
> Where Allua of songs rushes forth as an arrow;
> In deep-vallied Desmond – a thousand wild fountains
> Come down to that lake, from their home in the mountains.[16]

The lake itself is the receptor of the wild streams of the mountains around; it is a dark bowl of richness, of energy, that natural energy into which the recluse of Inchydoney wishes to be drawn. According to legend, Saint Finbarr had a hermitage on the

'green island' in the lake. From there he set out, following the
Lee to its mouth where he founded the city of Cork.

Callanan imaginatively reverses this journey, and seeks out the
native origin of the city which is now the scene of his frustration
and inactivity:

> How oft when the summer sun rested on Clara,
> And lit the dark heath on the hills of Ivera,
> Have I sought thee, sweet spot, from my home by the ocean,
> And trod all thy wilds with a Minstrel's devotion,
> And thought of thy bards, when assembling together,
> In the cleft of thy rocks, or the depth of thy heather,
> They fled from the Saxon's dark bondage and slaughter,
> And waked their lost song by the rush of thy water.

Here, by this lake, Callanan says, he once used to achieve an
imaginative communion with the lost Gaelic bards. This communion meant that his 'harp' could give voice to the nature
around it, that it was Aeolian in fact. Callanan *says* that there
once was a time when the sense of alienation from nature, which
is the theme of 'The Recluse of Inchydoney', did not exist.
'Gougane Barra' laments the passing of those days. All Callanan
can do is remember and catch a faint echo of that once
magnificent song that mixed landscape with life and emotion:

> Though loftier Minstrels green Erin can number,
> I only awoke your wild harp from its slumber,
> And mingled once more with the voice of those fountains,
> The songs even echo forgot on her mountains,
> And gleaned each grey legend that darkly was sleeping
> Where the mist and the rain o'er their beauty was creeping.

It is all in the past, the 'grey legends' are here seen to have been
an organic part of the landscape of the place, in a manner
comparable to the way in which, at the end of 'The Recluse'
the poem is said to be 'the wild voice of Desmond'. He is
romanticising his own past, is in fact, creating a version of Celtic
pastoral. But he is not unaware of this, because the second
section of the poem, following immediately on the sweet recollection of that impossible past union, veers off on a huge,
complex, conditional clause:

Least bard of the hills! were it mine to inherit
The fire of thy harp, and the wing of thy spirit,
With the wrongs which like thee to our country has bound me,
Did your mantle of song fling its radiance around me,
Still, still in those wilds may young liberty rally
And send her strong shout over mountain and valley,
The star of the west may yet rise in its glory,
And the land that was darkest, be brightest in story.

The last four lines are nerveless rhetoric. They lack conviction, a lack made evident by that big word 'liberty'. Also, from 'Still, still' on (itself a mere metrical stutter) there is hopeless confusion in the tenses. The exclamation of the opening and the huge conditional clause are leading up to a statement which never comes. Callanan has put himself in the unfortunate position where he has committed himself to saying what he would do if he were to inherit the spirit of the 'least bard of the hills', and he cannot say. The best he can drag up out of the conventional thought of his time is 'young liberty', and the rhetorical tension disintegrates in a mess of slack tenses.

The conclusion of the poem is appropriate to this failure to say anything. He imagines himself dead, back near the ocean, at the mouth of the Owenbue, which flows into the Lee's estuary at Crosshaven. When Ireland is free some other 'Minstrel' will come

And bend o'er my grave with a tear of emotion,
Where calm Avon Buee seeks the kisses of ocean,
Or plant a wild wreath, from the banks of that river,
O'er the heart, and the harp, that are sleeping forever.

The 'wild wreath' is appropriate, the thought having become so loose, the emotion so slack that the best Callanan can do is draw up an image of his own death, or rather, of his having died. The Gaelic bards he imagines inhabiting the wild terrain of the Gougane Barra poem had a violence and energy, a sense of belonging to a tradition from which he feels cut off. The poem on the one hand declares Callanan's determination to inherit their wild spirit, and so become some kind of Irish Byron, but on the other hand, its sad, ineffectual conclusion confesses his own sense of alienation from the power that naturally came to them. All he can hope for is some future eccentric 'minstrel', who will lay a wild wreath at his forlorn grave at the mouth of the Lee, far away from its source, the true fount of Gaelic life.

In a letter he wrote to Alicia Fisher from Everton near Carlow (where he taught school in 1825/26) he speaks of 'Gougane Barra', of the bards, of the 'grey legends', of his resolve to dedicate himself to 'Irish subjects', and of his own consciousness that he lacks talent and energy:

> You like 'Gougane Barra'. Then I was on the Island during the most fearful hurricane I ever experienced. Perhaps you think the allusion to the Bards a mere poetical fiction. I certainly have no positive authority for it but the historical fact that the whole range of mountains at that side of the County Cork were the retreat of the Irish when driven from the low-lands by the flint-hearted Saxons, and the probability of the thing. As for the grey legends 'tis quite true, no poet has in this country at least been as industrious in that way as myself. I mean, please God, to confine whatever share of talent I may possess to Irish subjects. No poet has yet done so because it would not be his interest. If I do nothing more than point out the unexplored region to some able successor I shall have rendered my country some service. Is not Scott a wonderful man? What miracle his single mind has performed for his country. I wish I had a small portion of his talent and industry – 'tis because he and Byron were the two first masters I went to school to I admire them so much.[17]

As 'The Recluse of Inchydoney' shows, Callanan wished to become involved with the forces of nature like many another Romantic; more than that, he felt that if he could achieve this he would have greater liberty, energy, a fuller, more authentic creative life. These forces were to be found outside Cork city, which became for him a place of frustration, waste, dissipated energy. Nature became associated in his mind with the shattered remnants of the bardic order, the shards of which could be found in folk songs, stories, the 'grey legends' of West Cork. They were the imagined sources of his creative freedom. He wanted to exchange his real self, and its traditions (such as they were) of business, banks, and dramatic societies, for a kind of anti-self composed of wild bardic energy, Byronic vitality, and romantic

Celticism. His translations from the Irish were the closest he came
to this curiously Yeatsian exchange; what John Windele said of
his original work is substantially true: 'in general nothing can be
more desultory, broken or unconnected'.[18]

VI

Six of Callanan's translations appeared in *Blackwood's
Magazine* for 1823 – these being 'The Dirge of O'Sullivan Bear'
(praised by Croker in his *Researches* of the following year),[19] 'The
Girl I Love', 'The Convict of Clonmel', 'O Say my Brown
Drimin', 'The White Cockade' and 'The Avenger'. Of his remaining translations, 'On the Last Day' appeared in *Bolster's Quarterly
Magazine* for August 1826 and 'The Lament of O'Gnive' in the
January 1827 volume of the same journal. The May 1828 edition
contained his famous 'The Outlaw of Loch Lene'. There are
fragments of other translations in the Windele manuscript, from
Irish and from other languages. And there is a section on Irish
prosody, showing that he studied the metrical systems of Gaelic
poetry quite closely, a study which influenced the metrical style
of his translations.[20] Curiously enough, the section which contains
his study of Irish prosody (called, rather grandly, 'Folia Sybillina')
is followed by a call for the abandonment of Gaelic in Irish
education.

Whatever doubts he entertained about the pragmatic value of
Irish in the modern world, he was nevertheless drawn to its
poetry, especially to the poetry and song of folk tradition, a
tradition still comparatively strong in the 1820s. When we think
of the richness of Hyde's gleanings at the end of the century in
the *Love Songs of Connacht* and in the *Religious Songs of Connacht*, we cannot but regret that Callanan did not do for the
poetry of the South West of Munster what Croker did for the
folk tales. Though he pretended to Croker and Windele that he
had made a 'great harvest' (which *may* have been stored in his
memory) he was not by temperament a collector or arranger.
This was a pity, because what attracted him in folk poetry was
the very essence of the thing, the wildness, the sudden exotic
images, the revelling in the impossible, the odd thought sequences
and the intensity:

> I'd drain the sea
> I'd turn back the stream
> I'd leap over the mountain to meet her
> I'd burn Mangerton
> I'd measure the sun
> I'd put to the sword the Fiana Eirin[21]

We find this on page 86 of the Windele manuscript. It is no more than a preliminary literal version of a Gaelic love song (there are many with similar sequences of images) but it does indicate for us those aspects of folk poetry which attracted Callanan, as they were to attract Ferguson after him, and, later on in the century, Hyde, Yeats and Synge.

Callanan desired poetic intensity. He says as much in a note in the Windele manuscript, where he speaks of emotion and poetry. He uses the unfortunate word 'distress' in attempting to express what he wishes to say, which shows that for him personal feeling tended to be all. To its intensity he was inclined to forsake the necessary coldness attendant on aesthetic emotion, that coldness that gives its own life to a poetic structure:

> The more distress there is introduced in a poem the more forcibly is the reader's attention arrested and the more intense is his pleasure, tho' that pleasure be of a painful kind – is this the case?[22]

In Gaelic folk song he found this intensity expressed in stark vivid images, which were frequently surprising in their strangeness and far-fetchedness. He liked the extremes of rhetorical declamation, his Romantic temperament glorying in the passion that could make a lover exclaim: 'I'd burn Mangerton'. Their fire could be made his in translation, and so could their structure.

Callanan also liked the interconnectedness of things he found in this verse: how a natural object became so effortlessly an image for an internal state, with no fuss or bluster or Wordsworthian mumblings about the influence these natural objects exert on the moral being. Indeed, when Yeats came later to write of this poetry as he came across it in Hyde's translations, he was overwhelmed by the almost paradisal absence of barrier between the emotion, the image, and the object upon which the image throws its net.

To Callanan it seemed as if the fusion between the subjective personality and external nature, that interfusion which was his dream, was a perfectly effortless and inherent quality in Gaelic folk poetry. A corollary of this interconnectedness was the imaginative looseness, the fluidity of this poetry, the ease with which the poet could fancy himself elsewhere, or in another shape. No doubt Callanan simplified, as Hyde did later, and Yeats, and Synge. Indeed many of the most startling images in Irish folk poetry only appear startling when translated into English: in Irish they are often part of traditional and rather insignificantly conventional tropes. But perhaps the conviction that something is the case is what matters in questions like this. Certainly, the idea that Gaelic folk poetry was fresh, original, paradisal, was a useful myth for Callanan and for the writers of the Irish literary revival at the close of the century.

Callanan, however, was writing in the 1820s, and did not have the confidence of these later men: for one thing Matthew Arnold's *On the Study of Celtic Literature* was still a long way off and for another the great German philological movement which gave Irish an ancient linguistic and cultural prestige had not yet properly begun. So when Callanan published his first six translations from the Irish in *Blackwood's Magazine* he was very unsure of himself and of his material. He makes it clear in an introductory note to the translations that he is concerned with 'popular Irish poetry, during the last century, or century and a half'. Irish, he says, had not been used 'as his common language' by a gentleman for generations, it being 'left to the lower orders exclusively, and they were depressed and uneducated, and consequently wild and illiterate'. In saying this he does not wish to impeach the fame of the 'bards', 'Seanachies' or the 'Ossianic fragments'. He will leave these to the 'wrangling antiquarians' whom his fellow-Corkman, Croker, also found 'marvellously cumbersome'. He wishes to give his attention to the 'popular songs of the lower orders', which are neither numerous, nor possessed of much beauty.[23]

Needless to say, Callanan is conscious of the fact that he is writing for an English audience here, many of whom would be unsympathetic to any whiff of Irish Chauvinism on his part. Further, some of the translations in *Blackwood's Magazine* contained strong stuff, which Callanan in no way attempted to dilute; – indeed it could be said that he fairly revelled in the more violent passages. In this he was radically unlike the translators James Hardiman had working for him on his *Irish Minstrelsy* eight years later, in that they tempered everything, trying to smooth out all eccentricities, sometimes with ludicrous results. Callanan let the whole thing through, Jacobite warts and all, then prefaced his versions with a note relegating the sentiments they expressed to 'the lower orders', and assuring the English public that songs like these were not too numerous:

> When the Prince, now an exile, shall come for his own,
> The isles of his father, his rights and his throne,
> My people in battle the Saxon will meet,
> And kick them before, like old shoes from their feet.[24]

There is a combination of vividness, swiftness and intensity here we find nowhere in Callanan's original poetry: we have had the intensity before, but it was blurred, diffused over too wide an area of feeling. Here the focus is sharp, clear, just right. There is a rhythmic inevitability about it also, which we certainly do not find in the sluggish stanzas of 'The Recluse' or the nervous, scarcely sustained energy of 'Gougane Barra'. Clearly, like Mangan after him, Callanan frequently found another poem's structure accommodated, contained, and gave point to his energy. The rhythmic excitement of the lines quoted above shows that Callanan was thoroughly enjoying himself. Momentarily he has ceased to be Callanan, the spoiled priest, failed poet, Corkman, and has become the Jacobite poet in the fastnesses of the mountains, looking forward to the coming of Louis in his strength:

> O! where art thou Louis, our eyes are on thee?
> Are thy lofty ships walking in strength o'er the sea?

Callanan's talent as a translator, (and it may be a talent especially characteristic of a writer lacking in original poetic nerve) is that he is capable of an extraordinary degree of imaginative identification. It is as if his imagination becomes possessed with the poem upon which he is working to such an extent that to all intents and purposes the poem writes itself anew through him. It is a mediumistic art. Mangan also had this talent, but he put much more of his own impress on the product. In Callanan's case it is almost as if the Irish poems rewrite themselves in another language, almost as if we encounter the impossible: Gaelic poetry in English.

To complicate matters further, the question of Callanan's originals is a very vexed one. In fact, of Callanan's nine translations from the Irish, only one of them has a verifiable original, with which it accords in all points. This is 'The Lament of O'Gnive', which is a version of Fearflatha Ó Gnímh's 'Mo Thruaighe mar atáid Gaoidhil', a well-known late bardic poem of the sixteenth century. It is Callanan's least interesting translation. With regard to his other eight versions, Irish poems have been found which match in certain of their lines with Callanan's translations. Sometimes, as with 'The Girl I Love' he seems to have borrowed from two or more Irish poems, but even here there is material in the English version which has not as yet been assigned a definite original. One way of explaining this is to posit Irish poems, now lost, which Callanan translated conscientiously, line by line. The fact that the Irish poems which accord with Callanan's versions are folk poems lends credence to this interpretation of what happened, because folk verse, by its very nature, is constantly changing, and it could be that his originals, in the form he knew them, have disappeared. The question would be much simplified had Callanan been more forthcoming about his originals, but, not being a disciplined folklorist, he took no trouble about sources.

In the case of one poem we can inspect a certain amount of evidence for Gaelic source material. 'The Girl I Love', bears the subtitle 'Súd í síos an caoin ban álain óg', which substantially resembles the first line of the *sixth* verse of a version of 'An raibh tú ag an gCarraig?' which Edward Walsh (another Corkman) gave in his *Irish Popular Songs* (1847):

> Siúd é síos an Ríogh-bhean álainn óg,
> A bhfuil a gruaig leí scaoilte síos go béal a bróg,
> 'S í an eala í mar an lítis do shíolruigh an tsárfhuil mhór,
> Charaid geal mo chroídhe, céad míle fáilte romhat!

Walsh translates these lines as follows:

> Lo! yonder the maiden illustrious, queen-like, high,
> With long flowing tresses adown to her sandal-tie –

Swan, fair as the lily, descended of high degree
A myriad of welcomes, dear maid of my heart to thee.[25]

The two opening lines of Callanan's version resemble the first
two of Walsh's 'An Raibh tú ag an gCarraig', praising the girl's
queenliness and the length of her hair. After that Callanan's
version goes off in a different direction:

The girl I love is comely, straight and tall,
Down her white neck her auburn tresses fall,
Her dress is neat, her carriage light and free –
Here's a health to that charming maid who-e'er she be.[26]

And the poem continues in this vein: joyous, contented, celebra-
tory. Whatever the original, it is certainly not a version of
the poem Walsh printed, which, despite the verse quoted praising
the girl's beauty, is crowded with melancholy images, of white
flowers breaking through the rotten timber of the lover's coffin,
and so on. Callanan's subtitle 'Súd í síos an caoin ban álain óg'
is the sort of line that might easily have been a kind of trope,
a conventional formula which could be introduced into any folk
poem of the love type. In which case the most we can say is that
Callanan's version and Walsh's poem are related, by their both
making use of a similar, admittedly arresting, formula.

Another clue which might appear promising is the phrase
that concludes each stanza of Callanan's version (except the
last): 'who-e'er she be', which points towards the Irish phrase
'pé in Éirinn Í', in meaning ('whoever in Ireland she be'), and
in aural correspondence. The trouble is that 'pé in Éirinn Í' in
Irish love poetry is a marvellously ubiquitous phrase, another
convenient trope for musically concluding a line, which we find
used in very many poems.

It is possible that Callanan worked from a lost original which
did contain the 'Súd í síos' line and was of the 'pé in Éirinn Í'
group of love songs. But it is less cumbersome and more satisfactory to admit the possibility that there may have been no one
original at all. Where does Callanan's version come from then?
The probable answer is that Callanan became moved to write a
love poem ('The Girl I Love') by listening to, or reading tran-
scripts of, Gaelic love songs of various types, which included a
'pé in Éirinn Í' song and a song containing the 'Súd í síos' line.

It would be natural for various phrases from the *different* songs to strike him as being particularly effective: these he would translate fairly literally, thus laying traps for later scholars. What we have in the end is a wonderful evocation of a certain *sort* of Gaelic love poem: of the contented, carefree type. It is almost as if Callanan created an English species of love song drawing on different Gaelic genera. In the best of his 'translations', (if we can now allow that term to cover this kind of intricate imaginative regrafting) this is what he does. It is almost as if Callanan's versions are themselves variants of Irish folk songs, with the vital qualification that they are in English. What he does is to participate in the process of ramification, extension, and variation all folk-song undergoes, but he does it in English. It is not quite the real thing, but it is close enough to a true 'negative capability', and the self-abnegation that implies, as makes no difference. The Irish songs, their images and rhythms, inhabit his syntax, and are alive. He is much more a transmitter of Gaelic folk tradition than a literary translator.

The 'Dirge of O'Sullivan Bear' is no more and no less than an Irish *caoineadh* in English. There are any number of poems about the death of Morty Oge O'Sullivan. O'Sullivan was a man of considerable influence in Castletownbere and the surrounding area of West Cork in the middle of the eighteenth century. He was an agent for the French and Spanish governments and enlisted local men for service overseas. The Secretary of State came to know of these activities through a local landowner, Puxley, who was shot by O'Sullivan on his way home from church. The military then moved in on O'Sullivan's house but according to Callanan, in a note prefixed to the 'Dirge', a servant named Scully had wet his gunpowder. He then tried to escape over the wall but was shot in the back. After that his body was tied to a boat and dragged through the sea from Castletownbere to Cork, where his head was stuck on a spike on the county jail, and there it remained for several years. Such a career, and such an ignominious death seized the imagination of the people of the area and their stories and songs about him are legion. Even now in Adrigole and in the countryside around Castletownbere stories of his exploits can still be heard, and I have listened to a man sing Gaelic stanzas about Morty Oge O'Sullivan which he himself did not understand.

Once again there are various lines in Callanan's 'Dirge' which

accord with lines in known poems and keens about O'Sullivan,
but there is no single original. Callanan has used material from
various sources to write his own *caoineadh* and he does it very
powerfully indeed. It has all the characteristics of the Irish
caoineadh, the praise of the dead man's physical beauty; the
fierce and violent curse on those who have caused his death, and
on all the circumstances connected with it; the way in which the
poem addresses the dead man, as if a loved one or near-relation
were the speaker (which in the *caoineadh* was always the case);
the style of the poem, its short, packed lines of two stresses, each
one the length of a breath-phrase, and its vivid startling imagery[27]:

> Long may the curse
>   Of his people pursue him;
> Scully that sold him,
>   And soldier that slew him,
> One glimpse of heaven's light
>   May they see never;
> May the hearth-stone of hell
>   Be their best bed for ever!

> Dear head of my darling,
>   How gory and pale,
> These aged eyes saw thee
>   High spiked on the gaol;
> That cheek in the summer sun
>   Ne'er shall grow warm,
> Nor that eye e'er catch light
>   But the flash of the storm.

> A curse, blessed ocean,
>   Is on thy green water,
> From the haven of Cork
>   To Ivera of slaughter,
> Since the billows were dyed
>   With the red wounds of fear,
> Of Muiertach Oge,
>   Our O'Sullivan Bear.[28]

To a reader ignorant of Irish, this 'translation' gives the best impression of what the Irish *caoineadh* feels like, in its swift breathless pace, its passion, and its vivid life.

And so we come at last to Callanan's masterpiece, and one of the best Irish lyrics of the nineteenth century before Yeats, 'The Outlaw of Loch Lene'. It is a mysterious poem, full of what Arnold would have called the 'Celtic note', a shifting magic and a yearning for what lies beyond earthly experience. It is even more obscure in its origins than Callanan's other versions. As has been suggested by Michael Curren,[29] it may have been a by-product of the projected poem 'The Outlaw of Caom-ané', a poem which never got beyond a few lines and various somewhat vague annotations. But Caom-ané (Céim an Fhiaidh) is in West Cork, while Loch Lene is near Killarney in Co. Kerry. Another source, suggested by Dr. Donal O'Sullivan in the *Journal of the Irish Folk Song Society* for 1927 is the poem 'Muna b'é an t-ól', printed in the same journal.[30] Undoubtedly there is some correspondence here, but it does not seem to go very much beyond the fact that Callanan's first line:

O many a day have I made good ale in the glen

could be an almost literal translation of the first line of the third verse of 'Muna b'é an t-ól: '

Is fada mé féin ag déanamh leanna sa ghleann.

For one thing the spirit and atmosphere of the two poems are entirely different: the Irish poem is rakish, frank, even lewd – Dr O'Sullivan leaves an indecent half-line unprinted, preferring asterisks – whereas Callanan's poem is 'high-minded' (a word he used to describe the Irish chiefs in the notes to 'The Outlaw of Caom-ané'), intense, melancholy, and very beautiful.

The process of germination involved here was probably very like that described in connection with the other translations. A line from one poem, attractive for its strange imagery, and emotional ambiguity ('ag déanamh leanna' in Irish can mean both 'making ale' or 'being melancholy', black bile being a property of both melancholy and ale, presumably) merged with lines from others, now lost or untraced. These fragments of actual poems merged with or were whetted into fresh sharpness by impressions derived from other Gaelic love laments, impressions of atmosphere, style of thought, of image sequence and so on. The result is a poem that seems to float like ectoplasm out of the life of Gaelic love poetry itself, transforming itself into English. It transforms itself because Callanan, for all his temperament and jarred personality, here kept personal intrusion to a minimum. He allows the poem its own life in a new language.

'The Outlaw of Loch Lene' is a Gaelic folk song in English, impossible as that may sound. It is what we might call an almost perfect translation, were it not for the irony that there is no original:

O many a day have I made good ale in the glen,
That came not of stream, or malt, like the brewing of men.
My bed was the ground, my roof, the greenwood above,
And the wealth that I sought – one far kind glance from
     my love.

'Tis down by the lake where the wild tree fringes its sides,
The maid of my heart, the fair one of Heaven resides –
I think as at eve she wanders its mazes along,
The birds go to sleep at the sweet wild twist of her song.[31]

The nature of Celtic folk tradition has been well described by the Welsh poet David Jones in his essay, 'The Myth of Arthur':

The folk-tradition of the insular Celts seems to present to the mind a half-aquatic world – it is one of its most fascinating characteristics – it introduces a feeling of transparency and interpenetration of one element with another, of transposition and metamorphosis.[32]

This not only describes 'the folk-tradition of the insular Celts', it also in doing so describes the imaginative quality of 'The Outlaw of Loch Lene': details clarify then shift out of focus just as quickly, the emotion transposes itself through a range of different images, and through this shift it defines itself, just as the quality of a melody may become more apparent through modulation. The rhythms Callanan employs have a flexibility and strength derived from their actual contact with Gaelic poetry, unlike Moore's similar rhythms, somewhat enervated by their own musicality.

The strength and flexibility of Callanan's rhythms give him verbal confidence, allow the interpenetration of one element with another, of actuality and wish, of visible and invisible, of the heard and unheard. The girl who haunts the outlaw's imagination is heard singing so sweetly that the birds go to sleep to the sound, though of course she is not there at all.

But there is another kind of imaginative flexibility in 'The Outlaw of Loch Lene' and throughout his 'translations', that shows in his sympathetic receptivity to Gaelic folk tradition. In these poems Callanan achieves a kind of annulment of his own tortured personality, through creative participation in the process of folk-song transmission, except that in his case transmission involved taking the qualities of certain types of folk song into another language, extending the scope of the genus by allowing it a radically different species. The transmission of a folk song from singer to singer, generation to generation is a process that has much in common with the process of organic nature itself, even to the extent of sometimes exhibiting a tendency towards deformity. In imaginatively participating in this process, Callanan came closest to realising his deep wish for depersonalisation, that wish to be drawn into the natural energies themselves which lies behind 'The Recluse of Inchydoney'.

VII

Nine translations, a handful of failed poems: it is not very much, but at his best Callanan has an intensity, vividness and strength very much his own. Even his failures are interesting ones. They are of a piece with his few successes. Because he wished to bring poetry in English into the second decade of the nineteenth century, and yet, somehow, remain distinctly Irish, he treated his themes in new, experimental ways, ways that involved a going out of the self to encounter the reality of his experience of West Cork.

3

James Clarence Mangan:
'Apples from the Dead Sea Shore'

I

Mangan was something of a Bohemian figure in the Dublin of his time. His haunts were the grimier parts of the city where he took opium and drank heavily. Often he would vanish for days on end, and then re-appear looking more wasted, more blanched than ever. He fascinated his contemporaries in spite of his disreputable appearance and his irregular habits. O'Donoghue's useful and still stimulating biography has many contemporary descriptions of the poet's appearance, with his tall witch-like hat, short black cloak, green spectacles, and prematurely snow white hair. The general picture that emerges is of an Irish urban version of the poet of *Alastor.* His contemporaries liked to feel that his preternaturally blue eyes had seen strange sights, had looked into unfathomable darknesses, and this was an image that Mangan went to some trouble to corroborate, writing articles about 'Ghostcraft' for the *Dublin University Magazine,* and generally displaying an interest on all possible opportunities for the arcane and the deliberately Gothic. Unlike his great contemporary, Baudelaire, however, (with whom he is similar in some respects) he never indulged in blasphemy, never abandoned himself to the latter's exotic Satanism. He seems to have avoided any kind of sensuality completely, and his friend and confessor in later life, Fr Meehan, has written of his purity, saying that he 'never lowered himself to ordinary debaucheries or sensuality of any sort.'[1]

Mangan's Catholicism, compounded with his own tendencies towards nervous self-scrutiny, created a temperament almost incapable of going out to encounter 'the reality of experience' as Stephen Dedalus has it. Some such encounter, some such going out from the prison of the self is fundamental to the imaginative process as we understand it since Coleridge. Mangan's poetry is often a poetry of failure, a sort of prolonged 'Ode to Dejection', because a constant theme is the failure to engage sufficiently with the world outside, and so the failure to find images for his interior condition. It is not for nothing that some of Mangan's most potent images involve freezing, dumbness, inarticulateness, a cluster we have already encountered in Thomas Moore.

J. J. Callanan found an imaginative freedom in the landscape and folk lore of West Cork; Mangan in his *Autobiography* (written towards the end of his life at the request of Fr Meehan) makes it quite clear that natural things have, for him, no power to bless, 'to chasten or subdue' his inner torments. This *Autobiography* is a curious document. Fr Meehan possibly thought that the setting out of the calamities of his own life might sharpen the poet's understanding of them: might perhaps even exorcise some of the things that troubled his mind. In the event the incomplete *Autobiography* is almost entirely phantasmagoric with little regard for fact. What facts there are have become distorted under the pressure of Mangan's capacity for transforming recollection into nightmare.

In Chapter III Mangan gives a vivid account of 'a tottering old fragment of a house' in Chancery Lane into which, he says, his family moved when he was fifteen or thereabouts. This hovel, according to Mangan, consisted of two rooms, one over the other, connected by a ladder. The lower room had no window or door, 'the place of the latter in particular being supplied, not very elegantly by a huge chasm in the bare and broken brick wall.'[2] By this time the family had certainly come down in the world, through (if his son's account be believed) the elder Mangan's fatal generosity to anyone outside the family. Fr Meehan questioned Mangan about the veracity of this description of the house in Chancery Lane, at the time a fairly respectable street, and Mangan replied that he had dreamt it, showing his disregard for the facts. Commenting astutely on this particular passage in the *Autobiography* O'Donoghue quotes from a sketch Mangan wrote of George Petrie, the antiquarian. Mangan is discussing how he arrives at an opinion:

I take a few facts, not caring to be overwhelmed by too many proofs that they are facts; with them I mix up a dish of the marvellous – perhaps an old wife's tale – perhaps a half-remembered dream or mesmeric experience of my own – and the business is done.[3]

So much for the facts. In this Mangan could not be further removed from his contemporary Samuel Ferguson, whose respect for facts, 'set down in strict not dry detail'[4] gives his verse solidity, substance, and at times also, stolidity and heaviness. For Mangan the factual, the quotidian, the flash of light on leaves, the here and now, were always that which he wished to fly from, because an adjustment to the contour and texture of what goes on in front of the eye involves an acceptance of one's own presence in time, an acceptance of the self. Mangan was always in flight from the self, wishing to go from the 'here' to the 'there', as M. Chuto has perceptively argued.[5] The 'there' could be anywhere, Weimar, medieval Baghdad, or bardic Ireland, anywhere as long as it temporarily gave him the illusion of release from his tortured imaginings and his wracked body.

At one time, he tells us, in order to quieten himself he tried long walks in the suburbs, but a medical friend, a Mr Graham of Thomas Street, advised him against these on the grounds that 'while your limbs walked one way your mind walked the other'. Graham suggested he try 'the foil or the racket' on the grounds that with these more absorbing exercises he might stand a better chance of forgetting himself. For a time, at least, they worked, and he felt his energies renewed.

Long walks failed to restore his spirits because natural things failed to interest him. He had no 'negative capability', his mind had no facility for moving freely outwards, mixing with, engaging with, the otherness of the life around it. His difficulty was not so much the 'irritable striving after fact and reason' that Keats saw as being opposed to negative capability, but a predominating self-consciousness, 'an impatience of life and its commonplace pursuits'. This he called his 'grand moral malady'.[6] He had no joy in things, in their essential qualities. He was incapable of the joy Coleridge expresses in contemplating the little cone of sand revolving at the bottom of a clear spring in the 'Inscription for a Fountain on a Heath':

> Long may the spring,
> Quietly as a sleeping infant's breath,
> Send up cold waters to the traveller
> With soft and even pulse! Nor ever cease
> Yon tiny cone of sand its soundless dance,
> Which at the bottom, like a Fairy's Page,
> As merry and no taller, dances still,
> Nor wrinkles the smooth surface of the Fount.[7]

This joy, this stillness, this outgoing of the mind is something we do not find in Mangan; it is something of which he was temperamentally incapable. At the end of the incomplete *Autobiography* there is a conversation between Mangan and an unnamed stranger. Mangan has wandered into the countryside near Rathfarnham and is lying, as he puts it, 'on a long knoll of grass by a stream-side'. It is a June evening and he is reading, typically, Pascal's *Les Pensées*. The stranger, after the opening exchange, remarks to Mangan that what he is reading 'is a very unhealthy work'. Mangan's reply is that 'everything in this world is unhealthy'.

> 'The stranger smiled. 'And yet', said he, 'you feel pleasure, I am sure, in the contemplation of this beautiful scenery; and you admire the glory of the setting sun'.
> 'I have pleasure in nothing, and I admire nothing', answered I. 'I hate scenery and suns. I see nothing in Creation but what is fallen and ruined'.[8]

This is a clumsy statement of a feeling central to Romanticism, that the world is fallen, innocence lost, that nature herself, instead of being a tranquillizing thing, is an enemy, a distraction, a complexity that impedes the flight of the spirit to its true peace. Coleridge knew this mood very well, and indeed it forms the crux of 'The Ancient Mariner'. But the strength of that poem, and what makes Coleridge a greater poet than Mangan, is that 'The Ancient Mariner' moves through this mood of disassociation, of being estranged from natural things, to a blessing of them that takes place 'unaware'. The mariner blesses the water-snakes:

> A spring of love gushed from my heart,
> And I blessed them unaware:

Sure my kind saint took pity on me
And I blessed them unaware.[9]

For all Mangan's scrupulous Catholicism (and perhaps because
of it) such blessing was rarely a visitant. His self-absorption was
so acute, his personality so hopelessly ruined by an anguished
personal history that the blessing of natural things, and the joyous
acceptance of them for what they are was not something about
which he could write. Instead, external reality became a daily
horror, a phantasmagoria to be gone through. The solicitor's
office he worked in for a time, became 'a cavern with serpents
and scorpions and all hideous and monstrous things, which writhed
and hissed around me, and discharged their slime and venom over
my person'.[10]

He is, of course, enjoying himself hugely in the above passage,
perhaps even indulging in a fit of pique against his erstwhile office
companions, but there is in it an intolerance of the actual, of the
here and now, and a sense that external things can even be
malevolent, that runs through all Mangan's writings.

An intolerance of what happens, of the actual, involves a basic
intolerance of the present tense, of the personality's fluid structure moving through time. 'Hold to the now, the here', (Stephen
Dedalus says in defiance of what he understands of George
Russell's mysticism in *Ulysses*) 'through which all future plunges
to the past'. In Mangan the here and now is felt to be oppressive,
a weight and a heaviness on his mind, to be escaped from, either
through fantasy, alcohol, or opium, or by the attempt at imagining the personality to be different from what it is. The latter is
the process we see most often at work in the poetry; it is why
Mangan expends so much poetic energy on translation, or pretended translation. His fantasy we often see at work in the prose
and one process involves the other. We have seen how in the
Autobiography, fantasy displaces historical fact, so that it is only
of use in charting the character of the poet's mind rather than in
providing the biographer with verifiable information. In the *Autobiography,* however, Mangan is ostensibly dealing with his own
distant past, (though it is a past very much distorted by the
pressure of how he felt at the moment of writing); in a prose
piece published in *The Comet* for 20 and 27 January 1833 called
'An Extraordinary Adventure in the Shades' he addresses himself
to a recent occurrence and recounts it in a first person narrative

which unfolds the 'extraordinary adventure' for the reader as it happens.

In fact nothing very much happens at all save that Mangan gets drunk. He opens the article with a mysterious paragraph which he calls 'exclusively personal' to himself, and in which he vows to abandon the entanglements of 'Fancy' for the beaten path of 'Reason', the 'burning imagery of the past for the frozen realities of the present and the future'. What follows in the article is an experiment with reality, an attempt to establish some relationship between subject and object. It is an attempt that fails hopelessly, the actual becomes more and more intangible in an increasingly articulate confused eloquence.

'The Shades', apparently, was a tavern in College Green, where Mangan was to meet an acquaintance at six thirty on the evening of 1 April 1832. The acquaintance fails to turn up and Mangan describes himself becoming absorbed with a figure seated at an opposite table reading a newspaper. Presently, as he drinks more port, the absorption becomes fascination, and the conviction grows on Mangan that he must have known this stranger in a previous reincarnation, or, as he puts it, they must have been 'fraternized members of the aboriginal Tuzenbund'. He feels linked to him through an 'electrical chain' that runs dimly back to 'the measureless deep of primary creation, the unknown, the unimaginably infinite. There is nothing incredible if we believe life to be a reality; for, to a psychologist the very consciousness that he exists at all is a mystery unfathomable to this world'.[11] If identity is such a mystery, how can anything be certain or fixed, least of all identity itself. This growing sense of the unreality of things has a marked effect on Mangan's observation of the stranger. Even his minutest actions, such as the shifting of his hat on his head become events of momentous importance. It is almost as if we are, for a moment, transported into the world of the 'Ithaca' episode in *Ulysses:*

The unknown had altered the position of his hat. What was the inference spontaneously deducible from the occurrence of such a circumstance? Firstly that anterior to the motion which preceded the change, the unknown had conceived that his hat did not properly sit on his head; secondly that he must be gifted with the organ of order in a high degree.

The difference between this and Joyce's catechetical interrogations in the 'Ithaca' episode is that Joyce's minutiae are a celebration of the multiplicity of things, and the variety of angles from which they can be looked at; here the complexity of external things, their mysteriousness, is a kind of threat to the existence of the psyche itself.

Mangan eventually concludes, purely on the basis of subjective impression, that the man before him must be Dr Roland Bowring, a famous translator of the day and someone to whom he would like to introduce himself. But how can this be done? How can one simply go over and speak to someone, how can mystery speak to mystery? Eventually, after further interior monologue, Mangan decides that the only possible way to approach the stranger is by adopting 'mannerism'. 'Mannerism' he says, 'is the genuine ore, the ingot itself. Every other thing is jelly and soapsuds. You shall tramp the earth in vain for a more pitiable object than a man with genius, with nothing else to back it with. Destitute of Mannerism we are walking humbugs.'

In other words it is impossible to present oneself publicly as oneself; the affectation of some role, some manner, is the only means by which the mysteries that are separate identities can come into contact. Here we have a primitive version of Yeats's theories of the mask, but Mangan's affectation lacks the heroism and power of Yeats's idea that the poet must adopt the mask of that which is most unlike himself, most challenging to his inherited tendencies. For Mangan the mask, or mannerism, is a carapace, and a frail one at that.

In the event Mangan never actually speaks to the man he imagines to be Bowring; in fact he changes his mind, and decides he is Maugraby, an 'oriental necromancer'. As Mangan continues to drink he imagines Maugraby's nose swelling, and, in Ionesco fashion, extending itself through College Green down Grafton Street. The next morning Dr Stokes tells him it was Joseph L'Estrange ('Brasspen') of *The Comet,* the newspaper for which the sketch was written, whom Mangan probably knew.

The *Autobiography* and the 'Extraordinary Adventure' have been looked at because they show Mangan's unease with external reality, his inability to lose himself in the contemplation and poetic celebration of the otherness of things and people. At root it is an unease with the self, with the process of his own personality evolving, changing, second by second. This goes much of the way towards accounting for the kind of poetry he wrote.

II

A good deal of Mangan's poetry is translation of one kind or another. With him it sometimes becomes a kind of literary impersonation, where he passes off what is in fact an entirely original poem (such as the well-known 'Twenty Golden Years Ago') as the translated composition of some minor or (as in this case), non-existent German or Persian poet. It is clear that for him translation was not the accurate and faithful transmission into another language of something worth linguistically re-creating for its own sake. It was a way of making money; he was cashing in on the taste for German and Oriental poetry created by Carlyle and by the setting and atmosphere of Byron's *The Corsair* and Moore's *Lallah Rookh.* But there was more to it than that. Translation was a convenient mode of composition because it allowed him a freedom he found it difficult to realize *in propria persona.* Jacques Chuto, in an essay on Mangan's translations from the German, tellingly quotes two passages from an article on himself that the poet wrote shortly before his death for *The Irishman,* a newspaper founded after the suppression of the *Nation.* This article by Mangan on himself is written in the third person, and signed E.W., perhaps alluding to the Cork poet and translator Edward Walsh:

It is a strange fault, no doubt, and one that I cannot under-stand, that Mangan should entertain a deep diffidence of his own capacity to amuse or attract others by anything emanating from himself. But it is the fact. I do not comprehend it, but he has mentioned it to me times without number. People have called him a singular man but he is rather a plural one – a Proteus, as the *Dublin Review* designates him. I confess that I cannot make him out; and I incline strongly to suspect that there must be a somewhat, that is dark and troubled, in his mind – perhaps a something very sore and very heavy on his conscience.

M. Chuto goes on to suggest that translation for Mangan was a means of depersonalizing himself, that he tried 'to drown his singularity in literary plurality'.[12] If the self is an incomprehensible mystery, so fearfully unknown and unknowable that the creative energies are gripped in a paralysis of fear and silence, then the poet is perched on the edge of an abyss, an abyss of confusion, frustration, but worst of all, inarticulacy, dumbness. The tongue is stuck to the roof of the mouth by a nameless incomprehensible terror, 'something very sore and very heavy'. Dumbness, paralysis, the abyss, these are images we encounter continually in those few personal poems he wrote in his own voice, the frozen brain and cloven tongue of 'Siberia', the 'pit abysmal' of the significantly titled 'The Nameless One'. Translation was a means of circumventing the abyss, of breaking the silence of creative paralysis through adopting the mask of a Rückert or a Freiligrath, a Meseehi or an Eochaidh Ó Heodhussa. Translation is a species of 'Mannerism', a means of presenting himself to the world, seeing that it is all but impossible to present himself as himself. The world is like the stranger in the 'Shades' tavern, it keeps on shifting and changing, appearing to be natural then transforming itself into grotesque and terrifying shapes. To encounter such a Proteus, according to Mangan's way of thinking, you have to be a Proteus yourself, you have to be 'plural', rather than 'singular'. Furthermore, his own personality, his feeling of what it was to be him, was so distasteful that translation offered a means of release. What natural things were for Keats, other poets (mostly German and Irish) were for Mangan.

Mangan did not have the imaginative freedom, the necessary joy, to surrender himself totally to the poets he translated in the way Keats surrendered himself to the clarity of natural things; had he been able to do so he would have been a great translator. As it is he *uses* those poets in order to express himself because they are different to him. He never submits to them, or co-operates with them in the way a true translator will do; he is like what Dryden would call the 'imitator', who uses the original as the 'groundwork', which he 'runs division on' as he pleases.[13] Instead of giving us versions of Rückert, Rückert, in the rehandling, becomes a version of Mangan. Or, as Chuto has put it: 'we believe that we are reading Wetzel translated by Mangan, whereas we are actually reading Mangan disguised as Wetzel'.[14] In other words he never truly gets away from himself, despite the illusion translation gave him of doing so. But the illusion was necessary. It freed him from the creative paralysis to which his self-disgust made him prone, but it also offered a means of expressing an interest in literary traditions other than the English one, which was so flourishing and so uncomfortably close as well.

We know that in the 1840s Mangan explicitly identified himself with the nationalist cause, but even in the early 'thirties he was writing for the *Comet,* a paper founded in support of the anti-tithe campaign, and so, radical, reformist, a kind of precursor to the *Nation.* For an Irish poet writing in English, yet wishing to preserve a sense of separateness from the traditions of that language, translations from other languages were more than simply literary exercises. They were a way of keeping one's distance from the great and perhaps overwhelming richness of English Romantic tradition. The irony was, of course, that that tradition itself enshrined a strong radical temper, and one well disposed to the cause of Irish nationalism. We know that Mangan read Byron, and his biographer tells us that he would sometimes recite long passages from him. He also knew Coleridge, and presumably Wordsworth, and he would almost certainly have read some Shelley, yet their intellectual toughness, their seriousness, seems to have left him unaffected. The Byron he admired was not the essentially compassionate poet of *Don Juan* but the image of him that had become graven in the popular mind. A closer reading of Coleridge would have helped Mangan in dealing with and comprehending those destructive moods Coleridge himself knew so well. But, on the whole, Mangan wished to keep his distance from a tradition so close and so intellectually extensive. When he was drawn to that tradition he was attracted by its more exotic, more sentimental side. We find him constantly referring to William Godwin's *St. Leon,* the hero of which has the elixir of life, and he also admired Beckford's *Vathek,* predictably enough.

III

When Mangan began contributing his *Anthologia Germanica* to the *Dublin University Magazine* in 1835, he opened the first two numbers with fairly extensive selections from Schiller. For Schiller, Mangan has nothing but praise. He admires his rooted-

ness in himself, his 'individuality', setting it against what he
describes as the 'Protean, Voltairean faculty of metamorphosis and
self-multiplication possessed by Goethe', a description which could
almost be a self-description.[15] In praising Schiller's lyrics he says
that their 'great hallowing charm is the captivating, rather than
faithful resemblance, they bear with the realities they profess to
be images of'. It is difficult to know what Mangan means by this,
but he seems to be implying that Schiller could at one and the
same time both personalize reality, draw it into himself, and yet
not become so lost in the labyrinth of the self that all contact
with the 'shapes and sounds' of natural things was severed. One
of Mangan's finest poems, and also one of his most faithful translations is his version of Schiller's 'Die Ideale'. The poem opens in
dejection, the imaginative power is spent, and cannot arrest the
flow of life:

> Can nought avail to curb thine onward motion?
> In vain! The river of my years is flowing
> And soon shall mingle with the eternal ocean.

At this stage he is sunk within himself, no light can break
through:

> Extinguished in dead darkness lies the sun
> That lighted up my shivered world of wonder . . .

The sensitivity of the word 'shivered' in the above, its fragility,
shows that not only is Mangan translating well, he is also rendering a state he himself knows a good deal about, the state of
imaginative sterility. For him this means being oppressed by the
barbaric unknowableness of the here and now. He finds this sentiment in Schiller's second stanza and finds magnificent English
for it:

> Gone, gone for ever is the fine belief
> The all-too-generous trust in the Ideal;
> All my Divinities have died of grief,
> And left me wedded to the Rude and Real.

However, his Schiller translations were exceptions; not for long
was he content to wear what Rudi Holzapfel has called the 'lyric

straitjacket' of fidelity.[16] He felt much freer with the minor German poets of the eighteenth and nineteenth centuries; they were less well known for one thing, and so translating them allowed him the opportunity of showing off his acquaintance with the more unfamiliar nooks and crannies of modern German writing. Furthermore, he felt a kinship with the sentimentalist poets of the late eighteenth century, such as Friedrich Klopstock, who indulged their moods and states of mind in a luxuriant, passive manner. Melancholy world-weariness is the favourite attitude that this poetry likes to strike. He was also drawn to the poets of the *Stürm und Drang*. They have a fiercer more active attitude to things, and their poetry, while often indulgent, has an energy and restlessness about it that appealed to one side of Mangan's character.

Mangan was temperamentally close to these two strains in near contemporary German poetry. Writing to Goethe in 1797 Schiller is disdainful of those poets who fail to control their lives and their feelings; 'these Schmids, Richters and Hölderlins' allowed themselves to become *überspannt* (unnaturally strained), locked into their own tensions, thereby cutting themselves off from the healing forces of nature, disabling themselves for the pursuits of normal life.[17] The word *überspannt* applies with uncanny accuracy to Mangan's case. In the essay 'On Simple and Sentimental Poetry' Schiller discusses the dangers to which the sentimental, indulgent, idealist poet lays himself open. He is inclined to attempt too much, to overstrain himself, and so become the victim of dream, retiring more and more from the real into a more and more desperate subjectivity. This, Schiller says, can lead eventually to the annihilation of character entirely, the fall into the abyss of madness. Schiller is here to some extent exorcising fears which beset himself – 'one feels', as Alan Menhennet writes, that he had 'looked into this pit' – but he is also thinking of the ruined lives and wasted talents of some of his contemporaries, such as Gottfried Bürger and Jacob Lenz.[18] Like them, Mangan, some forty years later, living in Dublin (a city which in its semi-cultured respectability was very like the German cities where those poets to whom he was drawn passed their frequently frustrated lives), was also a victim of excessive subjectivity. The urban life around him was dead to his eyes, the closest he got to the country was suburbia; what was most real to him was his own over-scrutinised and over-intense inner life.

It is not surprising then to find that when Mangan writes about the sentimentalists and *Stürmer und Dranger* he likes to adopt a superior and condescending attitude towards them, as if they have pitiably come unstuck in difficulties which he has overcome. His attitude towards them is Schillerian, one to which he is totally unentitled. 'Deutschland's bardlings' he calls them in 'Twenty Golden Years Ago', an original poem which he fathered on a non-existent German poet whom he called 'Selber' (himself):

> Yet may Deutschland's bardlings flourish long!
> Me, I tweak no beak among them; – hawks
> Must not pounce on hawks: besides, in song
> I could once beat all of them by chalks.
> Though you find me as I near my goal,
> Sentimentalizing like Rousseau,
> O! I had a grand Byronian soul
> Twenty golden years ago.[19]

In the *Dublin University Magazine* for October 1835, in a preface to his versions of the poems of Matthison and Salis, Mangan confidently enunciates the prevailing defect of German poetry, that it is 'too adventurous an attempt to assimilate the creations of the ideal with the forms of the actual world'. He goes on, in terms that seem to echo Schiller's, to expatiate on the dangers of too radical a severance between actuality and the world of the imagination. The imagination, if not 'sentinelled with Jealous vigilance by Reason and Precedent', has an all too fateful tendency to lose itself 'in an abyss'. He continues:

It would appear that there lies somewhere in the geography of the human soul a *terra incognita,* which hardy speculators have been in all ages ambitious to penetrate. The possible existence of this Land of Shadow we are not prepared to deny; but the hazards of a voyage to explore it, to establish its boundaries and analyse its mysteries, come to us, we confess, unrecommended by any rational prospect of a counterbalancing remuneration. Not so, however, have thought the German metaphysicians and poets.[20]

They have sought out the depths and many of them have 'perished'. We can see that in theory at least Mangan is lining himself up on the side of Schiller, and of classical restraint. Nevertheless most of his German translations are from those very poets who cultivate emotionalism and sentimentality. Mangan himself was entirely without any touch of Schiller's restraint. He revels in the self-indulgence of Klopstock's 'To Ebert', where the German poet imagines himself the sole survivor of all his friends. He is drawn to the way in which Justinus Kerner evokes a *Stimmung* (mood, atmosphere) of melancholy weariness despite the fact that he tries to make fun of him: 'Kerner', he says, 'does little else than weep, listen to birds and brooks, hide himself in hedges, and apostrophise the zodiac'.[21]

In the *Anthologia Germanica – No. VII* in the *Dublin University Magazine* for August 1836 Mangan has a translation from Ludwig Tieck, to which he gives the title 'Life is the Desert and the Solitude'. It is a clear and direct statement of the German *Sehnsucht,* the yearning to be out of the process of time, and to find some paradisal sweetness:

> Whence this fever?
> Whence this burning
> Love and Longing?
> Ah! for ever,
> Ever turning
> Ever thronging
> Tow'rds the Distance,
> Roams each fonder
> Yearning yonder,
> There where wander
> Golden stars in blest existence . . .

For a moment the 'undeveloped Land' where these stars wander, where 'fair forms' flit through 'green glades', seems to draw closer. He asks a spirit to 'rive' his chain, but 'the vision fades' and he wakes once more to weeping:

> Hence this fever;
> Hence this burning
> Love and Longing.[22]

Despite the fact that in 1837 he wrote an article on Tieck for the same magazine, in which he affects to mock at his vagueness and emotionalism, calling him a 'man-milliner to the Muses', never-

the less the original of 'Life is the Desert and the Solitude' provoked in Mangan a version which states unequivocally one of his
central pre-occupations, the desire to be out of time, away from
the personality, which, in its ever-changingness, is subject at all
times to unpredictable surges from the unconscious, and so is
essentially unknowable. Translation, then, from a poet whom he
later takes the trouble to mock, calling him a 'Jackpudding under
the mask of a Howling Dervish' is a way of having his cake and
eating it.[23]

The centrality of the Tieck translation is testified to by the fact
that Mangan had in July 1833 contributed to the *Comet* an
original poem which had exactly the same title.[24] This poem, like
the later translation, is about the anguish of life, save that here
the paradise is not some other 'undeveloped Land' outside of the
poet's time, as it is in the translation; it is the summer that lies
before his eyes but from which he is hopelessly cut off:

> I behold around
> Enough of summer's power to mould
> The breast not altogether bound
> By grief to thoughts whose uncontrolled
> Fervour leaves feeling dumb and human utterance cold.[25]

But he *is* 'bound', of course:

> Yet I am far – oh! far from feeling
> The life, the thrilling glow, the power
> Which have their dwelling in the healing
> And holy influence of the hour . . .

External things and their beauty only mock at him, wound him
with the inaccessibility of their 'voiceless beauty':

> And all that glances on my vision,
> Inanimate or breathing, rife
> With voiceless beauty, half Elysian,
> Of youthful and exuberant life,
> Serves but to nurse the sleepless strife
> Within – arousing the keen thought,
> Quick-born, which stabbeth like a knife,
> And wakes anticipations fraught
> With heaviest hues of gloom from memory's pictures wrought.

When this state is reached what is needed is a kind of casting out of the inner dark, an exorcism, and the imagination must actively assert itself, and not just lie a-bleeding, bewailing its lot. To cast out the inner dark it is necessary to name it, and this is precisely what Mangan cannot do. He cannot dramatize his conflict, and so make poetry out of it. Out of the quarrel with ourselves, Yeats was later to say, we make poetry. But the quarrel cannot be with some amorphous darkness, with a mood. Mangan's poem moves into futile questionings which remain unanswered, and then, eventually, into the quicksands of self-pity:

> What slakeless strife is still consuming
> This martyred heart from day to day?
> Lies not the bower where love was blooming
> Time-trampled into long decay?

Had he dreamed when younger that time would 'paralyse and bow' him so, then he should have killed himself. As it is, anything he attempts is spoiled by a 'something sore and heavy' as he calls it elsewhere. At the end of the poem he finds a weak image for it, 'A cankering worm whose work is slow', which in its obviousness is totally inadequate for the weight of emotional pressure it has to bear. This poem appeared in 1833; three years later in the translation to which he gave the same title he found another name for the dark inside: he called it Ludwig Tieck, and subsequently laughed it off in the essay on Tieck a year after that again. But the 1833 poem did not leave him; he published it again in the *Dublin University Magazine* for 1839 under the title 'Stanzas Which Ought Not to Have Been Written in Midsummer'.

Like Tieck, Ferdinand Freiligrath was a poet who was writing and publishing during Mangan's own lifetime. Both of them outlived their Irish translator. Freiligrath's intense exoticism attracted Mangan. He wrote of lions in African deserts, the blue volcanic fires of Iceland, of the King of the Congo with his hundred wives. In 'My Themes' Freiligrath accounts for his exoticism, and his explanation (as translated by Mangan) is very illuminating about Mangan himself, and about his taste for the exotic.

In the poem there are unnamed interlocutors who ask the poet, Freiligrath/Mangan, why he wanders 'ever thus in prolix rhymes/ Through snows and stony wastes', while they come toiling after.

They urge him to get out of his 'willow zumbul' on his imaginary camel and 'study Mankind', but chiefly to look into his own 'bosom,' and take his marvels from there. They wish him to reveal all his secrets, to give up his vital energies:

> 'Unlock the life-gates of the flood
> That rushes through thy veins! Like Vultures, we delight
> To glut our appetites with blood'.[26]

The poet, however, will not take their barbaric advice:

> Those far arctic tracts of ice,
> Those wildernesses
>   Of wavy sands,
> Are the only home I have. They must suffice
> For one whose lonely hearth no smiling Peri blesses.

But he is not to be pitied; the imaginative wildernesses he exults in are not as stark as the desert within, a desert he would give himself up to were he to take the advice of the interlocutors:

> Pity me not. Oh, no!
> The heart laid waste by Grief or Scorn,
>   Which only knoweth
>   Its own deep woe,
> Is the only desert. *There* no spring is born
> Amid the sands – in *that* no shady Palm-tree groweth.

So the rich crimsons and blues of Arabia, the sultriness of the tropics, the vast bleakness of Iceland, are an imaginative escape for Freiligrath, and for Mangan too through translation.

A discussion of Mangan's versions of Freiligrath, where the strange hues of imagined countries are a distraction from the pressures of the self, leads naturally to a brief consideration of Mangan's most exotic compositions, his 'Oriental Versions and Perversions', as O'Donoghue titled them in his 1903 selection.

As Jacques Chuto has pointed out, Mangan's exoticism has a stress on the 'exo' element in that word; for him it was a way out of the here and now into an imagined 'There', where 'the un-reached Paradise of our despair' may be at last attainable.[27] It is an attempt at capturing the timeless, the paradisal, the impossible

beauty Yeats would later call antithetical, in that it is the
opposite of all that troubles, confuses and hampers the spirit in
daily life.

But nowhere in Mangan is the timeless moment of apprehended
beauty presented with such strange and vivid completeness as
in Yeats's *The Only Jealousy of Emer* or in the last section of
'Meditations in Time of Civil War'. For Yeats the moment of
purity only comes after great struggle and toil, and the struggle is
with the complexity of daily life and the self's relationship to it.
Mangan's Oriental paradise attempts to be a way out of this, an
avoidance of the struggle. So that the beauty he achieves has
little veracity or conviction because it arises out of no real
encounter with or victory over the daily self, but out of little
more than the wish for life to be other than it is. It is a muffled
beauty, sustained by the adroit manipulation of vowel sounds and
refrains, an adroitness owing a good deal to Moore's presentation
of mood through word music in the *Irish Melodies:*

> Morning is blushing; the gay nightingales
> Warble their exquisite songs in the vales;
> Spring, like a spirit, floats everywhere,
> Shaking sweet spice-flowers loose from her hair,
> Murmurs half-musical sounds from the stream,
> Breathes in the valley and shines in the beam.
> In, in at the portals that Youth encloses,
> It hastes, it wastes, the Time of the Roses! [28]

Here too, as in most of the *Melodies,* there is a great overarching
sadness, a sense of grief unuttered, or so generalized (as in the last
two lines above) that it undergoes the dilution of cliché. If we try
to dispel the verbal inattention induced by the torpor of the heavy
rhythms, we see that the paradise the languourous words attempt
to conjure is itself dissolving even as it is being invoked. The
'Time of the Roses', which is supposed to be outside time as we
experience it, is, it turns out, subject to decay. So there is a tension in the poem, between the timelessness for which the poem
strives, and the evanescence insisted on in the last line of each
stanza throughout, but it is a tension muffled by verbal conjuring.
The music of words for their own sake, the delight in their
rhythm and movement is a feature of all Romantic poetry, but in
Irish poetry of the nineteenth century it often proved a distrac-

tion, and what should be a part of an overall effect occupied too central a position. This is why Ferguson, with his rough, if sometimes awkward clarity, his casualness with regard to metrics as long as he got the facts straight, is such a welcome irruption in Anglo-Irish poetry. His example was (or could have been, had it been heeded more carefully) a corrective to that of Moore.

It would, however, be an injustice to Mangan to over-estimate the influence of Moore, although we can see it operating quite clearly in 'The Time of the Roses', and in 'The Time of the Barmicides', another of his Oriental pieces. Self-intoxicated word music suited the mood of suspended amimation, of beautiful stasis, these poems strive towards. But not all of Mangan's Oriental pieces try to evoke this unattainable paradise, where can be found

> the young lilies, their scymitar-petals
> Glancing like silver 'mid earthier metals.

The *Literae Orientales* (which he called his selections of translated Eastern verse) began like this, as an attempt at 'realizing the Unreal'.[29] It was, in other words, yet another attempt at self-forgetting, at abandoning the here and now of his anguished and harassed life in Dublin. It did not take too long, however, before he 'peopled his imaginary East with his own obsessions'.[30] Even in 'The Time of the Roses' there is a consciousness that that 'Time' is hasting away, but in 'The Howling Song of Al-Mohara' there is a contrast between the beauty of the world which Al-Mohara inhabits, and his state of mind. The richness around him, the sweet odour of the musk roses in his Egyptian vases, are a torment to a mind riddled with guilt. Something 'sore and heavy' lies on Al-Mohara's conscience, as it did on Mangan's:

> The silks that swathe my hall deewan
>   Are damascened with moons of gold;
>   Allah, Allah hu!
> Musk-roses from my Gulistan (garden)
>   Fill vases of Egyptian mould;
>   Allah, Allah hu!
> The Koran's treasures lie unrolled
> Near where my radiant night-lamp burns;
> Around me rows of silver urns

> Perfume the air with odours old;
>   Allah, Allah hu!
> But what avail these luxuries?
> The blood of him I slew
> Burns red on all – I cry therefore,
> All night long, on my knees,
>   Evermore,
>   Allah, Allah hu! [31]

The darkness inside darkens all the brightness of the world out-side; in the same way Mangan's Eastern imaginings are darkened by the shadow he casts himself. There is no anaesthesia of the self's forebodings.

Mangan's versions from the German and from the Oriental allowed him a means of circumventing the abyss of his own mind, with its fears, guilts and hesitancies. Essentially, translation was a means of fleeing the quarrel with the self, a way out of the confrontation with his own complexity (and absurdity) he would have to face for his poetry to have conviction. As it is, there is a sense of the peripheral about much that he wrote, sometimes maddeningly so, when he is being impishly inane in a schoolboyish way. He had the disabilities of a great poet, but did not have the imaginative drive to make coherence out of his inner chaos.

He was further disabled by the fact that Irish poetry in the nineteenth century lacked a tradition in English, a tradition that would be recognisably different from the English poetry of the day. What was needed was poetry that would impinge upon areas of feeling and thought that seemed especially Irish, or at least different from those areas of thought and feeling that English poetry expressed. For better or for worse, Irish poetry would have to be national before it became anything else. Mangan found German poetry of the eighteenth century immensely attractive because it was secure in its own tradition and it was far from English. Furthermore, German poetry of this period was intensely nationalist in feeling and tone, in ways that Irish writers and readers (judging from the popularity of Mangan's translations in their day), found irresistible.

There were reasons, then, other than purely psychological ones, why so much of Mangan's work was in translation. He wanted to make his poetry different, partly through a delight in oddity for its own sake, but also because he wished to set himself apart from

contemporary English writing. It is for this reason that his
versions of Irish poems are so important; here was material that
was as strange and as exotic as any 'apples from the Dead Sea
shore' (Freiligrath, 'My Themes'), but which was Irish, was, in
some sense or other, his, by right of inheritance. The surging
waves of energy and excitement we find in these poems are an
index of how much they meant to him. Because these poems were
Irish, and so somehow his, he may have felt that through them
he would escape from himself into knowledge of himself, as part
of some kind of national being.

IV

As early as 1832 Mangan had been interested in Irish literature.
In the *Dublin Penny Journal* for 15 September of that year he
says he intends to enter 'the MINE of ancient Irish literature, and
bring out from the obscurity of oblivion those treasures of
intellect and genius and antiquarian curiosity there to be found'.
Here he is echoing the claims made for Irish writing and Irish
culture generally by such as Joseph Cooper Walker, Charlotte
Brooke, Theophilus O'Flanagan (secretary to the Gaelic Society
of 1808) and more recently by James Hardiman in his *Irish
Minstrelsy* of 1831. Indeed by now it had become something of a
literary cliche to make these kinds of assertions about the 'hidden
treasures' of Gaelic culture, assertions that were bolstered by the
immense popularity of the *Irish Melodies*.

Irishmen continued to feel that they were the product of a
significant and ancient culture, and this was both consolation and
torment to them – if they thought that way they were invariably
English speaking, and so cut off from the very tradition of which
they liked to feel proud. Those who spoke Irish did not have the
luxury of such cultural consolations; their concerns were more
immediate and practical, earning a living and staying alive. In
the 1830s, not only did Irish literature lack adequate translators;
it lacked, first and foremost, adequate scholars. Up to now there
had been the admirable efforts of Charlotte Brooke in the late
eighties of the previous century; there had also been others, the
scholars of the Gaelic Society, for example, but the real beginning of Irish studies on a proper scholarly basis did not come

until the 1830s. Certain names stand out here; that of George Petrie, antiquarian and Gaelic scholar, John O'Donovan, future editor of *The Annals of the Four Masters,* and his brother-in-law, Eugene O'Curry, future author of the *Manuscript Materials of Irish History.* O'Donovan, O'Curry and Mangan, along with other scholars and antiquarians all contributed to the *Dublin Penny Journal,* founded by Petrie and Caesar Otway in 1832 with the express purpose of awakening the interest of the Irish public in its own past. It was Mangan's special fortune that he came to know these men, that their labours in attempting to clarify little patches of the Gaelic past stimulated Mangan's incandescent imagination into a version of that past all his own.

Mangan's contact with the Gaelic scholars was strengthened when in 1838, Petrie found Mangan a job on the Ordnance Survey team. In 1824 an English Parliamentary Committee had recommended that all Ireland be surveyed and remapped. Lieut. Thomas Larcom was put in charge of the project, and he employed Petrie to direct those working on the topographical material. Their office was at Petrie's own house, 21 Great Charles Street. There, from 1838 to 1841, Mangan was in frequent, sometimes daily contact with O'Curry, O'Donovan, Petrie, Samuel Ferguson, and W. F. Wakeman. O'Donovan, O'Curry, and W. F. Wakeman would wander the countryside, a county at a time, going from townland to townland, collecting as much topographical information as possible, along with other information as well. It was the duty of the Dublin office to collate this field-work and to relate it to historical sources and manuscripts to hand. It was work involving close scrutiny and comparison of maps and texts, and it was work which would make self-evident the close inter-relationship between the names of places in rural Ireland of the time and its ancient past, or pasts. It was this sense, that past and present should be inseparable in Ireland (as in any civilised country), that the English speaking part of the population should be made aware of the extent and depth of its roots in the past, that provoked the founding of the *Irish Penny Journal* in 1840, as it had provoked the founding of the *Dublin Penny Journal* in the early 'thirties. Petrie was editor of both these journals, and his intention was to raise national consciousness, not in any militant way (although his activities cannot be separated from the rising nationalism of the 'thirties), but in a way that would strengthen and give substance to an Irishman's sense of what it was to be Irish and so enable him more fully to be himself. Samuel Ferguson makes all this quite clear in a remarkable article he wrote on the *Dublin Penny Journal* in the *Dublin University Magazine* for January 1840.

Mangan, stimulated by his contact with Irish scholarship in the Ordnance Survey office in Petrie's house, and perhaps working under commission from Petrie himself, contributed four translations of Irish poetry to the *Irish Penny Journal*. At this stage Mangan almost certainly knew no Irish. He worked from literal versions supplied by Eugene O'Curry. His English reworkings of O'Curry's versions have a vigour and intensity, a sense of rhythmic stability and flourish that we find in little else by Mangan, save his own later translations from the Irish and one or two original poems. Hesitancy has gone; there is a stride and confidence, as in the tough, forceful rhythm of 'The Woman of Three Cows':

> O woman of Three Cows, *agra!* don't let your tongue
> thus rattle!
> O, don't be saucy, don't be stiff, because you may
> have cattle.
> I have seen – and here's my hand to you, I only say
> what's true –
> A many a one with twice your stock not half so proud
> as you.[32]

There is clarity here and even humour, but above all a creative, transforming energy; the original of this poem is dry, compressed, restrained, written in a much tighter, less vigorous rhythm than Mangan's version. O'Curry, when he gave Mangan the literal version to work on, may have made some remarks on the metre, but, if he did, Mangan chose to go his own way. The odd thing is that the metre Mangan used for his version has more in common with the *amhrán* or assonantal metres of later Gaelic poetry than with the curt syllabic metre of the original:

> Go réidh, a bhean na dtrí mbó!
> As do bhólacht ná bí teann.

Perhaps the idea of using a longer more flexible rhythm emerged in discussion with O'Curry; certainly O'Curry later tried to claim some of the credit for the existence of the translations.[33] Whatever the facts of the case it is clear that Mangan's use of the long line here is alert, energetic and alive, the rhythm having the property of conferring concreteness on the details handled. In this his long rhythms here are entirely unlike the long rhythms of his Oriental versions, where the metrical space allows time for languishing, and details get blurred. There is nothing blurred about the following:

> O'Ruark, Maguire, those souls of fire, whose names are
> >   shrined in story –
> Think how their high achievements once made Erin's
> >   glory –
> Yet now their bones lie mouldering under weeds and
> >   cypress boughs,
> And so, for all your pride, will yours, O Woman of
> >   Three Cows!

The contact with Irish poetry, through his personal contact with the leading Gaelic scholars of his day gave Mangan an imaginative alternative to the *Sehnsucht* and *Uberspannung* of German Romantic poetry. Yearning after an impossible ideal, the longing to be other than what he is, becomes a lament for a past that no longer exists, save that in his versions from Gaelic that past has a personal urgency and pressure, a sense that he is lamenting a life that once had some real substance. The Gaelic world has existed; evidence of its remnants came to his desk every day in the Ordnance Survey office. There had been a time when an Irish poet could count upon a community of understanding, when the imaginative artist was not always thrown back into the hell of the self. This was yet another version of pastoral, but it was a version of pastoral fraught with political overtones. If such a community had once existed, when the poet was not alone in his anguish, then those responsible for the break-up of that community were not just guilty of an unforgivable historical crime, they also became responsible for Mangan's own distress of spirit. So his country's history became a metaphor for his own anguish. In this, strangely enough, he was following the Gaelic poets of the seventeenth and eighteenth centuries, where the state of the country is always a personal matter.

Mangan was drawn to the great Gaelic lament, where the poet

mourns the passing of the sweetness of the old order, contrasting
it with the barbarity of the new, with its meanness and its clumsy
language. The lament became personal, not in any direct sense,
but in the sense that he too, like Erin, was in a 'breakless chain',
an 'iron thrall'. How easily the political metaphors gave vent to
his own state of mind can be seen in his version of Eoghan Ruadh
Mac an Bháird's poem 'A Bhean Fuair Faill ar an bhFeart'
written in 1609, in Rome, to Nuala, surviving sister of Rudh-
raidhe and Cathbharr O'Donnell. Young Hugh O'Neill, her
nephew, has also died, all of them in suspicious circumstances.
Mac an Bháird was chief poet to the O'Donnells, so his lament
for the dead chieftains is also a lament for the passing of the
order he has known. Mangan's translation, titled 'An Elegy on
the Tyronian and Tyrconnellian Princes, Buried at Rome' is
among the most powerful things that he wrote, and its power
derives from the intense personal energy that informs the
sonorous rhetoric Mangan puts in Mac an Bháird's mouth. But it
is no mindless sonority; it flexes and changes, to throw the highly
charged word or phrase into relief. It is a masterpiece of pace:

> O Woman of the Piercing Wail,
>   Who mournest o'er yon mound of clay
>   With sigh and moan,
> Would God thou wert among the Gael!
>   Thou would'st not then from day to day
>   Weep thus alone.
> 'Twere long before, around a grave
>   In green Tirconnell, one could find
>   This loneliness;
> Near where Beann-Boirche's banners wave
>   Such grief as thine could ne'er have pined
>   Companionless.[34]

The rhythmic hovering over the word 'loneliness', the way this
word plays against 'green Tirconnell' in the previous line shows
Mangan's wonderful metrical control. But it is not a matter of
mere facility; short phrases are used throughout the poem to
emphasise the desolation of spirit that Nuala and her poet are
going through.

In a letter to Charles Gavan Duffy on 15 September 1840,
Mangan tells him that he has completed what he calls 'a trans-

magnificanbandancial elegy of mine (a perversion from the Irish)
on the O'Neills and the O'Donnells of Ulster, which is admired
by myself and some other impartial judges'.[35] Mangan is speaking
of the poem just quoted; clearly he is excited by it, and he has
every right to be, it being one of the few great poems of the
nineteenth century in Ireland.

In what does its greatness lie? It is not just simply a matter of
rhetorical flourish; there had been and was to be plenty of that
in nineteenth century Irish poetry, but getting verbally exhilarated
was no proof against mediocrity. A measure of the poem's origin-
ality may be gained if we compare a literal version of one of the
stanzas with Mangan's refabrication. One of the verses O'Curry
supplied Mangan with would have read substantially like this.

Two of that three who happened there (were of)/ The race of
Hugh, the high prince of Aileach,/One of those (two) was
nephew to that Hugh – /A warrior not experienced in grief.

As material for poetry this does not look very promising, but
Mangan takes these meagre facts and erects a configuration of
lament around them:

> The youths whose relics moulder here
> Were sprung from Hugh, high Prince and Lord
>   Of Aileach's lands;
> Thy noble brothers, justly dear,
> Thy nephew, long to be deplored
>   By Ulster's bands.
> Theirs were not souls wherein dull Time
> Could domicile Decay or house
>   Decrepitude!
> They passed from earth ere Manhood's prime,
> Ere years had power to dim their brows
>   Or chill their blood.

This is translation transmogrified; out of the last phrase 'A
warrior not experienced in grief', Mangan creates the whole
second half of the stanza. The drive and swiftness of these lines,
the ease with which the rhetoric finds concretion, derives from a
sense of imaginative freedom which is not just here but runs
throughout the poem. Poetic freedom in the Romantic period (and
in the modern too) involves a going out from the self, a 'negative

capability'. Only then can the joy intrinsic to true creation come
about. All along, in Mangan's versions from the German and
from the Oriental we have seen various attempts on his part to
fly the terrors of the self, to achieve some kind of relationship
with the writers he translates and through them with their
different worlds. But the kind of writers to whom he was temperamentally drawn had themselves that unease with regard to the
self and its relation to the world about it that was Mangan's own.
His escape, then, was not really an escape, merely a pretended
one, embarked on, perhaps, in order that he might have something to sell to the next number of the *Dublin University
Magazine*. Here in these translations he made for Petrie's *Irish
Penny Journal,* a different spirit breathes, especially so in the
'Elegy'. There is a sense of freedom, of release, of joy, curiously
enough, despite the fact that the poem is all grief.

The fact that it is all grief is one of the reasons for its success.
This is a static poem, in that it follows the original in striking one
intense attitude and sustaining that throughout. There is no
development in the poem of the sort we expect in most modern
poems. It is a *caoineadh,* a lament, and its structure is the simplest
structure of all, the catalogue of things which were, of how
things might be had the lamented lived, the deeds of the dead.
This structure, which is hardly a structure at all in the Aristo-
telian sense, perfectly suits Mangan's poetic temperament. He,
like many an Irish poet, does not like structures that develop,
because that involves traffic with the movement of time, and so,
ineluctably, the self. He, like Stephen Dedalus after him, prefers
stasis, the frozen moment which is filled to overflowing with
significance. (Small wonder that the young Joyce liked Mangan
so much.) The 'Elegy' is one long suspended moment, an epiphany
of the Gaelic world now irretrievably lost, as Mac an Bháird
addresses Nuala, surviving sister of the O'Donnell, mourning the
dead in the graveyard of the church of S. Pietro on the Janiculum
in Rome. Mangan does not actually become Mac an Bháird in his
translation; such things do not happen outside the fancies of
literary critics. Rather does Mangan find a kinship with the
Elizabethan Irish poet, and it is this joy in fellow-feeling that
underlies the flexibility and concreteness of the poem's verbal
flourish.

Part of the excitement of this translation, and of the translations from the Irish that Mangan did intermittently from now on

until his death in 1849, was the sense they gave that there was such a thing as an Irish poetic inheritance. Mac an Bháird, Mac Liag, or Eochaidh Ó Heodhussa were part of him, however dimly apprehended, in ways that Schiller, Rückert or Meseehi could never be. The fact that they were but dimly apprehended, that O'Curry could only guess at the meanings of many of the stanzas he found in manuscript appealed to Mangan's love of the mysterious, the secret. The literal versions he worked from were skeletons of bodies, the beautiful lineaments of which he felt he was trying to re-establish. Translation was not just poetical work, it became a resurrection of the national imagination. It was no accident that Mangan wrote to Duffy (then editor of the *Belfast Vindicator*) telling him of the marvellous elegy he had just written. Duffy two years later was one of the founder members of the *Nation,* to which Mangan contributed extensively.

Mangan's work for the Ordnance Survey continued until 1841, when the government decided to end the researches of the topographical section on the grounds of cost. So Mangan was out of a job; the relative freedom from money worries a regular employment gave can perhaps be seen in the energetic, engaged translations he was writing for the *Irish Penny Journal* at the time. But the *Journal* itself lasted less than a year, and its last number appeared in June 1841.[36] James Henthorn Todd of Trinity College then got Mangan a job in the library there, cataloguing; this lasted until the end of 1846, by which time he had probably become unemployable.[37] However, the deterioration in his personal circumstances during 1846 (for that year he was only employed part time in the library) coincided with a resurgence of his poetic powers. During his spell at Trinity he had written little; now, with his life crumbling away, he comes into his *annus mirabilis.* In this year he contributed to the *Nation* some of the strongest poetry before Yeats, poems like 'Siberia', 'To the Ingleeze Khafir', 'Dark Rosaleen', 'A Vision of Connaught in the Thirteenth Century', 'A Lamentation for the Death of Sir Thomas Fitzgerald', 'A Farewell to Patrick Sarsfield'. Most of these were versions from the Irish, but his original poetry is also aflame with a patriotic zeal that sometimes approaches frenzy.

The *Nation* first appeared on 15 October 1842, under the editorship of Charles Gavan Duffy. The *Nation* was the newspaper of the Young Irelanders, as they came to be known, who, led by Thomas Davis, supported O'Connell in his movement for the

Repeal of the Act of Union. After a time they became critical of
O'Connell's downright refusal to consider physical force under
any circumstances. Their growing militancy must be seen against
the background of the desperate state of the country from 1845
to 1848; these were the Famine years. Mangan had published
pieces in the *Nation* from its very first number, but it is not until
1846, when the paper, after Davis's death, began, under the
influence of the incandescent Unitarian John Mitchel to advocate
physical force openly, that his contributions take fire. He and
Mitchel, the one a self-obsessed Dublin Catholic, and the other a
fire-eating Dissenter from County Down, had in common a taste
for the extreme, the violent. In the *Autobiography*, Mangan tells
us that in his reading he had a strong taste for the 'wonderful in
art, nature and society'. He revelled in descriptions of earth-
quakes, inundations, rebellions, he had a craving for the sensa-
tional. The poems he wrote for the *Nation* in 1846 have a strong
apocalyptic strain, but it would be foolish to dismiss this as mere
sensationalism. It was a violent response, encouraged by the
increasing militancy of Mitchel, to a present that had become
nightmarish. A sense of that violence may be gained from the
poem 'To the Ingleeze Khafir, Calling Himself Djaun Bool
Djenkinson', (for 'Ingleeze' read English, for 'Djaun Bool' read
'John Bull'). It is a scream of nationalist hatred, despite the fact
that it has often been read as an 'extravaganza':

> I hate thee Djaun Bool,
> Worse than Marid or Afrit,
> Or corpse-eating Ghoul!
> I hate thee like sin,
>   For thy mop-head of hair,
> Thy snub nose and bald chin,
> And thy turkey-cock air.[38]

This appeared in an issue of the *Nation* (18 April 1846) which
contained accounts of families living in caves, slowly dying of
starvation.

Mangan had always found it difficult to adjust to the present,
to the actuality taking place before his eyes. In its cumbrous
unfathomability it threatened to engulf the frail self, as
Maugraby's nose threatened to suffocate Dublin. Mangan, to
whom day to day reality was difficult enough, had the misfortune

to live through one of the most chilling periods of Irish history.
What is extraordinary is that he tried, for a few months, to
measure up to it, and in doing so became something of a spokesman for the afflicted and starving. Unlike most of the other
Nation poets he became national, even nationalistic, without failing to be a poet as well.

The issue that contained the 'Ingleeze' poem also contained one
of Mangan's strongest poems, 'Siberia', a poem about a desolate
frozen landscape, which possibly owes something to Mangan's
versions of Freiligrath's poem about Iceland and its bleakness.
The bleakness in 'Siberia' is a profound metaphor for the state of
Ireland in 1846, and for the state of Mangan's own personal condition. It is, strangely, for one so locked up in himself, a public
poem, which strengthens its political overtones by the intensity of
its personal content. Not until Yeats was such a marriage to take
place so effectively again;

> In Siberia's wastes
>   The Ice-wind's breath
> Woundeth like the toothed steel;
> Lost Siberia doth reveal
>   Only blight and death.
>
> Blight and death alone.
> No summer shines.[39]

Tears are impossible in this frozen place, 'they freeze within the
brain'. Here

> man lives, and doth not live,
> Doth not live – nor die.

The inhabitant of Siberia, the 'exile' as Mangan calls him, is one
with the place; its desolation has got into him, killing his spirit,
his capacity for life:

> And the exile there
>   Is one with those;
> They are part, and he is part,
> For the sands are in his heart,
>   And the killing snows.

The exiles here do not have the energy left even to curse the man who has condemned them to this place, the 'Czar':

> Therefore, in those wastes
>   None curse the Czar.
> Each man's tongue is cloven by
> The North Blast, that heweth nigh
>   With sharp scymitar.

Exposure to the sharpness of the Northern cold has cleaved the tongue, so not only are the exiles condemned to a landscape of desolation, they are also condemned to silence, being unable to voice their feelings about what is happening to them. This is a powerful and complex image in that it expresses at once Mangan's awareness of the way things were in the country at the time, and his sense of futility about them, for political reasons; but it also shows the psychological difficulty Mangan had about expressing himself in his own voice. National disaster and personal frustration, political and creative, are fused in the metaphor of Siberia. The metaphor is a manoeuvre, almost certainly unconscious, to enable him to deal with the reality of Ireland in 1846, and his own response to it. In a way it is a sophisticated version of the 'mannerism' we saw Mangan considering when about to approach the man whom he thinks is Magrauby in the Shades tavern in 1832. Reality cannot be approached directly, but sometimes, as here, the indirection is profound.

Another kind of manoeuvring is to be found in 'A Vision of Connaught in the Thirteenth Century', where the indirection is a means of finding expression for the self, and its relationship with reality. The poem is supposed to be written by a German poet about a dream he had 'one Autumn eve' by the side of 'the castled Maine', a dream 'Of the time and reign/Of Cahal Mor of the Wine-red Hand'. It is a supposedly Teutonic vision by one of Deutschland's 'bardlings' of Ireland in the thirteenth century. As such it is a kind of transported *Sehnsucht*; the German's dream of Ireland is as paradisal, at first, as Mangan's dreams of the Orient were. This mythical Ireland is a composite of Teutonic longing, Oriental paradise and Romantic nationalism:

> I walked entranced
>   Through a land of Morn;

> The sun, with wondrous excess of light,
> Shone down and glanced
>   Over seas of corn
> And lustrous gardens aleft and right.
>   Even in the clime
>   Of resplendent Spain,
> Beams no such sun upon such a land;
>   But it was the time
>   'Twas in the reign,
> Of Cahal Mor of the Wine-red Hand.[40]

There is 'no such sun' as this in reality; Cahal Mor's time is out-side time as it is lived through. The land is a place of unity, where it is possible to speak and be answered without 'mannerism'. The place also evokes the dream of a 'Palace of Art', in that the minstrels here are not alone, eating out their hearts in secret, but are joined together in a unity of music that seems to flow out of the landscape itself. It is Blake's 'The Lost Traveller's Dream under the Hill', transferred to a semi-mythical Irish context:

> Then saw I thrones,
>   And circling fires,
>   And a Dome rose near me as by a spell,
> Whence flowed the tones
>   Of silver lyres,
>   And many voices in wreathed swell;
>   And their thrilling chime
>   Fell on my ears.
>
> As the heavenly hymn of the angel-band –
>   'It is now the time,
>   These be the years,
> Of Cahal Mor of the Wine-red Hand!'

The dreamer tries to enter the Dome which has risen magically out of the landscape, and from which comes the woven, total music he hears, but

> behold! – a change
> From light to darkness, joy to woe!
>   King, nobles, all,

> Looked aghast and strange;
> The minstrel-group sate in dumbest show!
> Had some great crime
> Wrought this dread amaze,
> This terror? None seemed to understand.

The dread amaze is brought about by man's fallen nature, and as such is a common Romantic theme; the dumbness, the silencing of the 'wreathed swell' of the minstrels is a consequence of man's sense of his separateness from others, cut off for ever from that complete music of which he can only dream. But the setting is Ireland, and the Romantic imagery has a further, harsher resonance. It is not just man's fallen nature that has silenced the music. It is the Saxon too, the alien, who has made the minstrel group dumb, in that they now have no language to speak. The Irish language, and so (according to Davis, and many others after him), the Irish identity, had been suppressed. Their tongues, borrowing the 'Siberia' metaphor, are 'cloven'. So then, curiously, the poem establishes a strange equivalence between the coming of the Saxon to Ireland and the Fall of man. The dreamer again goes forth:

> But lo! the sky
> Showed flecked with blood, and an alien sun
> Glared from the North,
> And there stood on high,
> Amid his shorn beams, a skeleton!

This grisly sentinel, under the 'alien' sun, presiding over the ruined wastes, all the pleasure domes gone, is a generalised image of death, but it is also an image of Famine. The poem appeared in the *Nation* on 11 July 1846, when during the hot and unnaturally humid summer it was beginning to be apparent that the potato crop that year was to be a total failure.[41] The final outcome of the Saxon invasion is famine, his emblem death. The minstrel group can no longer sing a total music, as the tongue of the minstrel is cut down the middle, one half Irish, the other English. (The tongue that has difficulty in articulating is a dominant image in the contemporary writing of Thomas Kinsella, John Montague, and in the Gaelic verse of Seán Ó Ríordáin). It is the Saxon who has done this injury: it is a kind of cultural emasculation.

It is not surprising, considering the context of poems like 'Siberia' and 'A Vision of Connaught', that Mangan's strongest verse moved, in 1846, towards greater militancy, violence, and actual hatred. Frenzy became a release for the tensions he attempted to mask by translating from German poets he was temperamentally very close to, and then mocking them in prose for their vagueness and their self-absorption. Frenzy was another kind of exoticism, a way of flying out from the hell of self. The Saxon becomes the embodiment of the inner hell, it is his presence that has corrupted daylight, that has darkened perception; it is he who has created the abyss inside, and made it impossible for there to be a correspondence between the mind and the world outside it, because he has made that filthy also. The great domes of woven music have gone; instead there is Dublin castle, and the slums of the city. For Mangan the Saxon is very like Blake's Urizen, and in this comparison we recognise the simplicity of Mangan's view. The presence of the English in Ireland cannot explain all that was corrupt in mid-nineteenth century Ireland, but it was a simplification Mangan made, and one made by many cultural nationalists after him. Hatred has its own attractions, not least among them an easy access to intensity, and intensity was something Mangan's irresolute and neurotic imagination would gladly acquire. Better to be hectic than dumb:

> But O'Kelly still remains, to defy and to toil;
>   He has memories that hell won't permit him to forget,
> And a sword that will make the blue blood flow like oil
>   Upon many an Aughrim yet! –
>   Och, ochone! [42]

That is from Mangan's version of 'A Farewell to Patrick Sarsfield, Earl of Lucan', and it appeared in the *Nation* on 24 October 1846. A similar note is struck in Mangan's famous poem 'Dark Rosaleen', (the *Nation*, 30 May 1846), where the mood is one of intense devotion to Ireland conceived as a stainless woman held in thrall. Her 'holy, delicate white hands' will, however, 'girdle' him with 'steel'; in her secret emerald bowers she will pray for him while he performs incredible feats fired with the thought of her. She, Ireland, gives him energy, and this energy translates itself to the poem, which is a masterpiece of rhetoric and incantation. The phrase 'Dark Rosaleen' becomes a talisman which the rhythm of the poem returns to, lingers on, and repeats over and over as a kind of energy-giving mantra for violence:

> You'll pray for me, my flower of flowers,
>   My Dark Rosaleen.
>   My fond Rosaleen.
> You'll think of me through Daylight's hours,
> My virgin flower, my flower of flowers,
>   My Dark Rosaleen.
>
> I could scale the blue air,
>   I could plough the high hills,
> Oh! I could kneel all night in prayer,
>   To heal your many ills.[43]

He is prepared to do more than that when the time comes. The last stanza of the poem reaches a blood-drenched apocalyptic intensity; the imagery is that of total insurrection:

> O! the Erne shall run red
>   With redundance of blood,
> The earth shall rock beneath our tread,
>   And flames wrap hill and wood,
> And gun-peal, and slogan cry
>   Wake many a glen serene,
> Ere you shall fade, ere you shall die,
>   My Dark Rosaleen!
>   My own Rosaleen!
> The judgement hour must first be nigh,
> Ere you can fade, ere you can die,
>   My Dark Rosaleen!

This Rosaleen is dark in more senses than one; her imagined innocence, ceaselessly beset by Saxon hordes, is an incitement to violence, and the thought of that violence to come is a comfort in affliction, a consolation to a mind tortured by the living images of famine, and by the unnameable misery of its own depths. The process we see at work here is intensity through moral and political simplification, rather than the 'simplification through intensity' that the poet of Yeats's phase 17 strives towards. Yeats's poet must encounter the dark within, and not be distracted by the gestures of political rhetoric, whereas Mangan's rhetorical frenzy is a flight from that very dark.

'Dark Rosaleen' does envisage an encounter, but it is a revolutionary one, and it is sometime in the distant future. When we push aside the rich folds of rhetoric we see that there is a strong suggestion that the hour of reckoning may never come at all. The earth will rock beneath the tread of the revolutionaries *before* Rosaleen will fade; that, it is felt, will never happen; the day of Judgement will have to come first, so that in a sense there never will be a need for that fearsome martial tread in actuality. But it gives a savage comfort just to contemplate it. Patrick Pearse's conception of Ireland as the beautiful, holy girl perhaps owes something to Mangan's incantation about her, but Pearse was prepared to let the blood run in his own life. Mangan was not but he liked to think about it.

'Dark Rosaleen' is a transfiguration of a prose translation of the Irish poem 'Róisín Dubh', which Mangan found in Samuel Ferguson's second article on James Hardiman's *Irish Minstrelsy* in the *Dublin University Magazine* for August 1834. In the stanza just dealt with Mangan found the images of carnage and of natural disturbance in his original, but the martial 'tread' is entirely Mangan's as is the gun-peal and slogan cry, and the mention of the day of Judgement. The original says that these perturbations will come about before Róisín Dubh dies, and seeing that in the original she is less of an allegorical type and much more human, this is felt to be not too far off. In other words, the wild geese will come home, led by the Stuart, in the foreseeable future. Mangan ignores the immediacy of this and goes for apocalyptic ambivalence.

'O'Hussey's Ode to the Maguire' was also written in 1846. According to O'Donoghue, this was written for the *Dublin University Magazine,* but for one reason or another this journal did not publish it. It appeared later in the year in H. R. Montgomery's *Specimens of the Early Native Poetry of Ireland.* This, like 'Dark Rosaleen', was based on a prose rendering by Ferguson in the *Dublin University Magazine,* this time from Ferguson's third Hardiman article in October 1834.

The original was written by Eochaidh Ó Heodhussa, chief bard of the Maguire sept of Fermanagh, while his chieftain, Hugh, was on a war-campaign in Munster under O'Neill in 1600. Ó Heodhussa imagines the hardships his patron must be encounter-

ing. For Ferguson in 1834 the affection Ó Heodhussa feels for the
Maguire, the concern for his well-being, is testimony to the great
capacity for loyalty in the native Irish, a trait, which, he maintains, England should understand and utilise for the extension of
the material prosperity of both Ireland *and* England. In 1846,
twelve years later, when the country was in the grip of famine,
Mangan's re-working of Ferguson's prose could not have a more
different import. Here is the first stanza from Ferguson:

> Cold weather I consider this night to be for Hugh!
> A cause of grief is the rigor of its showery drops;
> Alas, insufferable is
> The venom of this night's cold.

Out of this Mangan makes:

> Where is my Chief, my master, this bleak night, mavrone!
>   O, cold, cold, miserably cold is this bleak night for Hugh,
>   Its showery, arrowy, speary sleet pierceth one through and
>   through,
> Pierceth one to the very bone! [44]

Whereas in 'Dark Rosaleen' the rhythm moved towards incanta-
tory refrain, here it stretches and flexes itself, restlessly discovering
new shapes and contours. It is a syntax that attempts to capture
emotional intensity, and indeed it is quite successful in doing that.
As with the 1840 version from Eoghan Ruadh mac an Bháird
Mangan feels a kinship with what he imagines it was like to be
Eochaidh Ó Heodhussa, and from that imagined kinship he
derives a creative energy, save that in 'O Woman of the Piercing
Wail' that energy is deep, musical and concretive, whereas here in
'O'Hussey's Ode' it is disruptive, anarchic, explosive. The frozen
landscape, in Mangan's rehandling of Ferguson's prose, is a translation of the psychic landscape of 'Siberia' to Munster. Here the
'pitiless ice-wind streams' also, but that, bad as it is, is not so bad
as the 'hate that persecutes him' (Maguire). In 'Siberia' we saw
that this cold is a metaphor for the iron Saxon, that it paralyses
grief, the tears freeze within the brain. Here Maguire's hand is
paralysed by the same frost:

That his great hand, so oft the avenger of the oppressed,
> Should this chill, churlish night, perchance, be paralysed by
> frost –
> While through some icicle-hung thicket – as one lorn and
> lost –
He walks and wanders without rest.

The complete inactivity of 'Siberia' has gone; though the hand is paralysed, Maguire is ceaseless in his wandering, but that wandering is felt to be futile.

Another effect of the fierce cold of 'Siberia' was to cleave the tongue, to render speech impossible, so that none can curse the 'Czar' who is responsible for sending the exiles there. Here, in 'O'Hussey's Ode' the restlessness of the rhythm, its wayward, yet always exact expansions and contractions, its fiery eloquence, seems a defiance against the silence a cloven tongue imposes. It is a syntax of desperate articulateness and of revolutionary zeal. Despite the 'white ice-gauntlets' that 'glove his fine fair fingers o'er', Maguire has an invisible protective sheath, a sheath of lightning, the same lightning that lightens through the blood of the chanter of 'Dark Rosaleen':

> A warm dress is to him that lightning garb he ever wore,
> The lightning of the soul, not skies.

And he has yet another consolation, the thought of the destruction he has made in the past, the mansions he has burnt to ashes. If ever there was revolutionary poetry this is it:

> . . . To-night he wanders frozen, rain-drenched, sad, betrayed –
> *But the memory of the lime-white mansions his right hand hath*
> *laid*
> *In ashes warms the hero's heart!*

Mangan, following his prose source, italicised the last two lines. How pleased Mitchel would have been with the stress thus laid on them.

Throughout this year of 1846 Mangan continued to do work for the *Dublin University Magazine* in German and Oriental poetry. In 1847 he began an *Anthologia Hibernica* for the same journal, and he began work for John O'Daly, the publisher, trans-

lating Irish Jacobite poetry, following O'Daly's success with
Edward Walsh's versions of that material. But from now on there
is a falling off in his work; he was writing to live, and the despera-
tion and unhappiness swamp the poems, making them laboured,
tortuous. He died in 1849.

V

Mangan was an urban poet with an over-acute sensibility. He was
a self-absorbed man, and this tendency to introspection was
increased by his over-scrupulous brand of Irish Catholicism. For
him, the inter-relationship between self and other upon which the
laws that govern our day to day activity rest, was frequently on
the point of breaking down. Life, then, was a mystery, but not a
stimulating or invigorating one; it was threatening, oppressive.
Existential reality, the process by which the future becomes the
past, the second by second felt pulse of existence, was unbearable
to him, darkened by fear and guilt.

The self and its processes (what Yeats called the 'complexity of
human veins') being unbearable to him he sought various ways
out of that circumstantial hell. Some of them at least could be
under the head of that 'mannerism' he thinks of employing in the
Shades tavern to approach the stranger sitting in the corner. How
can one possibly present oneself as oneself? That would mean a
security in the self, and that is evaporating second by second. So
Mangan, unsure about appearance and reality, chose masks,
personae, to present himself in his poetry, like Eliot and Pound
after him. Translation was a series of these masks whereby he
could pretend to appropriate the moods, sentiments and thoughts
of other poets.

Mangan's mannerism differs from Yeats's mask theory, in that
for Yeats the assumption of the mask involves a struggle with the
self to make it different, more effective, more effortless. Mangan's
mannerism is posturing, and leads inevitably to rhetoric rather
than poetry. This rhetoric is sometimes astonishingly good as in
his versions from the Irish made from 1840 to 1846, and in a few
original poems ('Siberia', 'A Vision of Connaught') where we see
a merging of Mangan's own state with that of his country. In the
1846 poems, his sense of kinship with the dead and dying Gaelic

world, fired by his sense of outrage at the Irish famine, makes the poetry militant and revolutionary. Frenzy has momentarily taken the place of mannerism as a way of flying the self and its complexities.

There are one or two poems where Mangan tries to lay bare the toil and agony of his soul in his own voice, poems such as 'The Nameless One', 'A Broken Hearted Lay', 'The Groans of Despair'. Apart from 'The Nameless One' these are boring. 'The Nameless One' is saved from groaning diffuseness by a tight stanza form. Even so, we learn very little from it, nor, we can be sure, did Mangan:

> Tell how this Nameless, condemned for years long
>   To herd with demons from hell beneath,
> Saw things that made him, with groans and tears, long
>   For even death. . . .
>
> And he fell far through that pit abysmal,
>   The gulf and grave of Maginn and Burns,
> And pawned his soul for the devil's dismal
>   Stock of returns –
>
> But yet redeemed it in days of darkness,
>   And shapes and signs of the final wrath.[45]

No one can write poetry like that for very long without the protection of irony, a protection he found, briefly, in his small, haunting masterpiece, 'Twenty Golden Years Ago'. The last stanza presents us with the only instance in Mangan's poetry of the present rendered existentially, as it passes:

> Tick-tick, tick-tick! – Not a sound save Time's,
>   And the windgust, as it drives the rain –
> Tortured torturer of reluctant rhymes,
>   Go to bed, and rest thine aching brain!
> Sleep! – no more the dupe of hopes or schemes;
>   Soon thou sleepest where the thistles blow –
> Curious anticlimax to thy dreams
>   Twenty golden years ago.

4

Sir Samuel Ferguson:
The Two Races of Ireland

I

Unlike Mangan, Sir Samuel Ferguson had a wholeness and simplicity in his life and work. The men were contemporaries and slight acquaintances. Ferguson was a Protestant, and a Northern loyalist one at that, proud of his descent from one of the oldest of the Highland clans, the 'Mhic Fhearghuis' of Athole, who came to Ireland in the early seventeenth century. He was by temperament and persuasion conservative, distrustful of all social instability, convinced of the rightness and godliness of his religious faith. He believed implicitly, along with many Victorians, in the efficacy of material progress; he saw mankind as advancing into a saner, more reasonable order of things, where sweetness of temper and moral seriousness would be the humane codes by which people could live. The difficulty was that his life spanned perhaps the most turbulent century of Irish history, a century where sectarian hatred and political upheaval was a constant reality. His long life (1810-1886) saw Catholic Emancipation, the Reform Bill, the Tithe War of the 'thirties, Repeal, the Young Ireland Movement and its abortive rising, Fenianism and the Land War. At its close it even saw, dimly, the first stirrings of the Irish Literary Revival. One of the poets to write a commemorative article on Ferguson was the young W. B. Yeats, to whom the older poet was a key figure in his fabrication of something like a literary tradition out of the scattered achievements of nineteenth century Anglo-Irish writing.

116

Ferguson lived a quiet life: the first chapter of Lady Ferguson's book on her husband has the title 'The Events of an Uneventful Life'. It was, however, a full life and a happy one. He was brought up in the beautiful countryside around Lough Neagh, in the valley of the Six-Mile-Water, not far away from the earth-work of Rathmore Moy-Linny, once the seat of the seventh century king about whom he was to write his most ambitious poem, Congal Claen. He was educated at Belfast, in the Academical Institution (which had a Professor of Irish), Trinity College, Dublin, and later in London, in Lincoln's Inn, where he studied for the bar. He had to make his own way, as his father had run through the family property, and he did this by writing, mostly on Irish subjects. He was called to the Irish bar in 1838 and ten years later married into the Guinness family and thus into the Ascendancy. He subsequently became a Queen's Counsel and in 1867 Deputy Keeper of the Public Records of Ireland. He was knighted in 1878 and in 1881 was elected President of the Royal Irish Academy.

He participated fully in the civilised life of the Dublin of his day, which became his home after he was called to the bar. He was an early contributor to the *Dublin University Magazine,* writing criticism on Irish topics, short semi-novellas on Irish historical themes, and archaeological pieces. He came to know George Petrie quite early (in 1833) and their letters written in this period give an impression of the enthusiasm and cautious scholarship Petrie brought to the unearthing of the Irish past in a way that would be stimulating and exact.[1] Petrie recognised the same energy and attention to detail in Ferguson as he constantly sought after himself, and expected of others. The painstaking and patient attention to detail, the attunement of all the faculties to the task in hand, was a marked feature of all of Ferguson's work, historical and imaginative, and explains how for him there could be a vital link between poetry and archaeology.

He enjoyed writing verse for its own sake, and his patient archaeological toil also totally absorbed him, but behind both these pursuits, and his other imaginative and historical ones, there was one great purpose which he shared with Petrie, with Thomas Davis and indeed to some extent with Mangan. This was the advancement of Ireland on the scale of nations, by making first Irishmen, and afterwards the rest of the world, conscious of the rights of Ireland to an ancestry as old as that of Rome, even

older. His archaeological work, his painstaking work over manuscripts in the British Museum and in the Royal Irish Academy,
aimed at getting the facts as straight as possible about the native
heritage. His imaginative work, his poetry, was an attempt to
make those scenes he had lived through in his mind's eye the
substance and fibre of the intellectual equipment of the Victorian
Irishman. Congal Claen should become as Arthur was to England,
though set forth in a much rougher (therefore to Ferguson's way
of thinking, more accurate) equipage than Tennyson's *Idylls.*

II

Whence came this attachment to Ireland, this patriotism of
literature and scholarship? Here we encounter a paradox, but
one familiar to anyone interested in the complexity of Irish
history. Ferguson was a Northern Unionist, absolutely convinced
of the rightness of his own Protestant faith, and of the abomina-
tion of Popery. 'Priestcraft' he regarded as rebellious, seditious,
and despite his admiration of Moore, found him wanting in his
attachment to the Catholic cause. To him Popery traded in lies,
deceit, and had for its ultimate aim the extermination of what
he regarded as the great strength of Ireland, its Protestant middle
class. This, for him, is 'the depository of Ireland's fate for good
or evil', whereas the Catholic activists (he is here thinking of
O'Connell, the year is 1834), led by 'the scheming, jesuitical,
ambitious priest' are a

> perverse rabble, on whom the mire in which they have wallowed
> for the last quarter of a century, has caked into a crust like
> the armour of the Egyptian beast, till they are case-hardened
> invulnerably in the filth of habitual impudence, ingratitude,
> hypocrisy, envy and malice; so that it were but a vain defile-
> ment of aught manly or honourable to advance it against such
> panoply of every foul component.[2]

The young Ferguson is undoubtedly enjoying himself hugely
here, and at the same time making the right noises for the
journal for which he happens to be writing, the *Dublin University
Magazine,* which addressed itself to the Protestant Irish, outlining
their cause and what they considered to be their rights and

responsibilities. Here Ferguson is attacking the rabble-rousing Catholic radicals, but his distrust of Popery went deeper; he considered it a threat to stability and ordered progress, a modern re-creation of primitive barbarism and cunning. And those Protestants who tried to conciliate the Catholic radicals he considered well-meaning but foolish dreamers.

In a sympathetic essay he wrote in 1840 on Petrie's *Dublin Penny Journal* of the early 'thirties he praised it for its antiquarian interests, and its promotion of the national literature, but disapproved of its conciliatory attitude towards the 'Roman party' by, for example, failing to mention in a life of John Scotus Eriugena, a fact of which every Irish Protestant ought to be proud, that Eriugena was 'the foremost to oppose the Romish novelty of transubstantiation' when first broached to the western churches by Paschasius Radbert. Worse, the *Journal* eulogised the 'zeal and intrepidity' of those Catholic bishops and others who obtained an 'unenviable martyrdom' in the Irish civil wars, and so 'culpably ministered to the pride and self-exaltation of the Roman party'.[3] In Ferguson's eyes, the *Journal* failed to realise the implications of what it was doing; the Irish Catholics were inflammable enough without the encouragement of intellectual tolerance.

There are times, indeed, when Ferguson's prose reads like bigotted rant; all the more paradoxical then that he, like the contributors to the *Dublin Penny Journal,* was often drawn in imagination to those rebels he found so pernicious with one part of his mind. Ferguson was no secret schizophrenic, but he was conscious of a tension (if not a conflict) in himself between what his convictions told him was injurious to Irish progress and civilisation (which he equated with the spread of Protestant enlightment illuminating Papist darkness) and an imaginative sympathy for those centuries when Ireland was practically free of English domination. The dilemma is set forth, none too clearly, perhaps, in a piece he wrote for the *Dublin University Magazine* for 1833 at the very beginning of his writing career, entitled 'A Dialogue Between the Head and the Heart of an Irish Protestant'.

After Catholic Emancipation and the Reform Bill (brought in by the Whigs under Lord Grey) it seems to the 'Head' that the way now lies open for Repeal of the Union. Its logic is panic-stricken and apocalyptic:

if Catholic Emancipation produce repeal, so surely will repeal
produce ultimate separation; and so sure as we have a separation, so surely will there be war levied, estates confiscated, and
the Popish church established.[4]

And, with the establishment of a Popish church, the implication
is, the Protestants will be at worst exterminated, at best pushed
from their positions of privilege where they, and only they, can
benefit their country. But the Protestant too has a deep attachment to Ireland. As the 'head' puts it eloquently:

> Yet stripped as we are of power and privilege, neither Whig
> tyranny nor Popish malice can deprive us of our birthright,
> which is the love of Ireland.

At the mention of this, the 'heart' is stirred in ways it cannot
really comprehend:

> I know not whence my blood may have been drawn, but it
> circulates with a swifter liveliness at the name of this country,
> and I feel and know that I am the heart of an Irishman.

In fact, so strongly does the 'heart' sympathize with Ireland that
it even begins to allow itself to think like a rebel, and begins to
comprehend the native Irish attachment to the priesthood, and
to the Catholic faith, so much have they 'fasted for it, fought
for it, suffered confiscation, exile and death for it'. The heart
cannot deny a proper charity to such devotion. To the 'head'
though, such 'apologetic, compromising, prurient, rebellious
sympathies' are extremely dangerous. Indulged in, they would
lead Irish Protestantism into active sympathy with the Catholics
and the English radicals, and so against their best interests, and
in the end the best interests of their country. Irish Protestants
must retain their independence, despite the fact they are 'deserted
by the Tories, insulted by the Whigs, threatened by the radicals
. . . told that (they) are neither English nor Irish, fish nor flesh'.
Their independence is vitally important to their survival. The
'heart' may very well say:

I love this land better than any other. I cannot believe it a
hostile country. I love the people of it, in spite of themselves,
and cannot feel towards them as enemies.

But such intensity of affection can be dangerous; it must not lead
to any alignment of sympathy with the Catholic cause, because,
as the 'head' caustically points out 'it is one of the necessities of
your existence that they should feel as enemies towards you'.
Why? Because a sympathy with the Catholics means, as Ferguson
saw it, sympathy with the anarchy of radicalism, which might
call France or America to its assistance, and it could lead to the
complete overthrow of the Empire.

This essay, the 'Dialogue', is a remarkable analysis of the
intellectual and emotional dilemma confronting an intelligent and
responsible Protestant in the 1830s, with regard to his sense of
what his relationship should be with his native country in the
context of his religious and political convictions. Above all, he
is proud of his Protestant (indeed Northern) independence; there
will be 'no surrender' to the turbulence of the 'filthy modern tide'
of radicalism and apologetic sympathizing with dangerous causes.
Even at the end of his life his basic sympathies have not altered
a great deal: in a letter to the Irish poet William Allingham,
lamenting the lack of a proper 'school of letters' in Ireland, he
complains of the fecklessness of the Irish people, their imaginative
laziness in wanting to create history according to their own
prejudices. He goes on to say that they need 'strong hands over
them – even Orangemen for want of better, if the Orangemen
could only be made to feel Irish. I don't think the Whig Liberals
will ever understand them.'[5]

Ferguson then was deeply conservative, but as is often the case
this word conceals more than it reveals. Being so conservative,
loyalist, anti-papistical, what drew him to the literature, history
and antiquities of Ireland when he was so ambiguous about the
religious and emotional convictions of the majority of its people?
We could say that being brought up in the beautiful countryside
of the eastern shore of Lough Neagh, in the valleys of the Six-
Mile-Water, instilled in him a love of the countryside together
with a curiosity about its associations in legend and history that
stayed with him throughout his life. And there would be some
truth in this; he has said himself that the impressions he received
in these places when a child 'influenced all my habits of thought

and sentiment in after life'.[6] His imagination constantly returned
to that area and its environs. Congal Claen comes from there, so
do Sweeney, the sub-king on Congal's side who went mad, and
the mythical herdsman Borcha, who keeps watch over the
fortunes of Ulster on 'craggy Bingian's top'. 'Willy Gilliland', one
of Ferguson's earliest poems, tells how the Covenanter Gilliland
fled to Antrim after Bothwell Bridge, laid low in Glenwhirry,
lived in a cave, and fished for food at a time when

> all the valley pastoral held neither house nor tree,
> But spread abroad and open all, a full fair sight to see,
> From Slemish foot to Collon top lay one unbroken green,
> Save where in many a silver coil the river glanced between.[7]

Little thought the outlawed Covenanter, reflects Ferguson at the
close of this 'Ulster Ballad', that where he had been a hunted
brute there would yet be 'broad lands and yeoman tenantry':

> still from him descendants not a few
> Draw birth and lands and, let me trust, draw love of
> freedom too.

According to Lady Ferguson, the poet's great-grandmother was
descended from this Willy, so Ferguson in the last line of the
poem is (like Yeats after him) proudly celebrating the independence of an ancestor's blood, linking his love of freedom with the
quietness of the outlaw in his pastoral retreat, and with his
ferocity when his horse is killed by troopers from Carrickfergus.
(Gilliland kills the trooper with the sharpened butt end of his
fishing rod.) But Ferguson was more than a local poet, celebrating the stories and traditions of his own locality, although he had
a great respect for the weaver poets of Ulster.

Before going to Trinity College he was educated at Belfast,
and Belfast in the opening decades of the nineteenth century
still retained some of the interest in Gaelic tradition that had
characterized it before the '98 rebellion. The Belfast Harp
Festival had taken place there; it was from there that Bunting
embarked on his tours through the counties of Ireland (not just
Ulster) collecting those Irish airs that he had made his life's
work, many of which lie behind Moore's *Melodies*. Belfast was

the city of the McCracken family, a rebel family, but one which had subsidised Bunting in his researches, keeping him for most of his life. In late eighteenth century Belfast, there was a strong connection between the tradition of Protestant Dissent, the radical republicanism of Wolfe Tone and the United Irishmen, and Gaelic song and culture. The violence and atrocities of the rebellion dissolved that connection, but an interest in Gaelic culture in manuscript, song and music continued to be a feature of the life of some of the city's middle class.

A Belfast Harp Society was founded in 1809, and in the early 1820s William Neilson taught Irish in the Belfast Academical Institution.[8] In 1830 the Ulster Gaelic Society was founded, with the Marquis of Downshire for President, having among its members Samuel Ferguson, and his friends Thomas O'Hagan and George Fox. They formed a private class for the study of Irish, probably using the Irish grammar of Neilson, published in 1808, and very quickly Ferguson realized that under the Ulster dialect spoken in his native glens, under the memories of Covenanters fighting for freedom, there were other strata of historical experience, going right down to ancient times, about which he and his fellow Protestants knew practically nothing. It was his life's work to excavate those strata, to bring to light the details of the Irish past, and not just the Ulster past, although that, for him, is where it all began. As an Ulster Protestant, proud of his independent tradition, absolutely convinced (like most conservatives of his day) of the need for orderly progress, he set out, in his imaginative and historical work, to place himself and what he stood for in some kind of living relationship with the Irish past, Anglo-Irish *and* Gaelic. If the vitality of such a relationship could be secured, then, he thought, Ireland had a chance of becoming a truly great nation. Ireland's history, for Ferguson, was absolutely vital for Ireland's future; only by establishing the facts as they really were could Irishmen come to see clearly. The scales of prejudice would drop from the eyes, the shriek of the demagogue would be silenced by understanding. Eventually, led by the light of plain sense and reason, Irishmen would develop independence of judgement, and so, inevitably, become Protestants in one sense or another, as had two notable converts of the day, William Carleton and the Reverend Mortimer O'Sullivan.

III

In a series of essays contributed to the *Dublin University Magazine* for 1834, essays based on James Hardiman's *Irish Minstrelsy* (1831), Ferguson set out to accomplish something he considered essential for Irish stability and progress: that was 'to make the people of Ireland better acquainted with one another'. Only by fostering a true understanding between the two races of Ireland, 'two of the finest races of men in the world, the Catholic and the Protestant, or the Milesian and Anglo-Irish', can her eight millions eventually rise out of the obscurity to which mutual hatred and discord has condemned them. Ireland is a country of enormous potential: the capital city is 'no circle of log huts', the royal road 'no green forest pass, no ragged mountain highway', and the northern line not unsuitable for 'the peaceful pomp of regal or vice-regal progress'.[9] If the Catholic Irish were educated properly in the scriptures, then Ireland would become

> a nation of enlightened, liberal, and prosperous people – assertors of our own rights, respectors of the rights of others – a truly integral and influential portion of the empire, repudiating alike the insolent violence of civil degradation and the hideous impiety of spiritual thraldom – in the fullest sense of the words, bold men, honoured by others and respected by ourselves.

In the pages of the *Dublin University Magazine* he is addressing the Irish Protestants, and he is very keen, as the spokesman of his class, to declare that he, too, despite the fact that there are those who claim to have exclusive rights to Catholic goodwill (he is thinking of O'Connell and Hardiman) can feel for the misery of 'the poor Papist whether drudging on the wharfs of London, or eating limpets, and sea-weed on the rocks of Erris'. He can even extend his 'indignant commiseration' (like the 'heart' can in the 'Dialogue') to the 'ruffian conspirator' and 'marching marauders' confident of the people's good-will at last. Literature (that which he is engaged in at present), history which does not attempt to distort the facts, and the study of antiquities will not only cultivate self-respect and so conduce to progress; the proper application of an enquiring and honest mind to Ireland's past will produce a literature that will be a 'reconciling strength' between a 'disgusted proprietary and a revolted population'.[10] Landlord and peasant, once the peasant has been educated into truth (and that education we have seen would be a scriptural one), will be able to move forward in mutual regard and understanding. This 'dream of the noble and the beggar-man' bears a remarkable similarity to Yeats's idea that the aristocrat and the peasant had a great deal in common, save that in Ferguson's case the dream of a unified people was strongly related to the utilitarian progress which such a union of interests would make possible.

Ferguson, however, saw James Hardiman, compiler of the *Irish Minstrelsy,* of which this series of articles is an extended criticism, as directly opposed to all kinds of free and open knowledge, and its concomitant, material prosperity. Indeed he sees Hardiman as a kind of literary Ribbonman, fomenting discord by the unfair and unrepresentative selection of items for inclusion in the *Minstrelsy,* and by the frankly bigotted tone Hardiman adopts in his notes and commentary. An example Ferguson gives of the kind of seditious material Hardiman introduces is the following translation of a poem on seeing an Englishman hanging from a tree:

Pass on – 'tis cheering from yon stately tree,
A foe's vile form suspended thus to see:
Oh! may each tree that shades our soil, appear
Thick with such fruit throughout the lengthened year.[11]

This is frankly seditious stuff, translation or no translation; at the time (1831) it must have been inflammatory, and it is only a small example of the kind of material Hardiman was prepared to print. He prefixed the *Minstrelsy* with an apology that most of the material was written before the 'late conciliatory acts' (Catholic Emancipation), but Ferguson scoffs at this, pointing out that those acts were passed in 1829, while the book was not published until 1831.

But these articles are not one long diatribe against Hardiman's militant Catholicism, far from it; in laying before the public the songs and poems of a Gaelic world, Hardiman

however politically malignant and religiously fanatical, has yet
done such good service to his country in their collection and
preservation, that for her sake we half forgive him our own
quarrel, and consent to forego a great part of its vindication.[12]

In collecting and arranging the Gaelic songs and poems in the
most comprehensive anthology of Irish verse since that of
Charlotte Brooke in 1789, Hardiman provided, for the mind
inspired with the right kind of imaginative sympathy and protected by a judicious caution, the basic material for a study of
the leading characteristics of the native Irish nature. A knowledge of those characteristics, characteristics that Ferguson sums
up in the somewhat unsatisfying term 'sentiment', is essential if
the sane and reasonable union Ferguson envisages between the
two races of Ireland is to take place. The Irish Protestant must
know the 'texture and complexion' of the *'merus Hibernicus'*, and
where better to find it than in his poetry and song, for 'sentiment
is the soul of song, and sentiment is one imprescriptible property
of the common blood of all Irishmen'. Ferguson says *'all'* Irishmen, so the Protestant Anglo-Irishman, if he looks, will find
much in the native literature of Ireland that will speak directly
to him. Needless to say, Ferguson believes in the reality of a
national identity; the characteristics of a people are 'inherent,
not fictitious', and nothing, he says, could reduce an Irishman
to the 'stolid standard of a sober Saxon'. In this he anticipated
Matthew Arnold, Patrick Pearse, W. B. Yeats, and indeed many
Romantic writers and modern politicians. Here, in these articles,
he is attempting, no less, to delineate as clearly as possibly for
the Protestants of Ireland, the main co-ordinates of Irish
personality, a living geometry which he maintains involves them.
For a man of twenty four he makes an astonishingly good job
of it.

If Irish sentiment is to be adequately revealed, then, in dealing
with the material supplying the evidence for the inquiry, Hardiman's Gaelic poems, the 'strict severity of literal translation' is
absolutely necessary. The translators that Hardiman employed to
turn his versions into English verse made the mistake of thinking
that they could turn Irish poetry into polite literature. They are
not, Ferguson says, 'elegant additions' to this, they are more
valuable as 'keys to Irish sentiment', and if that is to be delineated
then the evidence must not be tampered with. Henry Grattan

Curran, one of Hardiman's versifiers, declares, says Ferguson, 'open war against the original'; he 'notches, buds, mortises, and mangles; sticks in a ramification of metaphors here, claps on a mistletoe-bough of parasite flowers there, and . . . , so metamorphoses the original, that it (the Roman Vision, for instance) comes out of his hands as unlike itself as an espalier stock that has been once a crab-tree'.[13] Clearly, Ferguson finds the crab-tree infinitely preferable to the espalier stock, because the crab-tree is historically more appropriate, as well as being a beautiful thing in itself. His ambition, which he realizes in an appendix at the end of his four Hardiman articles, is to make verse translations of these originals that will be true to the native sentiment that informs them.

What then are the main characteristics of Irish sentiment, unalloyed? Firstly, a 'languishing but savage sincerity', to be found mainly in the love songs. In this,

> in its association with the despondency of conscious degradation, and the recklessness of desperate content, is partly to be found the origin of that wild, mournful, incondite, yet not uncouth, sentiment which distinguishes the national songs of Ireland from those of perhaps any other nation in the world.[14]

The example he gives of this desperate wildness is a song called 'Uileacan Dubh O! ':

> If you would go with me to the County Leitrim,
>   Uileacan dubh O!
> I would give the honey of the bees and mead as food for you;
>   Uileacan dubh O!
> I shall give you the prospect of ships, and sails, and boats,
> Under the tops of the trees, and we returning from the strand,
> And I would not let any sorrow come upon you.
>   Oh! you are my Uileacan dubh O!
>
> I shall not go with you, and it is in vain you ask me;
>   Uileacan dubh O!
> For your words will not keep me alive without food:
>   Uileacan dubh O!
> A hundred times better for me to be always a maid,
> Than to be walking the dew and the wilderness with you:

My heart has not given to you love nor affection,
And you are not my Uileacan dubh O!

The starkness of this, all the more striking perhaps for the
hesitancy and strangeness of the literal version, (a strangeness
Synge was to transmute into finer metal seventy years later), sets
Ferguson's analytic temper and his imaginative sympathies
aflame. Such intensity, he says, would not be possible in 'the
comparatively artificial state of feeling induced by the influence
of wealth and refinement'. Yet that comparatively artificial state
is vital for the advance of conscious art, and Irish poetry and
song is wanting in 'the *ars poetica'*, especially 'in point of
arrangement'. If Ireland is to take her proper place as an integral
part of the empire, then her poetry will have to learn the travail,
not of passion, which it has in abundance, but of art and judgement. 'We know', says Ferguson magisterially, 'no Irish song
addressed to the judgement', but if Irish art could learn judgement and control, then the combination of that with the native
savage intensity would be potent indeed, perhaps even Homeric.
Ferguson himself, in his later re-tellings of Irish saga material
attempted this kind of amalgamation, combining moral seriousness with the rough alacrity of his native materials. Some even
called him Homeric, among them the early Yeats.

Leaving aside what he considers to be the artlessness of
'Uileacan dubh O', Ferguson imagines a personality behind the
love song, a topography, and an entire historical reality. He fills
out the dialogue with a Romanticised scenario, but it is an
imagining that has behind it Spenser, Fynes Morrison, and an
intimacy with the Irish (especially Northern) countryside.
'Uileacan dubh O', according to Ferguson, was composed by a
rebel:

We can imagine the gaunt wooer of Leitrim, year after year,
disputing his summer sustenance with the hives of hollow oaks,
fighting the wild boar for the mast and acorns of many a
successive autumn, and, winter after winter, descending like
a famished wolf on the pillaged border of the pale. We can
imagine him growing old in caves or thickets; his grizzled beard
purpled with the juice of berries, his thin locks bleached and
tanned by winter storms and summer heats, his limbs brown
from the marsh waters, his very language half-articulate from

disuse in the wilderness, his hand against every man, and every man's against his. Is this an overcharged picture of the old Irish outlaw? Alas! it is but a faint copy of that which history tells us was the dreadful original.

The veracity of this is irrelevant; what matters is its vivid circumstantiality, the ability Ferguson has to imagine, sympathetically, a breed of man to whom the Ribbonmen owe their ancestry. And he can sympathize because of the song he imagines the gaunt wooer declaiming in his misery. The imagination is, as it were, a free agent, independent of party or creed; it is, paradoxically, the duty of the modern Irish Protestant to exercise that faculty in attempting to recover a sense of the Gaelic past if the passionate intensity of native sentiment is to be harnessed, and so become a motive force in the empire. Such strength of feeling, if transferred to proper objects, could move mountains, even build railroads in impossible places, perhaps into the wilds of Leitrim itself.

The other great characteristic of Irish sentiment, according to Ferguson, is

> the excess of natural piety, developing itself in over loyal attachment to principles subversive of reason and independence.[15]

These are loyalty to clan and to church, the word 'piety' here carrying strong overtones of *pietas*. As Ferguson sees it Irish society has retained a primitive and fanatical sense of loyalty which attaches itself to local causes and private revenges. Hence the faction fights, the sectarian killings. It has missed out on the gradual civil evolution of England, so that there is a 'mixed crudeness and barbarity', creating tension and continual inefficient revolution (very unlike, of course, the Glorious Revolution of 1688 in England). The two races of Ireland are 'unable to amalgamate from the want of these intermediate steps upon the civil scale – steps forgotten by the one and never taken by the other'.

The duty of the Irish Protestant is 'to supply the lost links' between the two peoples, Irish and Anglo-Irish, seeing that they have (or should have) the leisure, wealth, independence of mind and intellectual charity to do so. They must build a bridge, and the bridge must be constructed from the stones of the past, resting on the sure foundations of unbiassed and exact history, painstaking archaeological research, but most of all, an acquaintance with Gaelic literature, with all its rugged and barbarous difficulty. For in the literature lay the true configurations of the Irish identity, to be read perhaps only with difficulty, but to be read, just as an ogham stone gave up its meaning after long decipherment. If the Protestant makes this effort to reach his 'less intellectual but more enthusiastic and devoted countryman' he will be making Irishmen 'know themselves and one another; this is the want, this is the worthiest labour of the age'. It would be hard to find an attitude towards literary activity further removed from the purely aesthetic than this. Nor is Ferguson interested in personal expression. Writing has more serious things to concern itself with than that.

So that when Ferguson turns to versifying a selection of poems from Hardiman's collection, his intention is in no way that of Mangan, who always wished to make his originals as expressive of himself as possible; Ferguson is not interested in that kind of coercion of his material. To him, such self-appropriation would be an insolence to the spirit of proper inquiry. Ferguson had that kind of personality which expresses itself in impersonality, in a kind of self-effacement, so that he makes an excellent translator, remaining absolutely true in as many particulars as possible, to the spirit, tone and rhythm of his originals, and to their curious, if at times chaotic image sequences.

We get, in the appendix affixed to the four Hardiman articles, twenty translations which are as faithful to their Irish originals as it is possible to get in English versions. Here, the act of the imagination is one of transparency, of self-denial, curiously analogous in its self-surrender to that 'negative capability' of which Mangan was incapable. In forgetting himself as much as possible, in attempting, successfully, to make his imagination a medium transparent to these 'uncouth' originals, Ferguson comes close, at times, to producing verse of Keatsian clarity and passion:

> I'd wed you without herds, without money, or rich array,
> And I'd wed you on a dewy morning at day-dawn grey;
> My bitter woe it is, love, that we are not far away
> In Cashel town, though the bare deal board were our marriage
>   bed this day . . .

My purse holds no red gold, no coin of the silver white,
No herds are mine to drive through the long twilight,
But the pretty girl that would take me, all bare though I be
    and alone,
Oh, I'd take her with me kindly to the county Tyrone.

One of the greatest difficulties in translating from the Irish
(and it is a difficulty as considerable now as it was in 1834), is that
of finding a style appropriate to the original, a style that will
neither be stiff and unresponsive to the idiomatic flavour of the
Irish on the one hand, nor curious and stage-Irishy on the other.
As Ferguson himself said, in a brief introduction to these
versions, the 'classic language of Pope' will not do, but the 'slang
of Donnybrook' will not either. Ferguson's conclusion is that it
is better to err on the side of quaintness than on that of formality,
to risk eccentricity in order to give the reader a more accurate
sense of what the originals read like in their own language. His
intention is to draw the reader into as close a linguistic relationship with the Irish poetry as English will allow him. This is seen
operating in the poem quoted above, where the rhythm re-enacts
the long curving rhythms of the original, especially in the last line
of the first stanza, in which the rhythm opens out to take in the
all-important concrete detail of the deal board as marriage bed.
All the time Ferguson's rhythm holds an undercurrent of strangeness, as if the other language, Irish, were just under the surface,
an impression he enhances by careful use of phrases and idioms
from Anglo-Irish speech: 'My bitter woe it is'; 'I'd take her with
me kindly'.
Ferguson concludes his selection of translations with a version
called 'The Fair Hills of Ireland', which is a vision of Ireland
as a place of abundance and plenty, a place untouched by Urizen
or by sectarian strife:

A plenteous place is Ireland for hospitable cheer,
        Uileacan dubh O!
Where the wholesome fruit is bursting from the yellow barley
    ear;
        Uileacan dubh O!
There is honey in the trees where her misty vales expand,
And her forest paths, in summer, are by falling waters fanned,

There is dew at high noontide there, and springs i' the yellow
  sand,
       On the fair hills of holy Ireland.

Curled he is and ringletted, and plaited to the knee,
       Uileacan dubh O!
Each captain who comes sailing across the Irish sea;
       Uileacan dubh O!
And I will make my journey, if life and health but stand,
Unto that pleasant country, that fresh and fragrant strand . . .

Large and profitable are the stacks upon the ground;
       Uileacan dubh O!
The butter and the cream do wondrously abound;
       Uileacan dubh O!

In writing of this landscape of plenty, Ferguson is doubtless
thinking of the rich glens of the Six-Mile-Water at a time of
harvest, but there is more to it than this. He is also thinking of
Ireland's potential for material prosperity; the stacks are large
and 'profitable'. This prosperity, this abundance, is not a vision
of a golden past, only to be shattered by the invasion of some
iron horde imposing silence and sterility, as happens in Mangan's
'A Vision of Connaught in the Thirteenth Century'; on the
contrary, this is a vision of the future, when the Irish captains,
with their characteristic 'glibs' of curled hair will return from
their service to foreign (Catholic) nations. Ferguson cannot mean
this literally, but what he implies is that if the native Gaelic past,
typified by the captains serving foreign powers, could be
assimilated by the people he is addressing (the Protestant gentry
of Ireland), if they could be brought to understand that it is in the
best interest of all for the two races to comprehend each other,
then Ireland would be a truly hospitable place, not torn by strife,
but a place of marvellous plenty. And mutual comprehension
must be initiated by the Protestants, they must show their good-
will. Once their intentions are plain, native Irish devotion, loyalty,
and sincerity will be at their service, and at the service of the
empire. Ireland will be England's pastoral dream made real.
    Ferguson's vision is a combination of idealism and utilitarian-
ism, all the more touching for its impossibility, but it is sincerely
held and seriously entertained. Progress towards a future when

the two races of Ireland will complement each other must rest
on Protestant understanding of the Gaelic past, so that when we
read the lines

> And I will make my journey, if life and health but stand,
> Unto that pleasant country, that fresh and fragrant strand,

we realise that Ferguson's journey is to be a journey into the
Irish past, the complex past of ogham inscriptions, Druidic rites,
saga, legend and poetry. It is no journey of antiquarian
dilettantism, but a journey that has to do with the discovery of
a national identity, and then, and only then, the discovery of
self. For Ferguson country comes first, personality second, and
this is what Yeats is alluding to in his essay of 1886, where he
praises Ferguson for his 'centrality', as he calls it. For Yeats,
writing then, he was Ireland's best poet, 'because the most central
and most Celtic'. He was the most central and most Celtic
because he put his conception of the national identity before
himself; he wished to express that before anything else. We might
now regard the image of Ireland Ferguson had as a piece of self-
expression in itself, but would we be entirely right to do so?

IV

Ferguson's attitude to the Irish past, his sense of it as being
necessary for national self-respect, and a contributory factor to
the growth of understanding and mutual respect between the two
races of Ireland, is further enlarged in an essay he wrote for the
Dublin University Magazine on Petrie's *Dublin Penny Journal* in
1840. It is a brilliant statement of how the past may become
truly operative in the present, in a positive reconciling way,
rather than in the divisive way it usually tends to operate in
Ireland. His view is that it is the task of men of scholarship and
imagination to rediscover the mislaid 'facts' (as he calls them) of
Irish history, custom and belief, and to lay them before the
public, in a careful but not boring way. Having done this, national
identity will be clarified and enhanced by a sense of the Gaelic
past as something that yields up its mystery to historical and
logical enquiry. This spirit of enquiry characterised Petrie's

journal of the early 'thirties, as it was to characterize his *Irish Penny Journal* of 1840, the year in which Ferguson wrote this essay.

It is Ferguson's conviction that there can be no true work of the imagination that does not root itself in 'matter of fact', either fact as it is now, or as it once was. In either case there must be, as David Jones was later to put it in his *In Parenthesis,* a 'correspondence with the actual'. Of course, actuality as it is now can never be severed from actuality as it was; that which has been becomes what is in the organism of time. The past is inescapable, that is why it must be comprehended, set down, understood; otherwise it may become a trap, or a source for convenient simplicities, that can be used to harden prejudice. It may also be a liberating, clarifying thing, if the enquiry is conducted properly, and strict truth adhered to in the presentation of what it yields. It can provide a sense of national identity, which Ferguson sees as being closely interwoven with self-respect and personal integrity. Ferguson writes:

> In reviewing the whole progress and prospects of Irish litera-
> ture, there is no event to which we would be disposed to attach
> so much importance, as an effectual revival of that taste for
> *facts* which prevailed in the times of Ware, Davis, and of
> Usher. It is a most prejudicial error to suppose that matter
> of fact, however the term may have been abused, is necessarily
> dry or uninteresting; on the contrary, there can be no true
> romance, no real poetry, nothing, in a word, that will
> effectually touch either the heart or the imagination, that has
> not its foundation in experience of existing facts, or in know-
> ledge of facts that have existed in times past . . . By the
> knowledge of the acts, opinions, and condition of our
> ancestors . . . we can extend the poor three score and ten years,
> which is our immediate portion in time, back and back as far
> as facts exist, for the support of speculation. It is this enlarging
> of our portion of space, of time, of feeling, that is the true
> source of all intellectual pleasure.[16]

In other words, through coming into closer contact with the facts of our ancestors, our own lives gain a flexibility, a sense of space, a sense of being released from the confines of the personality into

the larger continuum of the imagination, where the distinctions
we make between past and present begin to dissolve:

> And all this doubling, and trebling, and infinite multiplying of
> the shares of time, and space, and feeling, originally placed at
> our disposal, is the result of the observation and recording
> of facts. All must be set down at first in strict (not dry)
> detail . . . What we have to do with, and that to which these
> observations properly point, is the recovery of the mislaid, but
> not lost, records of the acts, and opinions, and condition of
> our ancestors – the disinterring and bringing back to the light
> of intellectual day, the already recorded *facts,* by which the
> people of Ireland will be able to *live back,* in the land they live
> *in,* with as ample and as interesting a field of retrospective
> enjoyment as any of the nations around us.

In Ferguson's mind there was no necessary disjunction between
his activities as a historical scholar, archaeologist, linguist and
poet. His duty as a poet was, as he saw it, to enlarge the scope
of contemporary realization of the Irish past, and this he could
faithfully do only if he were in some sort a scholar as well.
Only by being a scholar himself could he have that first-hand
experience of the facts of historical research his poems would
have to be based on if they were to have any authenticity. And
authenticity was something he was prepared to sacrifice finesse
and polish to; we have seen that in his verse translations from
Hardiman's collection he is prepared to err on the side of
eccentricity rather than on that of formality: better to be closer
to Donnybrook, than to Pope. In his poetry, especially in his
retellings of Irish saga, which are his major achievement, he
sacrifices the normal usages of polite English to achieve an effect
which he hopes will be analogous to the effect of the original
in Irish. He is frequently awkward, but it is an awkwardness
that has for its object authenticity; he wants to make Victorian
English expressive of the different qualities of Old Irish narrative,
whether it be its stark swiftness, or its elaborate rhetorical
flourish. He wants to draw his readers close to the stylistic 'facts'
of Old Irish narrative, as well as its content, so that they may be
better able to come into possession of their own past, a legacy
that he sees as contributing to the growth of self-knowledge, self-
respect, and understanding between the two races of Ireland.

This Protestant idealism drew Ferguson to Thomas Davis, leader of the Young Ireland movement, despite the fact that he had little sympathy with that movement, because of its support for O'Connell, its commitment to Repeal, and its overconciliatory attitude to Catholics. Even though Davis held such views, Ferguson tells us in an affectionate tribute written on him in the *Dublin University Magazine* in February 1847 that conservative opinion in Dublin was drawn to Davis, for his openness and frankness, and for his desire to impart 'a spirit of independence and manliness . . . in calling forth their genius and enlarging their intelligence' to the mass of the Irish people, through the *Nation*.[17] To the Irish ascendency Davis gave a new-found national pride, so that for Ferguson he was a stabilising influence, bent on drawing the aristocracy and the peasantry together in peaceful union. This is probably a reasonably fair interpretation of Davis, and it shows how much Ferguson had in common with him.

Ferguson wrote the Davis memoir after he had returned from a year abroad in 1846, a long break taken for health reasons. He came back to find the country in the grip of famine. Like many others he felt he should respond in some appropriate way, and he became a member of the Irish Council to advise the Government on measures to be taken. The advice given, that relief should be the common responsibility of the United Kingdom, if the Union were to have any meaning, was not heeded: in the words of Gavan Duffy, 'though there should not be a separate kingdom for Ireland for the purpose of self-protection, it must be peremptorily isolated in its afflictions'.[18] As a recent historian has put it, Whig famine policy was that 'Irish property should pay for Irish poverty'.[19]

The inhumanity of this doctrinaire economic attitude outraged not only the more militant nationalists, like John Mitchel; it also shocked more conservative opinion. Russell's government seemed like a machine, operating according to the laws of *laissez faire,* totally invincible to pity. It was remote from the actuality of Irish hunger, and remained so until it was too late. The panic of crisis also hardened English parliamentary attitudes towards Ireland into contempt, which again was something that did not go unnoticed by radical or by conservative opinion. The radical answer was the 1848 rising, the conservative answer was even more surprising in some respects, the formation of a Protestant

Repeal Association and a call for legislative independence for Ireland. It was, quite deliberately, a harking back to Grattan's Parliament of 1799, before the Union. The move received Ferguson's support. He was outraged at the contempt shown towards Ireland at Westminster, and in an address to the Protestant Repeal Association in May quotes a remark made in parliament, which he regards as symptomatic of the state of Anglo-Irish relations: 'If Nigger were not Nigger, Irishman would be Nigger'.[20] There seemed to be no regard in the English legislature for Irish pride, Irish independence of spirit, all those things for which he was toiling intellectually, and for which he had broken his health. So we find that by May 1848, responding to the pressure of events, Ferguson has taken up a political stance roughly analogous to that of the dead Davis: 'I have . . . seen reason lately to believe that the disadvantages of the Imperial connection greatly outweigh any advantages we might derive, and infinitely outweigh those which we hitherto have derived, from that source.'

The Whig policy of relieving the Irish distress by making Irish property foot the bill meant that the burden fell almost exclusively on the landed classes. This Ferguson saw as part of a deliberate 'plebeianising' policy on the part of the Whigs, which had for object, finally, the extermination of the Irish gentry, which he associated with the spirit of gentility and honour. It was the wish of the government at Westminster, as he saw it, that there should be no other class of people in Ireland save 'the mere tillers of the soil'. So, for a time, Repeal as envisaged by the Protestant Repeal Association received his active support, but that Association was short-lived and ineffective. The centre of gravity of Irish politics had shifted to the left, the reconciling tradition of Davis was overwhelmed by the more extreme tradition of militancy deriving from John Mitchel and Fintan Lalor. For a time in the 'forties it seemed that his scholarly and imaginative work had a real correspondence with the actualities of Irish life; he even went so far as to say that an art which does not root itself in some actuality, whether present or past, can have no substance, and present and past are held in equation. But the Irish famine changed the realities of Irish life out of all recognition. The present increased in intractability in the 'fifties and the 'sixties, with the growth of the revolutionary movement which came to be known as Fenianism. Apart from this the whole character of Irish society was changing; before the famine it was still possible to feel paternalistic towards the Catholic population, that they were misguided, and that given time and gentle treatment they would come round to a more 'independent' way of thinking. Now a Catholic middle class had begun to emerge, small shopkeepers, traders and the like, many of whom had done well out of the famine. They themselves were strongly conservative, had little sympathy with Fenianism, in that it threatened stability, and had a strong-minded leader in Cardinal Cullen.

Ireland, in other words, was beginning to become a modern mixed society, a society hardly amenable to the attractive simplicities of Ferguson's conservative patriotic idealism. From about 1850 onwards, for the rest of his long life, Ferguson could only feel a mixture of frustration, despair, and confusion when he allowed himself to contemplate the contemporary Irish scene. In this he was, curiously enough, very like the Fenian Charles J. Kickham, whose novel, *Knocknagow* (1873), laments an Irish rural society that has passed forever. For Kickham, as F. S. L. Lyons has pointed out, the famine was a watershed in that 'it wiped out a paternalism which, if sometimes vicious, could also be benevolent, and had substituted in its place the cash nexus'.[21]

The cultural interconnection between past and present, the idea that contemporary disunion between the Irish people can be modified if not healed by a clear understanding of the Gaelic past on the part of the Protestants, which is the burden of Ferguson's essay on the *Dublin Penny Journal* of 1840, became less tenable as Ferguson grew older. Not that his work in Irish history and archaeology ceased; if anything it increased, and it was in later life that he made his retellings of Irish saga, but the actualities of the past came to occupy the greater part of his attention. He became more and more inclined to distance himself from an unattractive and unpredictable present, and to rely on the company of a few civilised and like-minded friends for solace in the turbulence of contemporary life. He did not have a proto-Yeatsian contempt for the fury and complexity of the 'filthy modern tide'; he simply led a quiet, scholarly life, functioning in his administrative capacities efficiently and well. He was blessed with a happy marriage and was comfortably off.

V

Considering the quiet life he led, the content of much of his poetry is quite surprising, in that Ferguson had an astonishing sympathy with the more brutal and violent aspects of Irish literary tradition. As Terence Brown has pointed out, we might have expected him to be drawn to the medieval Irish devotional tradition, especially as he was inclined to regard modern Irish Protestantism as the true inheritor of the spirit of resistance to Papal authority, which was a feature of the Celtic church.[22] Scholarship in this area had not gone very far in Ferguson's lifetime, but there can be no doubt that he was more at home temperamentally in the wider – and wilder – spaces of pagan Ireland. In his essays on Hardiman we have seen that it was his object to determine what it was that constituted national sentiment, or identity. In his poetry this too was his object; he wanted the verse to respond to the intense, often savage sincerity of the Celtic nature, as he saw it. He wanted it to show forth the Irish capacity for devoted loyalty, (even when that loyalty was given to a wrong or brutal cause), its innate, if simple, heroism and nobility.

This romanticized view of the essential Celt is, as Terence Brown has shown, remarkably similar to the version of the Irish peasant Yeats and Synge were later to fashion, much to the anger of the newly-risen Catholic middle classes, many of whom had been peasants themselves only a generation or two before, and who resented Yeats's scorn at them for betraying what they considered themselves well out of.[23] Although Ferguson's Gaelic Ireland is a romanticization, it is not one done in soft lights and delicate hues and vague allusive word tones. On the contrary, it is a vividly rendered masculine world done in bold broad strokes, with little attention to the niceties of characterization. It is an energetic world, violent, bloody and unpredictable, with most of the action taking place outdoors. Nature is a constant backdrop to the events, and more often than not those events are given precise locations, imitating the topographical character of a good deal of Gaelic story.

All the time we are conscious of Ferguson's continuing preoccupation with the 'facts' of that Gaelic world he wished to re-present imaginatively in as faithful a manner as he could.

Often the effect is harsh, where he makes an attempt to present
in English an impression of what the original Irish was like,
stylistically. In 'Fergus Wry-Mouth', for example, he makes a
reasonably successful attempt at capturing the often terse, almost
sardonic quality of the dialogues in Irish saga as they survive
in manuscript. King Fergus has been given the power to walk
under water by the fairies, with the warning that he must never
attempt to explore Loch Rury. He does, and meets a monster,
called the Muirdris, who is so hideous that the sight of it

> Hung all his visage sideways with affright.
> He fled. He gained the bank. 'How seems my cheer,
> Oh Mwena?' 'Ill!' replied the Charioteer.
> 'But rest thee. Sleep thy wildness will compose'.
> He slept.[24]

This is awkward, but it is an awkwardness that has for its object
immediacy. Indeed, one of the qualities of Ferguson's original
poems is their freshness, their air of somewhat rough but alert
attention to detail. It is an objective poetry, delighting in the
externals of the old Irish world, its swift, energetic, often brutal
physicality. Congal, in the hall of Dunangay, where he has been
insulted by the Christian high king Domnal, describes how he, in
support of Domnal, killed Sweeney Menn, Domnal's predecessor
and lawful king:

> 'on the sunny sward
> Before the fort, sat Sweeney Menn, amid his royal guard,
> He and his nobles chess-playing. Right through the middle band
> I went, and no man's licence asked, Garr-Congail in my hand,
> And out through Sweeney's body, where he sat against the wall,
> 'Twas I that sent Garr-Congail in presence of them all.
> And out through Sweeney's body till the stone gave back the
>   blow,
> 'Twas I that day at Aileach made keen Garr-Congail go'.

He revels in the martial, savage imagery. These are a major
feature of his sources anyway, and as he points out in a note
to 'Mesgedra', they should no more repel the reader than Medea's
cauldron or the supper of Thyestes. The reader should not allow
the atrocities to blind him to what is behind them. Behind them

are the 'characteristic forms of grandeur' of the ancient Celt, his savage nobility and strength, and his capacity for direct energetic action. This energy, expressed in the martial imagery seems to be what Ferguson most associated with the essential temperament of the race. His verse is at its best when it strains in its excitement to catch that energy, and make it live again in a modern unsatisfactory language. In 'Conary' there is a passage which does this very successfully, a passage describing the effect of the war-pipe on fighting men. The piper is one of the three red pipers Conary, the high king, saw before him on his way to the hostel of Da Derga, and they are an evil omen for him. The pipers are of the sidhe, and have power over him because he has disregarded various taboos. Later, surrounded in Da Derga by invaders, he sends out a force of men on a circuit of the hostel in an attempt to repel the enemy, fatally asking one of the red pipers to lead them into combat. The piper excites their feelings so intensely that he can draw them away from the hostel:

>   'Yea, mighty king', said one,
> 'The strain I play ye shall remember long',
> And put the mouthpiece to his lips. At once –
> It seemed as earth and sky were sound alone,
> And every sound a maddening battle-call,
> So spread desire of fight through every breast and brain,
> And every arm to feat of combat strung.
> Forth went the sallying hosts: the hosts within
> Heard the enlarging tumult from their doors
> Roll outward; and the clash and clamour heard
> Of falling foes before; and, over it,
> The yelling pibroch; but, anon, the din
> Grew distant and more distant.[24a]

Ferguson had a horror of violence, of civil war, of anything that would disrupt the ordered pattern of things. He was drawn to the Protestant Repeal Association, because he thought that some measure of self-determination was the only way to avoid the complete collapse of Irish society, which would follow the extermination of the Irish gentry. English policy with regard to Ireland seemed intent on that extermination of the privileged. 'Conary' is a poem about a society breaking down, and there is nothing anyone can do about it, because Conary, the high king, is fated to break all his taboos. There is a malignancy around him, which his kindly, peace-loving nature cannot control. Among the invaders there are some Irish, foster-brothers of Conary, in fact, whom he failed to punish severely, sending them into exile instead of killing them. With them also are two of Conary's own brothers, who joined the others for the excitement of it. One of these, Lomna Druth, pleads with the British pirate Ingcel, not to attack the hostel where Conary is staying the night. In killing the inhabitants, he will be killing 'the life, the soul itself/Of our whole nation', because the people gathered in the hostel are all those who 'minister our loftier life':

> For, slay our reverend sages of the law,
> Slay him who puts the law they teach in act;
> Slay our sweet poets, and our sacred bards,
> Who keep the continuity of time
> By fame perpetual of renowned deeds;
> Slay our experienced captains who prepare
> The youth for martial manhood, and the charge
> Of public freedom, as befits a state
> Self-governed, self-sufficing, self-contained;
> Slay all that minister our loftier life,
> Now by this evil chance assembled here,
> You leave us but the carcass of a state,
> A rabble ripe to rot, and yield the land
> To foreign masters and perpetual shame.

The plea of Lomna Druth is a conservative plea in that he wishes to dissuade Ingcel from disrupting the established mode of life in Ireland, its hereditary, hierarchical nature. If he does invade, there will be but rabble left. All independence will be sacrificed forever; the state will no longer be able to govern itself. The conservatism of Lomna Druth has within it a desire to safeguard Ireland's self-determination. Lomna Druth is overruled, the British pirate Ingcel is interested only in plunder. He has no interest in Ireland's well-being.

Lomna Druth's futile plea expresses Ferguson's conservative nationalism, whereas the ruthlessness of Ingcel could stand for the exploitative and unsympathetic attitude of the British government towards Ireland, about which Ferguson frequently complained.

It is clear that Ferguson's re-tellings of Irish saga are no mere satisfying of a taste on his part for the archaic and barbaric. They show a desire to re-present, as faithfully as possible, those 'facts' of Gaelic history and legend which would enlarge the imaginative scope of the contemporary Irishman, and make his intellectual life more authentic, because more in contact with his own past.

There is a sense that this project can only hope to succeed partially, if succeed at all. In 'Aideen's Grave' the poet Ossian sings a burial dirge over the dead Aideen, who has died of grief on hearing of the death of Oscar, Ossian's son, at the battle of Gavra. They intern her at Howth under the great cromlec. Ossian's lament takes a strange turn halfway through and he imagines how the life he knows will pass away, how the language he is controlling now at this dramatic moment will fail. Even the marks on Aideen's stone will in time wear away. Then he imagines someone in some far distant time attempting to sympathize with the lay he is singing now, with his time and with his grief. The someone is, of course, Ferguson, but Ferguson's reviving of that grief can only be 'imperfect':

> The long forgotten lay I sing
>   May only ages hence revive,
> (As eagle with a wounded wing
>   To soar again might strive,)
>
> Imperfect, in an alien speech,
>   When, wandering here, some child of chance
> Through pangs of keen delight shall reach
>   The gift of utterance, –
>
> To speak the air, the sky to speak,
>   The freshness of the hill to tell,
> Who, roaming bare Ben Edar's peak
>   And Aideen's briary dell,
>
> And gazing on the Cromlech vast
>   And on the mountain and the sea,
> Shall catch communion with the past
>   And mix himself with me.[25]

There is something of Eliot's desire for impersonality here;

Ferguson wishes 'to speak the air', not to speak of himself, to mix himself with the dead hero, rather than assert his own uniqueness in the here and now. Self-assertion, energy, belonged to those men in the past. Now speech itself is imperfect. It is not the total speech of Ossian. Life has waned:

> Of Oscar and Aideen bereft,
>   So Ossian sang. The Fenians sped
> Three mighty shouts to heaven; and left
>   Ben Edar to the dead.

There is a strong feeling here that 'the dead' are all those who have followed the Fenians, those Dubliners of Joyce who go to Howth for day trips from time to time, those Dubliners of Ferguson's own day, and Ferguson himself, who used to go there to recover from his periodic breakdowns in health.

Ferguson, in his re-tellings of Gaelic saga, or episodes from Irish history (like for example, his well-known savage ballad, 'The Welshmen of Tirawley'), tried to re-invigorate the 'dead' imagination of his own time by re-creating the energetic vitality of the old Irish world, as he saw it. Whenever he speaks of the poets of his own day he is inclined to regard them as somewhat unhealthy and unmanly in their search for 'recondite thought and curious felicities of expression which of late in our literature, have become too much the fashion'.[26] His ideal was Burns, not because Burns made much of the ancient traditions of Scotland in the way that Ferguson was trying to do for Ireland, but because Burns, to Ferguson's mind, seemed in contact with the simple actualities of his own time, Burns 'spoke the air' of his own locality with an authenticity denied to most poets from the time of Ossian. His speech was less 'imperfect' than that of Ferguson, stronger, 'manlier' (one of Ferguson's favourite words) than the 'nosers of curious odours' (Edward Dowden's phrase) of his own time. An Irish poet could not hope for the kind of authenticity that Burns had, seeing that rural Irish society had not as yet progressed to the stage of civilisation needed for a poet like Burns to emerge.[27]

Urban poetry was by definition a diseased imposture, so it was necessary to retain as much contact as possible with the country-side, especially the countryside of one's upbringing. That for Ferguson was the countryside of county Antrim, especially those vales east of Lough Neagh, a territory that had, strangely enough, been colonized by Lowlands Scots, who still spoke the dialect of Burns up to Ferguson's time. It is not surprising then to find that his great epic hero comes from that area, Rathmore Moy-Linny. Like Yeats after him, Ferguson

> thought
> All that we did, all that we said or sang
> Must come from contact with the soil, from that
> Contact everything Antaeus–like grew strong.

But it seemed to Ferguson that in his time the soil had gone sour and dead, and so was incapable of such a flourishing growth as Burns. That soil had to be re-invigorated with memories of former growth, former energy, former richness. Thus Ferguson's Irish sagas attempted to 'raise the native elements of Irish story to a dignified level; and that ambition I think may be taken as the key to almost all the literary work of my . . . life'.[28] They were to fertilize the soil for the coming of the truly representative national poet, the Irish Burns. Thomas Moore was not he, not only because he was not a Protestant, and so lacking (as Ferguson saw it) the fearlessness and manliness such a poet would need, but because Ferguson recognized in him a lack of attack, a lack of the directness such a poet should have. In January 1845, in one of two essays on Burns, he accurately foretold that the representative Irish poet, when he would come, would come from the middle classes, not the farming class, as in Burns's case, as it would be only among the middle classes that sufficient independence of spirit would be bred into the man's bone.

What happened followed fairly exactly Ferguson's prediction: Yeats was of the Protestant middle classes, fiercely proud of his family's independence of spirit, and indeed using Ferguson's poetry as a seed bed for his own vigorous imagination, building Ferguson, especially in his early writing, into a kind of Homeric figure among the 'sybaritic' poets of his day, praising him for a kind of rough-hewn massiveness.

One thing that Ferguson would probably have disapproved of in Yeats's re-handling of him soon after his death was the way in which Yeats made him out to be a kind of revolutionary nationalist. This was a natural enough thing for Yeats to do, as Ferguson had laid so much stress on the essential nature of the

Celt, different in character and imagination from the 'stolid Saxon'. Such radical theorizing is dear to the hearts of all revolutionary nationalists, but we cannot make Ferguson out to be an unconscious Fenian (in the modern, political, not the Ossianic sense) in spite of all his superficial conservatism. His fascination with racial theorizing, while undoubtedly a contributory factor to the political outlook of Yeats and, later again, Pearse, was something he shared with many Victorians, among them Matthew Arnold, and no one could accuse the English public school inspector of being either an unconscious Fenian, or a proto-Fascist.

Terence Brown has argued that in his revelling in fierce martial imagery, Ferguson was unconsciously responding to the contemporary political forces of his time. War was what the Fenians were after, and here, in Ferguson's versions of saga, were images of war associated with racial purity.[29] Brown points out that civil disruption terrified Ferguson's conservative attitude (an attitude expressed in 'Conary'). It may be that Ferguson's attraction to the violent, the savage, the unpredictable in nature and humanity, was, as well as being a re-call of Celtic energy, also an exorcism of the violence of a turbulent present, with all its tensions and complexities.

This is not self-expression in the usual sense of the word; it has more in common with the 'objective correlative' of Eliot, where images and narrative, entirely separate from personality, carry the emotional charge which refuses to be stated directly. The narrative and its accompanying images (often images of violence in Ferguson's sagas) help to dissolve the tension of living in a turbulent present more completely than any attempt at direct statement of that tension. It is in the long poem *Congal,* in the complexities of its narrative structure, that we find the most complete and probably unconscious exegesis of the tensions in the mind of a conservative Irish Protestant in the latter half of the nineteenth century.

VI

Ferguson based *Congal* (1872) on the two historical tales, *Cath Muighe Rath,* and its introductory pre-tale *Fled Dúin na nGéd,* the *Battle of Moyra* and *The Banquet of Dunangay*. These historical tales were edited in 1842, by John O'Donovan and William Hennessy, and published by the Irish Archaeological Society. From then on the two tales occupied Ferguson's imagination. He was attracted to them for their broad theme, which had to do with the dis-establishment of the old, native order in Irish society by the forces of Christianity and progress. Congal, a sub-king of Ulster, ruling from Rathmore Moy-Linny near Antrim (Ferguson's own area) is drawn into conflict with Domnal, high king of Ireland ruling from Dunangay on the Boyne, because of an actual or imagined insult (it is left unclear in the poem) at the feast to which the high king has invited him. Congal cannot be simply equated with the old order, although all the poets in the first book of the poem are very eager to do so. Most of the poets, as preservers of the Gaelic order, have retired to Ulster, where they receive protection from Kellach the Halt, Chief of Mourne, and uncle to Congal. 'Erin's churls' (the followers of Domnal and the priests), have banished the poets, and they now have sanctuary in the 'sheltering, song-preserving hills' of Ulster, where they still teach 'the better Bardic utterance', awaiting the day of liberation.

Congal, on his way to the feast at Dunangay, is asked to stay the night at the court of Kellach the Halt, where the poets sing to him, in disdain of the high king's messenger who has accompanied him, songs that can only be called seditious. One of the poets, Cical, identifies Congal with Slanga, son of Partholan, one of the first invaders of Ireland. When he 'saw the sunshine flame /On Congal's crest' he knew him to be Slanga reborn. Ardan too, the chief-poet, claims Congal as the champion of Ulster's suppressed rights. He reminds him of the richness and extent of Ulster, of the magnificence of the tributes to which he is traditionally entitled, of his responsibility, as it were, to the landscape itself, the sense that 'abrupt Easroe /In many a tawny leap and whirl' belongs to him and he to it in ways that the new order represented by Domnal cannot comprehend. Ardan then looses a traditional curse on the high king, a curse wherein Ardan imagines the natural forces also leagued against Domnal. He makes himself out to be their spokesman:

'From livid lips of desperate men who bear enormous wrong,
Heaven cannot hold it; but the curse outbursting from on high

In blight and plague, on plant and man, blasts all beneath
the sky.
Burst, blackening clouds that hang aloof o'er perjured
Domnal's halls!
Dash down, with all your flaming bolts, the fraud-cemented
walls,
Till through your thunder-riven palls heaven's light anew
be poured
In Law and Justice, Wealth and Song, on Congal's throne
restored!'[30]

The heaven here is not the heaven of Domnal, but that other
pagan heaven of Ardan. Congal has mixed feelings about these
bardic tributes. To Ardan he says 'for thy lay /I thank thee and
I thank thee not'. He and Domnal have sworn peace, even though
his lands have been reduced. Furthermore, although Ferguson
does not go to any great trouble to give Congal any depth of
character, he is conspicuous for his independence from bardic
belief, and from Christian belief also. He simply wishes to get
on with the practical business of living, of settling down with
Lafinda, his betrothed. He would let the past be with the dead,
but those around him are intent on keeping the dead alive and
on invoking the unseen forces on all possible occasions. For this
reason, the dead will not stay dead, the unseen trouble the living.
When war is decided upon, Congal himself hears a tumult in the
mountains, 'as of immeasurable herds a-droving all around'. Then
there is a sound as of shale dislodged from the summit and Ardan
cries out with excitement that it is the herdsman-god Borcha,
climbing to his herd-seat as of old, where he sat and counted
the numbers of his flock. This, for Ardan, means that the
'Powers/ Unseen that round us live and move' are on their side,
the side of the poets, of Kellach and of Congal. However, Congal
wants nothing to do with these unseen forces. If he is to fight,
he wants to fight with manly arms alone.

The unseen forces, however, will not stay out of the action.
They haunt it and their intentions are inscrutable. It is almost
as if they themselves do not know what they are doing. To some
extent they are in the grip of the way events have gone in the
tangible Ireland of Congal and Domnal, to some extent they are
subject to incomprehensible laws of their own. Manannan Mac
Lir, ancient protector of Ireland, appears to Congal while he

and his army are encamped on the way to the battlefield of Moyra. The huge shape tramps around the camp, and Congal goes out to speak with it. He sees, vaguely, the great bulk striding through the white mist, 'like a man much grieved, who walks alone /Considering of a cruel wrong'.[31] Congal addresses it, asking it why it comes now to trouble his sleep before a battle, but there is no reply. Ardan later tells him that Manannan's power has now gone, but that he revisits Ireland when evil destinies threaten it, uselessly to haunt the outcome.

Crossing the river Ollarva the army are confronted with the horrifying spectre of the Washer of the Ford, laving blood-stained tunics and the limbs and heads of men in the water. The stream approaching her is 'tranquil, clear and bright' but downwards from her 'the blood-polluted flood rode turbid'. From the mess of tangled limbs she lifts up a head, saying, 'thine own head, oh Congal'. This episode, of the Washer of the Ford, Ferguson took from an account of the wars between two septs of the O'Briens entitled *The Wars of Turlogh* written in 1549 by one Mac Craith. It is discussed in the third of Ferguson's Hardiman articles and the hag's speech quoted there matches very closely the one she makes to Congal in the later poem. All that this shows is that the barbaric imagery fascinated Ferguson, and he was glad to incorporate it in a poem which revels in it. It also increases the reader's sense of the chaos of the unseen forces that surround the human actors in *Congal*. Congal who, despite the fact that he has his doubts about the ancestral argument for war of Ardan and Kellach the Halt, is nevertheless fighting for the old ways, finds himself confronted with manifestations out of native legend that threaten and terrify. Eventually he takes what is, under the circumstances, a fairly rationalist view, and maintains that all these 'phantasms' are in fact created by the curses of the priests that surround Domnal, to dishearten the just army of Congal. But, according to Congal, his men are independent, free, unsuperstitious; the 'weak ghosts' sent out by the priest-ridden Domnal can have no power over them. Their cause is just, they must win, and with that he and his men move on to 'Moyra's fated field'.[32]

They do not win, Congal is given his death wound from behind with a bill-hook by Cuanna, an idiot, son of Ultan-Long-Hand. He eventually swoons from loss of blood, and through a combination of the powers of Manannan and Borcha is spirited away

in a great storm back to his native Antrim. He finds that Ardan
also has been brought from the battle in the same way. They find
themselves in 'grassy Collin' outside a convent founded by Brigid,
where Lafinda has become a novice. She tends the dying hero
in his last moments, during which he is granted an extraordinary
vision from which Lafinda piously averts her eyes. It is a vision
of Manannan Mac Lir in benign aspect, a vision of blessed plenty,
of sweetness and release. The god reveals himself as the countryside is when it is beautiful, when there seems no distance between
perceiver and perceived:

> No longer soiled with stain of earth, what seemed his mantle
>   shone
> Rich with innumerable hues refulgent, such as one
> Beholds, and thankful-hearted he, who casts abroad his gaze
> O'er some rich tillage-country-side, when mellow Autumn days
> Gild all the sheafy foodful stooks; and broad before him
>   spread, –
> Bray or Ben-Edar – sees beneath, in silent pageant grand,
> Slow fields of sunshine spread o'er fields of rich corn-bearing
>   land;
> Red glebe and meadow-margin green commingling to the view
> With yellow stubble, browning woods, and upland tracts
>   of blue.[33]

The simile goes on for another fourteen lines, during which it
is revealed that the 'he' who looks out over this richness is a
citizen just recovered from an illness which has kept him 'long
indoors'. The simile is not simply a distraction, but helps to make
the vision granted to Congal at the end all the more vivid. He,
Congal, at the point of death, is like the modern citizen recovered
from a disease. All the beauty of the Irish countryside breaks
fresh upon the sight, and this freshness, this sweetness, is the
true Manannan Mac Lir, free from the toil, the blood, the fury
and complexity of human strife. It is an amazingly good close
to a very confused poem. Congal says:

> my deeds of strife and bloodshed seem
> No longer mine, but as the shapes and shadows of a dream:
> And I myself, as one oppressed with sleep's deceptive shows,
> Awaking only now to life, when life is at its close.

Congal, when he dies, is brought into the sacred enclosure; those who bring him in offer sanctuary to Ardan as well from the hosts of the approaching Domnal. He, however, his king having attained illumination outside the convent, decides to remain outside as well, 'while up the hill the hosts of Domnal came'.

A great deal has been said in the past about the faults of *Congal*. Many critics begin their demolition with the unsuitability of the metre for a sustained narrative which is self-consciously attempting to be dignified. It is a resurrection of the Chap-manesque fourteener, which has an irresistible tendency to degenerate into the sing-song of the ballad measure. Many of the criticisms levelled at the metre are just, but it does at times attain what Ferguson desired, a long loose flowing measure, with floating stresses, a nineteenth century version of what Ferguson imagined a bardic chant to be like.

To find fault with the poem's metre, however, is only to scratch the surface. More complicated is the fact that our sympathies are confused, and this confusion is hardly deliberate on Ferguson's part. It is, however, a very rich and suggestive confusion. Congal is the hero; that at least is clear. Lady Wilde recognised this immediately; writing in the year *Congal* was published she says:

> Congal seems to me to typify Ireland. He has the noble, pure, loving nature of his race – still clinging to the old, from instinctive faith and reverence, through all the shadowy fore-bodings that he is fighting for a lost cause; and the supernatural here has a weird reality and deep significance. It is the expression of our own presentiments . . . Yet he fights on, with the self-immolating zeal of a martyr, for the old prejudices of his nation, his fathers, his childhood, against the new ideas that overthrew all he reverenced . . . The death of Congal, too, has a pathetic significance . . . Here again I find a symbolism to our poor Irish cause; always led by a hero, always slain by a fool. I must talk over this, and a great deal more in the epic, when I see you.[34]

Terence Brown has recently argued that here Ferguson was (probably unconsciously) contributing to the growth of one of the favourite icons of later nationalists, the failed yet noble hero, whose failure testifies to his authenticity. There is truth in this, and certainly Ferguson wished his hero to stand for a central feature of the Irish identity. Congal is a martyr for a failed cause. Yet when we look more closely the picture loses some of this clarity, valuable though it is from the point of view of nineteenth century political history, and the growth of its dangerous iconographies.

Congal has something essentially Irish about him. But he is no credulous heathen. He is not drawn into the fight by the appeals to legendary rights of the bards, though he is touched by their eloquence. He is a pagan, but a very independent one. He will have no truck with their superstitions, though the narrative of the poem makes clear that there are unseen forces operating on human life. The bards think that these forces are on the side of the man who is trying to oppose the new order, an order that will surely be inimical to them, but the forces seem to have little sympathy either way. If anything they lean towards the new order of Domnal, making Congal's journey to Moyra so fraught with fatal omens. They seem to enjoy making appearances, and a march to a forthcoming battle presents a good opportunity for powerful manifestations. Congal remains suspicious of them, and attributes them to the priests that he sees as running King Domnal's life for him. Congal is a strange mixture of Celtic nobility (as Ferguson saw it) and Protestant independence of mind.

In the poem, however, that independence is doomed. The day is to be with the new order. The Ulstermen see Domnal as priest-ridden; according to the poets he is something of a proto-materialist, exiling the poets, so that their influence is confined. In their view he disregards 'life's needful charge of knowledge'.[35] From the Ulster point of view in the poem he looks like an image of the Victorian, middle class, Irish Catholicism against which Yeats was later to rage, that fearful Catholicism which 'dried the marrow from the bone'. But that is the Ulster point of view *in the poem*.

The total picture of Domnal that *Ferguson* gives us is not at all an unsympathetic one. Throughout the poem he behaves nobly, and indeed the insult that first occasioned the strife may not have been intended. Especially notable is his behaviour towards Cuanna, the idiot boy who killed Congal. Cuanna's stepmother would appear to be responsible for the boy's idiocy; she, when he was a boy, scared him out of his wits by showing him a doll dressed as a goblin, so that her own son could assume his place. Domnal takes the boy seriously and assures him of justice. In all Ferguson makes Domnal a noble opponent to Congal, but at the close it is Congal who has the true vision of Ireland, when Manannan Mac Lir puts off his shapeless indeterminateness (though not his silence) and shows him the blessedness of natural things, a blessedness he only comes to see on the point of death. And he sees it outside the convent where Lafinda, his loved one, has, to put it crudely, gone over to the enemy.

What are we to make of all this? Congal is the essential Celt (according to Ferguson), manly, noble, fearless, undaunted by the unseen and indeterminate forces of Ireland's legendary past. These forces are massive and violent, and no one has a satisfactory way of dealing with them. It might be argued that they are in the poem only because Ferguson delighted in the vague, the massive, that their chaos is merely a failure on Ferguson's part to organise his heathen machinery properly. Even so, such a failure would be a significant one, indicating Ferguson's powerlessness in the face of the massive and often brutal energy he saw as being characteristic of Irish identity, and of Irish art. It was an energy he at once tried to tame, and yet convey to the modern Irishman.

In the poem Congal regards these manifestations of power and violence as the 'weak' demons of priestcraft, but he is shown to be wrong; they are more than that. (As Lady Wilde said, they have 'a weird reality and deep significance! ') They are an energy underlying whatever it means to be Irish, and to be Irish is to be involved with them to some extent at least. To be a poet is to be especially susceptible to their power, as the poets in the poem are, except that they misinterpret them also. These great indeterminate shapes are powerful blurred images of the turbulence that underlies Irish history. They also seethe beneath the present, threatening to fracture whatever frail structures good-willed men try to erect on the basis of sanity and understanding. So their blurred outline in the poem is the terrified sketch of the violence that is constantly under the surface of Irish life, portrayed by a man who, more than anything, longed for stability.

Ferguson is fair to Domnal, although the Ulstermen are not; he and they are, after all, enemies. Although Domnal is just and noble according to his lights, it is to Congal that Manannan reveals himself at the end in benign aspect. This is the true vision

of Ireland. So, out of the great blur that surrounds the poem in
the persons of the native deities, out of the confusion of
sympathies deriving from Ferguson's fair-mindedness in dealing
with Domnal, a proposition begins to emerge, a proposition that
Ferguson held all his life: that the only true Irishman is a
Protestant, because only he has the independence of spirit that
can keep him clear of the turmoil of Irish life. He can give,
because he is free to refuse. He can serve Ireland because only
he can make that severance between head and heart necessary
to sane life and progress. Her Catholic sons, though their
desire to serve is also intense, always tend to lose themselves in
the blur of energy that Congal manages to hold at a distance.
That energy is violent, unpredictable, destructive. Only by holding it at a distance can normal life (and that is all that any sane
man wants) be possible. It is a curiously Augustan stance, but
Ferguson was not the only Victorian who by temperament
belonged to the age of Grattan's parliament.

VII

Before 1850 or thereabouts, it had been Ferguson's ambition to
establish a living equation between past and present in Ireland.
He saw it as his Protestant responsibility to make that past live
in a spirit of sane, free enquiry. That done, national self-respect
would be enhanced, and with it national independence. In *Congal,*
Ferguson's most ambitious poem, that independence is defeated,
although it is given a vision of the true Ireland at the close. The
future belongs to Domnal and his priests, his centralization and
his favourites. Even Lafinda herself has become a nun. Finally,
irony of ironies, Congal himself is to be interred in the convent
enclosure. The poem is, at root, a lament for the passing of
Ireland as Ferguson knew it, and that, for him, meant the best
of Ireland. The country is to pass over to the modern mixed
society, that will not be without justice, but the day of the
rabblement will have begun. The 'plebeianizing' tendency he
spoke of in 1848 is irreversible; Ireland is handed over to the
dead, the violent, and the democratic.

The poet Ardan stays outside the convent enclosure, to face certain death from Domnal's forces. He is the literary ancestor of the Yeatsian hero.

5

Aubrey de Vere:
An Attempt at a Catholic Humanity

I

Like Ferguson, Aubrey de Vere was deeply conservative in attitude; like him also he belonged to the Protestant Ascendancy. De Vere inherited his place in that class, whereas Ferguson came to it on his marriage to Mary Guinness. The de Vere family lived at Curragh Chase in County Limerick, and near it was Adare Manor, home of the Dunraven family, where the young de Veres used to go on holiday at Christmas. Life was relaxed and civilized in the big house; the children had tutors, one of whom, Edward Johnstone, drew the young Aubrey's attention to Wordsworth's poetry, his passion for which did not abate for the rest of his life. The children wandered about the large estate, or tended the little gardens their father had given each of them, and at night there were readings from novels, travels, and biographies, and from the speeches of Brougham or Canning.

Aubrey's father, Sir Aubrey de Vere, was a paternalistic landlord with liberal views. His son described him as a 'Liberal Tory' or 'Canningite'. He was in favour of Catholic Emancipation and he obviously communicated something of his enthusiasm for the movement to his son, for when the Bill was passed in 1829, Aubrey, then fifteen, climbed to the top of a pillar opposite the house, and waved a torch in the gathering darkness. Aubrey's older brother, Stephen, who eventually inherited the baronetcy, maintained his father's liberal traditions. During the famine of the late 'forties Stephen went so far as to accompany some of the peasants who had been under his supervision on the public works to Canada on an emigrant ship, sharing with them all the discomforts of the passage, in order than he might be able to report accurately to Parliament on the hardships involved in sailing on these vessels.[1] By the close of his life, Aubrey tells us, Stephen had reduced the rents on his estate to about three quarters of what would have been considered a fair rent. He also approved of Gladstone's Land Act of 1881, which led the way to peasant ownership, and thereby the eventual collapse of the land-owning class to which he himself belonged. Aubrey, though himself something of a 'Liberal Tory', like his father and brother, did not allow his radical sympathies to extend so far. Like Ferguson he believed in the importance of an elite in maintaining the vitality of a country, in keeping alive the best traditions of its past, and in allowing scope for individual effort. He despised what he thought of as the 'Jacobinical' tendencies of the later nineteenth century because they were destructive of sanity and inherited order.

De Vere came to maturity in a time of intense religious discussion. There were the Tractarians at Oxford, led by Newman, who insisted on the importance of tradition in religious practice, and on the need for maintaining a Church polity, a visible and comprehensive organization with its roots in the Christian practice of the past, as an antidote to the anarchy of contemporary individualism. Instead of making up one's own mind about matters of faith and belief, the church should take it upon itself to interpret for one, and in this way guard against the chaos of subjective judgement. It is easy to see that the natural progress of many Tractarians was towards the church of Rome, and indeed Newman himself became a convert in 1845. De Vere met Newman in Oxford in 1838 and was very impressed by his atmosphere of sanctity and otherworldiness, thinking him like some 'youthful ascetic of the middle ages'.[2]

Immediately after his visit to Oxford, de Vere went to Cambridge. At the time Cambridge was identified with the other side of the great contemporary debate on religious matters. Clearly the young Irishman was trying to expose his mind to as much of the evidence of faith as he possibly could. His cousin, Stephen Spring Rice, author of some bleakly introverted sonnets, was a member of the famous Apostles Club at Cambridge, where, the members claimed, everything was discussed with absolute freedom. Tennyson, and the theologian F. D. Maurice, had been members of this famous club. Both these men, especially Maurice, were to have a profound influence on de Vere. Here at Cambridge he found an entirely latitudinarian atmosphere where the only authority acknowledged in discussion was the tribunal of the individual judgement. Temperamentally he was more at home in the intellectual milieu of Oxford, and all which that implied, finding its reverence for tradition and for authority more congenial than the recklessness and daring of the arguments at Cambridge. There he felt that people were more inclined to delight in the brilliant flash of paradox for its own sake than, as his biographer Wilfrid Ward puts it in his flowery way, 'to strive for the renewal of the empire of revelation over the human heart'.[3] He found that the Cambridge men had what he described as a taste for irony, for playing around with theories, as if they were a matter for amusement. He thought them self-centred and they seemed to him to give encouragement to the modern disease of over-subjectivity and reliance on private judgements alone to sort out the true from the false in the interior life. In a letter to his cousin at Cambridge in 1841 he indulges in a mock-heroic denunciation of the Cambridge vices, as he sees them:

> I mean you Apostles or Apostolic men . . . Are you not, one and all, utterly profane and unclean? . . . Are you not ironical persons? Is not your creed that everything is everything else? Your practical code to try everything and hold fast to that which is bad? Your devotional system to burn incense to a 'many-sided' kaleidoscope, and raise an altar to your own centre of gravity.[4]

De Vere was impressed by the distinction which Samuel Taylor Coleridge made between the higher 'Reason' and the 'Understanding'. By the reason in this sense Coleridge meant that faculty in man through which he arrives at an intuitive grasp of those truths to which the understanding has no access. The mind, in other words, could come to truths which could not be explained by human logical processes, but these truths were none the less valid for that. The mistake the Cambridge men seemed to him to make was that they relied overmuch on the understanding, failing to realize that there were modes of knowing other than argument, logic, and private judgement.

They lacked a proper humility, a readiness to forsake the crazy mazes of dialectic in order to allow the footprints of a higher mind than theirs to reveal themselves in the tracks of the reason. When these footprints became clear (and Coleridge insisted that experience taught us that they could become clear) a man could forget the whirling colours of the subjective kaleido-scope and follow the track made by God in the universal mind for our guidance. For de Vere it was the duty of the church to teach its members how best to follow that spoor of the higher reason. It was her responsibility to be a touch-stone of reality in the chaos that modern self-consciousness had brought:

> Of all the thoughts at this moment going on, in the brains of men, not one in a thousand has anything that answers to it either in pure reason or the truth of things. What, then, if Religion, instead of holding forth a substance of Reality in the midst of this phantom dance, forgets her peculiar and positive function – watches the maniacs till she goes mad, catches the impulse and joins the rout?[5]

Now more than ever, in the chaos of modern intellectual egalitarianism, was it vitally necessary to have a church that held firmly to tradition, and disclaimed the right of the individual conscience to make up its mind about everything. Through what he saw as an undiscriminating dislike of anything that looked like a system, the very idea of religion itself was being lost. 'Is not "Religio", he asks, 'to *bind* again? and how can you bind except by Doctrines reduced to their orthodox form and Duties explained, applied and enforced'.[6] It is the binding that makes one free, just as the ligament makes the muscle free to move by its binding.

It is not surprising to find that de Vere, following Newman, was received into the Catholic church in 1851, at Avignon, on his way to Rome. Thus his conservatism became the radical con-servatism of nineteenth century English Catholicism, in sharp contradistinction to the tenacious Irish Anglicanism of his con-temporary and friend, Samuel Ferguson. Both men were deeply conservative, but their conservatism took very different forms. Ferguson saw religious issues always in their Irish context, and so held on fiercely to his Protestant traditions, in that they were, he believed, Ireland's best guarantee for an independent-minded, manly nation. De Vere, however, saw beyond the Irish context, was aware of the great theological issues of the mid-century, and this gives his Catholicism an obviously English flavour.

His brother Stephen seems to have been quite different in attitude. He became a convert to Catholicism some years before Aubrey, but he seems to have done so on the basis of reflection rather than reading – he said of the High Church writers that their books were 'all patchwork'[7] – reflection stimulated by the devoutness of the Irish peasantry in their trials during the famine years, when he worked closely with them. Aubrey did not disdain the peasantry, but he did feel a remoteness from them, a remoteness natural to someone of his class. To him the peasants never ceased to be children, charming more often than not, but also with the unpredictability of a people who had not yet arrived at maturity. They were easily influenced to violence by those who wished to topple the whole structure of society, but just as easily subdued by a word from the parish priest. He is full of praise for those priests, who, confident of their authority, spoke out against the destructive Jacobinism of the Fenians.

De Vere was an even more ardent disciple of Wordsworth than of Coleridge. Holding that the Irish as a race had not yet arrived at true adulthood, that they were yet as children, he was, as a good Wordsworthian, imaginatively attracted by their history. There, in Ireland's trials and glories, might be found the footprints of the higher reason as it acted on an entire race; history would present evidence of God's dealings with the Irish and his design for them. A prolonged meditation on Ireland's history would begin to clarify the lineaments of her true identity, and her identity was that of a child, pure, innocent, spontaneous. The great difficulty, as de Vere saw it, was to preserve that pristine innocence in the modern world of the nineteenth century, the century of steam, Benthamite economics, and the ceaseless Jacobinical surgings of democracy. His way out was to think of Ireland as having a special role assigned to her, a role entirely opposed to the forces of modernization. Whereas other nations were cast in the imperial role (Rome), the commercial role (England), or the artistic role (Greece), Ireland's vocation was, like that of Israel, a spiritual one.[8] For that reason she was called by her bards the 'Isle of Destiny', 'Inisfail', and de Vere gave that title to his most accomplished poem.

So, like Ferguson, and Yeats after him, de Vere wished to come to what he considered the essence of the Irish national being; and again, like Ferguson, what he came up with bore remarkable similarities to his own major preoccupations. Ireland's vocation was, as it always had been, an Apostolic one; she was to be a guiding light for European Christianity in the darkness of the nineteenth century. She might even reconvert England, through her quiet and patient suffering, to the one true faith. Ireland's trials, in this view, were visited on her by God in order to purify her, to refine away any attachment to the things of this world. She was a chosen nation, like Israel, and Israel had to go through her desolation in the desert. Her afflictions were not just calamities brought about by human cruelty and injustice; they were actual evidence of God's love. All was arranged according to a divine pattern; it was de Vere's function as a poet to re-interpret that pattern, that destiny, to show the footprints of the deity in native history, and to preserve the lineaments of innocence in the features of the national being. There is a strong touch of fatalism in all this, and this was something de Vere recognized, but it was a trait he ascribed to the Irish themselves:

> Her Fatalism meant simply a profound sense of Religion. The intense Theism which has ever belonged to the East survived in Ireland as an instinct no less than as a Faith. The Irish have commonly found it more easy to recognize the Divine hand than secondary causes. They have regarded Religion as the chief possession of man. Such nations are ever attached to the Past.[9]

The 'secondary causes' referred to here are human evil or inefficiency, but these mattered less than the design behind them. Life itself was something of a dream. He had a Victorian obsession with death, and the deaths of his father, of Wordsworth, Hartley Coleridge and Miss Fenwick, those friends of his at Rydal, made him think of life as a thing lacking in substance, so that 'to love, as well as to faith, it is the unseen things that become the realities'. To make the mistake of believing in the substance of things as they exist, and of devoting our energies to the pursuit of material satisfaction, was to forsake our nature and become 'dog-like . . . poking our nose into everything to discover whether it is good to eat'.[10] All things, even famine, had an invisible dimension and it was that which was the truth of things to the eyes of faith.

There was in this attitude a remoteness from the actual, a disdain of things, which inevitably created problems for a man who wished to think of himself as a poet. A poet has to deal with words, and words are earthy of the earth, carrying with them the smear of man's humanity and inhumanity, something another Victorian convert poet realized:

> all is seared with trade; bleared, smeared with toil;
> And wears man's smudge and shares man's smell.[11]

But this human stain is a kind of challenge for Hopkins, in that his poetry sets out to redeem the actual, to make his words respond to the 'dearest freshness deep down things', and so charge them with God's grandeur. Poetry then becomes an act imitative of the incarnation, in that the words are reborn in the context of the freshness that lies under all things. De Vere's aim, curiously enough, was remarkably similar to that of Hopkins, in that he too wished to discover and re-present God's continual presence in things, but somehow the things themselves, in their unredeemed cumbrousness, seem to get in the way. In our lives we come farther and farther away from the marvels of childhood until

> At last the charm is broken: day by day
> Drops some new veil, until the countenance bare
> Of that ice-idol, blank Reality,
> Confronts us full with cold and loveless eye.
> Then dies our heart, unless that faith we share
> Whose touch makes all things gold and gives us youth for aye.[12]

The trouble here is that such faith can be spoken of in the way he does here, but it cannot easily be presented in human language, and that is all any poet has to work with. Language is indissolubly knit to things, to actuality, so as a poet de Vere had to traffic in the material, the substantial, despite his feeling that all life was a dream, that the true reality was that which was invisible. He can be seen grimly spelling it out for himself in the following tortuous stanza from *May Carols*:

> The man who grasps not what is best
> In *creaturely* existence, he

> Is narrowest in the brain, and least
> Can grasp the thought of Deity.[13]

But the weary doggedness of this stanza tells us how reluctantly de Vere accepted this teaching. Yet he realized that this was a lesson he had to learn if he was to be a poet in any sense at all.

In a letter written in 1855 his friend Henry Taylor accused de Vere of a lack of poetic passion, saying that his verse had more intellectual and spiritual excitement than humanity. De Vere replied that this was true in his youth, that he then believed that poetry should be above human passion, 'perpetually inculcating a love which is the Antitype of all human and natural affection'.[14] Now, however, he thinks differently. Following Coleridge, he thinks that poetry should embody all of a man's being, that in it the material and the spiritual should be fused as one. The human and the passionate should then have a place, but, he goes on to say, they should be idealised 'at least to that extent to which poetry is itself an ideal art'. As the letter proceeds his ideas become more and more distrustful of the actual until at the end he says that any passion poetry includes should be 'of a more elevated nature than belongs to actual life'. In other words, poetry should be human and yet be above the human at the same time. In a mind like Coleridge's such contradictions could be fruitful, but in a mind like de Vere's they produced confusion, and, worse than that, a distrust and unease about the very business of writing poetry itself. His solution was to systematize, to plan his poetic projects in such a way as to include the human – with all the intractability forced on it by reality – in the theme itself, but in such a way as to beg the question by taking a theme which already had answered the difficulty. If in his verse we miss 'The roll, the rise, the carol, the creation', we find plenty of dogged persistence in pursuit of the poetic, and much earnest endeavour.

II

Having been received into the Catholic faith at Avignon in 1851, de Vere continued on to Rome in considerable exhilaration of spirit. While at Rome he had an audience with Pope Pius IX, whom he found fat, strong and genial. The Pope asked him about the kind of poetry he wrote, and urged upon him the desirability of writing poems in honour of the Blessed Virgin and the saints. De Vere took the Pope at his word and spent the next five years working on a series of poems on the Virgin entitled *May Carols or Ancilla Domini*. He was later to fulfil the second part of the Pope's injunction with his *Legends of Saint Patrick* and his *Legends of the Saxon Saints*. The serial form of *May Carols,* consisting of a long series of fairly short poems concentrating on a single theme, was one to which he was drawn. It had been the form of Tennyson's intense meditations on death in *In Memoriam,* a poem he greatly admired, which Tennyson himself had read to him with tears running down his cheeks. He was to use the form again in his best poem *Inisfail*.

His *May Carols* was an attempt at a poetry of spiritualised humanity. Mary, for de Vere, and for Catholic thought of the time, was 'Religion itself in its essence'.[15] Through her, de Vere wrote in the preface to the *Carols,* 'Holy Church keeps a perpetual Christmas'. She reconciles the material and the spiritual, just as she did in the Incarnation itself where the human became transfigured, where man and God became one. Through her the human became reassociated with the divine, the Word became flesh. In this sense Mary is perpetuated in the church itself, because this is precisely what the church sets out to do, all its endeavour being to draw the actual, the natural, into closer contact with the divine, the invisible. The Eucharist itself, at the centre of the sacrifice of the mass, is a recalling, or *anamnesis* of the Incarnation; bread becomes divine flesh, just as human tissue became divine substance in Mary's womb. To write then of Mary is to make one's theme the church itself, a fit theme for a convert flushed with enthusiasm for the obscurities of Catholic teaching. But in writing *May Carols* there was more involved than a delight in the arcana of Catholic analogical thought. To write of Mary, and so of the church itself, was to enter into a fuller, more integrated humanity, because a more spiritualised one. The church for de Vere was 'the great Representative of renewed and re-integrated Humanity', her system a system conducive to greater freedom. Through her teachings she drew the human closer to the divine, so that in her, as in Mary, there was a correspondence between the visible and the invisible. The human was thus enhanced by the continual presence of spirit.

May Carols is a celebration of Mary, and as such it is also a celebration of the church itself, of its capacity for spiritualising the human and the natural, so that all things become evidence of the omnipresence of God. The world, 'once but God's outer court, may . . . become His Temple, and may be destined to become His Holy of Holies'.[16] Such a theology appealed to a poet who once believed that poetry should somehow surpass the human; here, in this elaborate sacramentalism, the actual world could, theoretically at least, be made symbolic of God's eternal presence. The human, the natural, could be elevated and sanctified through the medium of poetry, itself to be a kind of imitation of the Eucharist, a recall of the Incarnation. All this elaborate theory was, he hoped, a way of making his poetry take more account of the human, the natural. It is ironical that such a carapace of contorted theology was necessary for him before he could begin to approach that reality which could so easily take on the aspect of an 'ice-idol', blank and inexpressive.

The sequence is not particularly successful. There is a good deal of pleasant if uninspired description, with the inevitable conclusion that all this earthly beauty is evidence of God's design for us, and is analogous to the beauty and purity of Mary:

> O Cowslips sweetening lawn and vale,
> O Harebells drenched in noontide dew,
> O moon-white Primrose, Wind-flower frail!
> The song should be of her, not you!
>
> The May breeze answered, whispering low,
> 'Not *thine*: they sing her praises best!
> The flowers her grace in theirs can show:
> Her claims they prove not, yet attest.
>
> 'Beneath all fair things round thee strewn
> *Her* beauty lurks, by sense unseen:
> Who lifts their veil uprears a throne
> In holy hearts to Beauty's Queen'.[17]

The thought here is fairly standard Catholic doctrine, and it is frequently echoed by Gerard Manley Hopkins, but the difference between the two convert poets is that Hopkins vivifies doctrine with a compelling freshness of realization, so that the idea is presented to us, dramatized, as it were, by the energy of Hopkins's language. To compare Hopkins's 'The Blessed Virgin Compared to the Air We Breathe' with de Vere's poem, is to compare a poem which is alert, vital, and energetic, to a poem which is dull, predictable, and pious, in a well-intentioned way. The cardinal point of difference between the two writers is not that Hopkins was a truer believer, and therefore a better poet: rather is it that Hopkins was, by nature, more interested in words themselves as a means of revealing certainties and truths than was de Vere. In Hopkins there is an excited sense of the rediscovery of words as potent things charged with alertness and meaning, in touch with that freshness and energy which is everywhere flowing through nature, like a 'Heraclitean fire'. De Vere, on the other hand, distrusted words, as he tended to distrust all earthly things. For him they could easily be deceitful appearances, distractions from the vision of faith, which should be pure. Being so distrustful of the medium of poetry itself, small wonder then that his verse is so tired, so lack-lustre, so laboured. It is made out of a pious desire to serve; there is little joy in it, and the verse is very often manufactured to suit the purpose, rather than having the inevitability of a thing being said in the way it has to be said.

De Vere's other papal projects were *The Legends of Saint Patrick* and the *Legends of the Saxon Saints,* companion pieces showing the progress of the faith in its earliest days in Ireland and England. The two countries, according to de Vere, 'are signally unlike':

> The Irish, as a race, are the more impulsive, more sanguine, more imaginative, tenderer in love, and fiercer in hate. The English are stronger, more reliable, and juster. The Irish are more sympathetic; the English more benevolent.[18]

While the early Irish were wilder and a good deal less predictable than the English (even, it might be said, barbaric), nevertheless they were a natural, spontaneous people, and while nature and grace could sometimes be fiercely opposed, they did also have a good deal in common. So that when Saint Patrick brought the faith to Ireland, his mission was a relatively easy one. As he says in 'The Children of Fochlut Wood' from the *Legends*:

> It was the time of Faith;
> Open then was man's ear, open his heart:
> Pride spurned not then that chiefest strength of man,
> The power, by Truth confronted, to believe.
> Not savage was that wild barbaric race:
> Spirit was in them.[19]

When, however, the Irish saints came to re-convert England to the faith, it having lapsed back into paganism, their job was not so simple. The English, according to de Vere, were not so receptive.

Apart from the desire to illustrate the difference in temperament between the two nations, the *Legends* had another purpose. They were to show the operation of spiritualized humanity (St. Patrick, St. Cuthbert etc.) on fallen humanity (the native Irish, the Anglo-Saxons).[20] So the *Legends* were a further attempt at making his poetry more human, less rarified, more in contact with the actualities among which people live and breathe. They are mostly unsuccessful, marred by inattention to the material with which he is working, the words themselves, their rhythms, their usage. One of the most striking passages in *The Legends of Saint Patrick* is one in which the apostle attacks poetry itself for its delusiveness. Despite the wisdom of the bards, and their knowledge of men's hearts,

> 'darksome is their life;
> Darksome their pride, their love, their joys, their hopes;
> Darksome, though gleams of happier lore they have,
> Their light! Seest thou that forest floor, and o'er it,
> The ivy's flash – earth-light? Such light is theirs:
> By such no man can walk! '[21]

A poet's illumination proceeds from a dark reflection of earthly light, whereas the true light is much more direct, coming straight from the source of all true light, God himself.

III

De Vere's most accomplished poem was *Inisfail* (1861), a lyrical chonicle of Ireland. Again, like *May Carols,* this is cast in serial form, save that it has greater firmness and continuity, each poem centering on an actual event or an aspect of an actual event in the history of Ireland, from the Norman conquest to the end of the penal laws. It is the most circumstantial of de Vere's poems, and one that takes most account of people and places. It had to do so, being a chronicle, and because it roots itself in the actual it is the most human of de Vere's poems, the least likely to veer off into the vaguely transcendental. Nevertheless, a systematic, religious design still persists. There is nothing wrong with having a design, but when the design involves a foregone conclusion (as it does here) the pattern, instead of stimulating, enervates.

To the Catholic, Ireland, like the Virgin, is an image of the church: at first the harbinger of faith, then the object of persecution, but eventually triumphant. The poem is to 'embody the *essence* of (her) history during a long period of that history', to 'be an echo of that voice which comes from the heart of a people', in all the different tones of that voice.[22] Hence the form, if it is faithful to the variegation of that voice must be fragmentary. Religion, however, will comprehend the fragmentary. 'The main scope . . . of a poem which illustrates the interior life of a Nation – the biography of a People – must be spiritual', de Vere says, and the meaning of that interior life, taken *in toto,* is completely clear to de Vere. Ireland's destiny is to renew her missionary calling; she is once more to be the instructress of her more advanced, more astute, but religiously inferior neighbour. She is the 'Isle of Destiny', 'Inisfail'. Her tribulations were but to prepare her for the great task ahead. There is some evidence to show that the Catholic Irish clergy seriously entertained this idea at the close of the nineteenth and the beginning of the twentieth centuries.

This design, however, ridiculous though it is, does not wrap the poem in a straitjacket of pious aspirations. Quite a number of the lyrics in this poem achieve an intensity, firmness, and authenticity above anything else we find in de Vere. This is owing to the fact that many of the themes, if they were to be treated at all, required an element of dramatization, of distancing, on the part of the poet. It is a long meditation on Ireland's troubles, focussing on dramatic situations which illustrate historical crises, managing, more or less, to avoid presenting us with the moralistic design (that Ireland's troubles are in fact her glory), at every hand's turn.

One of the features of *Inisfail* that contributes to its sense of
firmness is the fact that de Vere uses rhythms which have the aim
of representing Irish rhythms in English, something that was very
soon to occupy the attention of William Larminie, George
Sigerson, Douglas Hyde and John Todhunter, as it had occupied
the attention of the earlier poets, Callanan, Ferguson and Edward
Walsh. De Vere's idea of what Irish rhythms are like is mostly
based on impressionistic readings of Moore, on conversations with
Ferguson, perhaps, and on some acquaintance with his versions
of Gaelic poems, collected in *Lays of the Western Gael* (1864). He
knew little or no Gaelic himself, but what there was to be read
on Irish history he knew. He had, after all, plenty of time for
study; his brother had to administer the estate, he himself having
successfully managed in early life to avoid all persuasion by his
family to take up some profession.

'A Bard Song' from *Inisfail* has the long flowing rhythm of
Moore, but that vehicle for opacity and emotional suggestion is
hardened by a more realistic attitude to the Irish bard, learned
from Ferguson, from John O'Donovan's *Annals of the Four
Masters,* published in the 'forties and the 'fifties, and possibly
too from Eugene O'Curry, who was professor of Irish in
Newman's University, where de Vere himself was Honorary
Professor of English Literature for a time. The last two lines of
'A Bard Song' have the respect for the 'facts' that characterized
the Ordnance Survey group which gathered around Petrie in the
'thirties and 'forties. Clearly, even by 1861 the influence of that
group was still a force:

> There is nothing that lasts save the Pine and the Bard:
> I, Fintan the bard, was living then,
> Tall grows the Pine upon Slieve-Donard:
> It dies: in the loud harp it lives again.
> Give praise to the bard and a huge reward!
> Give praise to the bard that gives praise to men:
> My curse upon Aodh, the priest of Skard,
> Who jeers at the bard-songs of Ikerrin! [23]

This is somewhat melodramatic, and his re-creation of the Bard
Ethell, with his contradictory pagan and Christian sentiments,
while attempting to be a representation of the proud intensity

of native Ireland, succeeds only in being rather silly, with something of the quality of the Irish Bull about it:

> The men that were wicked to me and mine; –
> (Not quenching a wrong, nor in war nor wine)
> I forgive and absolve them all, save three:
> May Christ in His mercy be kind to me.[24]

'The Bard Ethell' is an extended monologue, but de Vere is more
successful over shorter ground, and where the theme is more
suitably pathetic, in a pre-Raphaelite way. In 'The Wedding of
the Clans' (which has the ludicrous sub-title 'A Girl's Babble') a
girl is speaking out of her distress at being married to a Norman
lord to knit up friendship between him and her own clan. This
has a circumstantiality, an entering into the young girl's fraught
state of mind that makes it memorable:

> I stepp'd from my little room down by the ladder,
> The ladder that never so shook before;
> I was sad last night: to-day I am sadder
> Because I go from my Mother's door . . .
>
> He has killed ten chiefs, this chief that plights me;
> His hand is like that of the giant Balor:
> But I fear his kiss; and his beard affrights me,
> And the great stone dragon above his door.[25]

There is an incompetence and inattention in the rhyme between
'ladder' and 'sadder' in the first quatrain, and we realise again
that this poet is not basically interested in words and the best
order they should be made to assume in expression. He is content
to be shoddy, as long as he can get the thing written, or, worse,
he does not even realize that he is being shoddy. If de Vere were
someone like Mangan, desperately writing to make a living, we
could understand the shoddiness and inattention, but the fact is
that de Vere had nothing else to do at Curragh Chase, save
perfect his verses. He was not idle: he wrote a vast amount,
but he lacked the capacity for slow toil that might have made
a true poet out of him, rather than one who by fits and starts
strikes thin veins of authenticity.

Nevertheless, there is an energy and an alertness in *Inisfail* not to be found in his other work. His 'War-Song of Tirconnell's Bard at the Battle of Blackwater' has considerable power. It is supposedly a bardic incitement to O'Neill and O'Donnell in their victorious encounter with Marshal Bagnal at the battle of the Blackwater in 1598. The bard reminds the soldiers of Ireland's wrongs at the hands of England:

> Sing, fierce Bards, the plains sword-wasted,
> Sing the cornfields burnt and blasted,
> That when waged the war no longer
> Kernes dog-chased might pine with hunger!
> Pour around their ears the groans
> Of half-human skeletons
> From wet cave or forest-cover
> Foodless deserts peering over,
> Or upon the roadside lying
> Infant dead and mother dying,
> On their mouth the grassy stain
> Of the wild weed gnaw'd in vain.[26]

The imagery here is not merely descriptive of Elizabethan ravagings of the countryside to starve the native Irish into submission; it is also the imagery of the nineteenth century famine, where the country was blighted by an act of God, but where people were allowed to die because of an economic theory. The passage, then, has a dual historicity. De Vere knew a good deal about the actualities of famine, actualities which provide the details for his sixteenth century 'War-Song'. In 1848 he published a book entitled *English Misrule and Irish Misdeeds* which accused England of a lack of sympathy towards Ireland, and advocated systematic emigration as a policy for alleviating Ireland's difficulties. During the famine itself he helped his brother to run the local relief committees, and at one time paid a visit to an especially badly-hit area in west Clare, near Kilkee. There he was appalled at the conditions in which people were living and dying. He, William Monsell (the future Lord Emly), Lord Arundel, and the Duke of Norfolk visited the moors and bogs of the area. One house they chanced into had in it only a baby in a cradle, the mother gone out, they presumed, to find some milk. They touched the cradle, and with a tiny shiver, the 'emaciated little face relapsed again into stillness'. Monsell burst into tears, and then de Vere, in his *Recollections,* has the curious remark that 'probably the mother returned to find her child dead'.[27] Obviously they did not wait to find out. Or perhaps the young men could not bear to. In any case these years went deep into de Vere's consciousness, as they did into the consciousness of almost every Irish writer of the time. Over ten years later we find the imagery of famine haunting the recall of the sixteenth century Irish wars in *Inisfail.*

Gradually, as we read through *Inisfail,* we come to realise that one of the main motives for its composition, was not just to present the dismal essence of Irish history, but also to expiate a sense of guilt that de Vere himself felt about the past, and about his privileged place in the present. This was not the great disruptive guilt of an Arnold or a Hopkins, but it was undoubtedly there. As a member of the Irish Ascendency he knew that his status was founded upon some decimation of the native population such as Tirconnell's bard recounts in his 'War-Song'. That guilt comes to the surface in a curious poem in *Inisfail,* entitled 'Sibylla Iernensis'. De Vere has been reading O'Donovan's translation of the *Annals of the Four Masters,* has been feeding on its 'tragic lore' as he has it. He sleeps and hears in dream the sound of great funeral bells tolling. The cries of wounded men are 'strangled' in the sound. He wakes, but the things of day have no power to bless a mind darkened with these grim reverberations:

> I woke. In vain the skylark sang
> Above the breezy cliff; in vain
> The golden iris flashed and swang
> In hollows of the sea-pink plain.[28]

The Sibyl of Ireland speaks through the history he has been reading:

> The Sibyl and that volume's spells
> Pursued me with those funeral bells!

De Vere actually makes the Sibyl speak at the end of the poem but her warning is a general one, not one particularly addressed to de Vere himself:

> 'His way who changes, not his will,
>   Is strong no more, but guilty still'.

Inisfail is a poem which attempts to respond to the dark injunctions of the sibyl of Ireland, to set down the inhumanities she has suffered under English 'misrule'. He wishes to give articulation to the 'strangled' cries from the Irish battlefields, her bogs, plains and wild places, to clarify them somehow from the tumult of the funeral bells that would drown out all else but their own dismal tolling. It is an attempt to comprehend imaginatively the great blur of Irish history, and the form he chose, the serial poem based on moments of lyric intensity, is a suitable one. The modern Irish poet, John Montague, in attempting a similar, but more localized, task has employed the same kind of formal organization in *The Rough Field.* But for de Vere the Catholic faith comprehends the fragmentary, making sense out of the broken shards of historical intensity he sets forth in the lyrics of *Inisfail.* So despite the chaos of the past, which the form of the poem goes to some length to imitate, nevertheless, for de Vere, the overall design of Ireland's destiny is clear. This design is summed up in 'The Wheel of Affliction', not a good poem in itself, but a wonderful example of nineteenth century imitation Gothic, with strong intermixtures of pastiche baroque. De Vere tells us that he has seen in sleep the saints, queens, kings and priests of vanquished Ireland,

> But the vision I saw when the deep I crossed,
>   When I crossed from Iorras to Donegal
> By night on the vigil of Pentecost
>   Was the saddest vision yet best of all.

> From the sea to the sky a Wheel rolled round:
>   It breathed a blast on the steadfast stars;
> 'Twas huge as that circle with marvels wound –
>   The marvels that reign o'er the Calendars.

> Then an angel spake, 'That Wheel is Earth;
>   It grinds the wheat of the Bread of God':
> And the Angel of Eire, with an Angel's mirth,
>   'The mill-stream from Heaven is the Martyr's blood'.[29]

So Ireland by her sufferings has become a kind of Eucharist, a conception which, in its passivity and acceptance of the way things were, must have pleased many of the Irish Catholic bishops who read the poem, but which must have exasperated many Fenian readers. However, not many would have read the poem when it appeared in 1861. Like Ferguson, de Vere was supremely conscious of the fact that there was little audience for Irish writing in the third quarter of the nineteenth century. And yet they both continued to work, indefatigably, each in his own way growing more and more remote from the actualities of Irish life, which were Fenianism and the Land War.

One poem towards the end of *Inisfail* seems to acknowledge de Vere's sense of remoteness, his bafflement at the absurdity of Irish history. For a moment the poetry escapes from the shackles of the pious, nun-like interpretation de Vere has clapped on Irish history. The poem 'Unrevealed' is one of the truest in the sequence, one of the truest indeed to be found among nineteenth century Irish poems. In it we are almost back to Moore, with his images of grief that cannot find a name, of rage that can find no expression, of intensity that cannot find the right words for whatever reason:

> Grey Harper, rest! – O maid, the Fates
>   On those sad lips have press'd their seal!
> Thy song's sweet rage but indicates
>   That mystery it can ne'er reveal.
>
> Take comfort! Vales and lakes and skies,
>   Blue skies, and sunset-girded shore,
> Love-beaming brows, love-lighted eyes,
>   Contend like thee. What can they more?[30]

Nature itself is in turmoil, just as the harper's song is; that wild turbulent beauty is but an index to a mystery that can never be spoken. Once again we are back at the uselessness of words themselves, but here that uselessness is the subject of the poem itself, not a hindrance to it. It becomes a kind of strength, just as in Beckett the impossibility of saying anything becomes a kind of lash to speech. But de Vere is no master of stoical despair, as Beckett is. He is a good Catholic and believes that the mystery will become comprehensible in the end. There is no great urgency

about expressing himself, as eventually the divine Word will work
through him in perfect peace:

> The Little Black Rose shall be red at last!
>   What made it black but the East wind dry
> And the tear of the widow that fell on it fast?
>   It shall redden the hills when June is nigh! [31]

This is no prophecy of the Easter Rising; it is a promise of the
Christian resurrection, when Ireland's trials shall all be made
'rational and acceptable' in the words of the Catholic liturgy.
Ireland's destiny is that she be redeemed; the poem looks forward
not to revolutionary liberation but to 'the resurrection of the
body, and the life of the world to come' in the words of the
Catechism. Already de Vere has been blessed with these intima-
tions of immortality:

> – This song is secret. Mine ear it pass'd
> In a wind o'er the stone-plain of Athenry.

This wind is an anamnesis (or re-call) of the wind that passed
through the upper room at Pentecost, rather than a wind of
change blowing through Ireland.

Inisfail, then, is a poem which attempts to accommodate itself
to the complexities, sufferings, and injustices of Irish history,
which de Vere, as a 'liberal Tory' in the tradition of his father,
was prepared to recognize. The fragmentary, lyric form is suitable
for the presentation of critical moments of intensity in that
history, but as a devout Catholic de Vere sees a divine providence
working through the tribulation, redeeming it, sanctifying it,
almost. The purposes and modes of that providence cannot
adequately be dealt with in human language, so that, oddly
enough, we are back with a poetry which like Moore's, can only
shadow forth its Platonic conception. Many of the Romantics
and the Victorians had gnawing doubts about the efficacies of
language, but de Vere's are sharpened by his strong tendency
towards a transcendental Catholicism, and by the fact that by
temperament and persuasion he was an Irish poet, whereas his
masters, those he found most compelling as examples, were the
very English Coleridge, Wordsworth, and J. H. Newman.

Inisfail was the high point of de Vere's career as a poet, but

he produced much work after this. *The Legends of St. Patrick*
and the *Legends of the Saxon Saints* came later than this, as did
The Foray of Queen Maeve which he published in 1882, at the
age of sixty eight. This he based on Professor Brian O'Looney's
manuscript translation of the *Táin Bó Cualnge* in the Royal Irish
Academy. He was drawn to the early saga for its heroism, as he
had been drawn to the lives of Alexander the Great and Thomas
à Beckett, both of whom he had made the subject of plays. More
compelling than the heroic quality of the saga, though, was the
stamp of reality it carried. Its compositors he saw as coming
'to the great drama of human life without preoccupations'.[32]
Here was a life which seemed to have the simplicity and rugged-
ness of nature itself, a humanity free from the perplexities of
late nineteenth century life, having about it the freshness of the
world newly born. Despite their barbarism, the great figures of
this saga, more like natural eminences than forerunners of puny
modern man, had all the essentials, to de Vere's way of seeing, of
the Christian code of life; honour, simplicity, graciousness
towards enemies, and steadfastness. Most of all they had a natural
humanity, and de Vere attempted to translate this strength into
late Victorian Miltonic blank verse, hoping he could do for them,
and the early Ireland for which they stood, what Wordsworth
had done for Windermere.

In a review of John Todhunter's *The Banshee and Other Poems*
in 1892 Yeats remarks of de Vere that despite *Inisfail* and *The
Foray of Queen Maeve* their author was better known as a poet
of the English Catholics than as an Irish writer.[33] Certainly de
Vere never became one of the litany of 'Davis, Mangan,
Ferguson', that Yeats was to intone to conjure out of a chaos
of semi-articulate, often would-be poets, something like an Irish
literary tradition in English. But de Vere has his interest; he was
the poet of that English Catholic movement that began in
Oxford: Newman appointed two of the *May Carols* to be sung at
the Oratory in Birmingham every May. While he wished to make
his verse as expressive of the Catholic faith as possible, de Vere
also wished to make his verse human as well. His *May Carols*
have an elaborate analogical theology behind them, to explain
the humanizing function of Mary in the church. Through the
church, as through Mary (who is emblematic of the church) the
spiritual becomes human. *Inisfail* is an attempt to present the
sufferings of Ireland's history, but also to offer a comprehensive

frame of providential order, so that her suffering will in the end be seen to have been all for the best. His *Legends* of Patrick and of the Saxon saints were to show the operation of humanity gifted with the spirit of Christianity, on fallen, but not ignoble humanity. Lastly, in *The Foray of Queen Maeve,* he set out to show the native nobility of Irish humanity, how ready it was for the leaven of Christianity to make it lift itself up to the Lord.

Set down like this, it all sounds drearily systematic, and indeed there is much dull stuff in de Vere. There are moments of intensity, but Yeats's telling criticism of 1895 must, eventually, stand:

Something may be due to a defect of genius, for he seems to me, despite his noble placidity, his manifold and moving exposition of Catholic doctrine and emotion, but seldom master of the inevitable words in the inevitable order, and I find myself constantly distinguishing, when I read him, between that calculable, considered, intelligible and pleasant thing we call the poetical, and that incalculable, instinctive, mysterious, and startling thing we call poetry.[34]

6

William Allingham:
'The power and zest of all appearance'

I

There was a tradition of nineteenth century Irish poetry: this tradition was unhealthier than most, beset as it was by so many uncertainties of language, politics and culture. The struggle of the artist to realize himself is nearly always a difficult one, upwards against the stream, but the currents of nineteenth century Irish life were so turbulent, their pressure so fierce that they tended to overwhelm the writer who would make his way through them.

It is with something like relief then that the reader comes to William Allingham in the tradition of nineteenth century Irish verse, after the muffled sadness of Moore, the frantic energy of Callanan, the kaleidoscopic selves of Mangan, the idealistic unionism of Ferguson and the unrealized piety of de Vere. Allingham's objectivity, his attention to exteriors, his love of common life, of detail, his political good sense, but above all, his warmth and humanity, are refreshing. He is the sanest of the nineteenth century poets, barring none, even Yeats.

This sympathetic sanity, this warmth, was something that was much prized by his contemporaries, more in England than in Ireland. Tennyson was his friend, so was Carlyle; they both had a high opinion of Allingham's character, but the friendship that exerted most influence on him was that with Dante Gabriel Rossetti. From Rossetti and from his friendships with the pre-Raphaelites he learnt to value his instinctive attachment to the actual, his love of colour and its shadings, and his feeling for the texture of the real.

As a child Allingham was drawn to colour and detail and

texture. In his unfinished *Autobiography* he tells us how struck he was as a child with the smallest details, preferring the mystery of the water-tub and the well, and that of the square red tiles in the kitchen, to the mountains and the great cataract near his house in Ballyshannon, Co. Donegal:

> The kitchen was floored with square red tiles. Its one tall window, with thick window sashes, beside which was the washing-tub on its stand, looked out on a little back-yard. Opposite the door stood a long 'dresser' with its rows of plates and dishes, tin porringers and strainers; and under this, in the corner next the window, was the place of a large tub of fresh water which, with its clear olive depth and round wooden dipper swimming like a boat on its tremulous surface, used to give me great delight, judging (as I do in this and similar ages) by my distinct impressions of forms and colours.[1]

This reads like a description of the background to a painting by John Millais in its fidelity to the actual. It is a relief to come to the 'clear olive depth' of the water-tub after the uncertain phantasmagorias of Mangan and the somewhat unwieldy medievalism of Ferguson. Allingham has a realistic touch that is welcome after the emotionalism and abstract politicising which is the burden of much nineteenth century Irish poetry. It is clear that he himself derived an emotional satisfaction from rendering things accurately in his writing. His work is full of an alert attention to the variegation of the exterior world. This is not just journalistic reportage, although it includes it; Allingham establishes a relationship with the surface of life, with its texture, with its primary vitality. He attempts a Chaucerian type of relationship with the real, and he acknowledges as much, when in *Laurence Bloomfield,* his long poem on the land trouble in Ireland, he says

> I have sometimes cried,
> 'Afford my verse a little touch of aid,
> 'Thou grave, good-humour'd, venerable Shade,
> 'Who once Comptroller of the Customs wast,
> '*Edwardo Rege!*' but my pray'r is lost.[2]

He invokes Chaucer, because he wishes to speak of 'every-day affairs', but admits that this is difficult in a time of telegraphs and policemen. He held the flow of life, the succession of impressions, to be a blessed thing, a thing worth celebrating. For him process did not hold anything like the terror that it held for Mangan, or indeed for Yeats. Primary life (as Yeats would later call it), life evolving moment to moment, he wished to regard as joyful, sweet. He felt none of Mangan's desire to escape from it through some kind of poetic ventriloquism; nor did he have de Vere's desire (or Yeats's), to develop a system that would confound process in its comprehensiveness. He wished to keep himself alive to the passage of life, to register its sounds and textures in his writing.

He is, needless to say, a very painterly writer. Rossetti once said to him, as they lay under an oak tree in a copse near Lymington, 'you ought to have been a landscape painter. You notice everything.' Allingham, however, in his diary entry added drily in parenthesis: 'Sometimes to the length of boredom, perhaps he meant'.[3]

We find this visual comprehensiveness throughout Allingham's work. His 'Invitation to a Painter' asks the painter to leave the 'jail of bricks and gas' that is London to come to the fuller life that awaits depiction in the West of Ireland. As always, his home town, Ballyshannon, on the mouth of the Erne, forms the basis of his Irish pastoral. But the pastoral here is an astringent one, with the tang of the real about it. Just before winter comes, the writer of the invitation says, he will take his English painter friend on the river to the 'water-house' where the eel-fishers work at night:

> When the nights are black and gusty, then do eels in myriads
>   glide
> Through the pools and down the rapids, hurrying to the
>   ocean-tide. . . .
> And the wearmen, on the platform of that pigmy water-house
> Built among the river-currents, with a dam to either bank,
> Pull the purse-nets heavy end to swing across their wooden
>   tank,
> Ere they loose the cord about it, then a slimy wriggling heap
> Falls with splashing.[4]

The writer of the invitation then describes how they will, the night's work done, eat a breakfast of fried eels hot from the pan with the fishermen in their tiny reeking water cabin.

Allingham always wanted his writing to be intermixed with the things of life: he was in no way an aesthete. He admired the poetry of the Dorset dialect poet, William Barnes, for the way in which the words there seemed to have an identity with the thing described. Early in his career, while still at Ballyshannon he had wanted his poems to be sung as ballads by the people of the locality without their knowing who the author was. For this reason, as John Hewitt has pointed out, he wrote words to folk airs he picked up here and there on his official duties as customs officer, sent them to Dublin to be printed anonymously in the way of the broadsheets, then had them sold at fairs and markets as the genuine article.[5] 'The Girl's Lamentation' is such a mock-ballad. He heard the air from a peasant boy in Ballyshannon and a part of the first three verses. The rest of the poem arises out of these. It is an act of imaginative impersonality, done in order that the poem should return to be a part of the local life out of which it had come:

> With grief and mourning I sit to spin;
> My love passed by, and he didn't come in;
> He passes me by, both day and night,
> And carries off my poor heart's delight.
>
> There is a tavern in yonder town,
> My love goes there and he spends a crown,
> He takes a strange girl upon his knee,
> And never more gives a thought to me.
>
> Says he, 'We'll wed without loss of time,
> And sure our love's but a little crime;' –
> My apron-string now it's wearing short
> And my love he seeks other girls to court.[6]

Allingham's desire, then, to adjust his writing to the actual, can be seen at work, not just in the journalistic detail of his descriptions of scenes and people, but also in his sense that poetry should somehow not be separate from the life about it, but should interact with it, making it more beautiful and also perhaps saner, juster. In other words his was (to use a phrase of our times) a 'poetry of the committed individual', committed, that is, to understanding, to better judgement, to deeper moral awareness. In his writing about Ireland, especially in *Laurence Bloomfield in Ireland,* we see that commitment at work.

II

In being committed to better, clearer understanding and deeper moral awareness, Allingham stood, as John Hewitt has said, 'in the great nineteenth century radical tradition of Ruskin and Morris'.[7] He had a good deal of sympathy for William Morris's aims, not just as a fellow pre-Raphaelite, but as a social reformer. In a diary entry for 1884 he tells us that he agrees with Morris's *Justice,* the socialist paper, but that he partly detests it as well. 'It is incendiary and atheistic, and would upset everything . . . I want reforms and thorough-going ones, but not by the hands of atheists and anarchists'.[8] In other words, he believes in evolution rather than revolution, in man's potential for sane rational advancement, rather than in the necessity for perpetual eruption in the social order. Once again Allingham's sympathy is for the texture of things as they are, for reality unfolding in its own way, moment to moment, epoch to epoch. The revolutionary would obliterate that texture in order to give substance to his apocalyptic vision. He would blow all to pieces, would make the earth rock beneath his tread, would revel in the 'gun-peal and slogan cry' of 'Dark Rosaleen'. For Allingham the valiant beauty of the passing thing was too precious, actuality too dear, to sell out on it for the frenzy of revolutionary intensity. In many ways he is Mangan's antithesis, for whom the passage of life was often so tortured as to make frenzy a welcome guest.

To Allingham reality was not an illusion hiding a fearsome chaos. A nose remained a nose, and it did not suddenly extend itself down the length of Grafton Street. The substantiality of the thing was an affirmation of the solidity and certainty of the world itself. And the world was a place where things were sanely and proportionately linked to each other, not a seething absurdity of lawless surges and troughs, where casual connections forged and unforged. In 'An Evil May-Day' he gives expression to his sense of the universe as a sanely ordered place:

What use is the Universe itself? . . .
At least we'll take for granted it exists,
Though questions may lack answers. 'Mother', 'Spirit',
What may these be? One thing, or separate? –
I care not which; for how should that concern?
All is, of need, connected, up and down,
And grossest link'd with subtlest. We must live
In a material world, must therein work,
Thereby be wrought upon. I am conjoined . . .
To my bodily organs first of all;
Related strictly to the beast, the bird,
The blade of grass, the clod of earth, the cloud,
The faintest haze of suns within the sky.
That nearest fiery orb makes flow my blood;
Electric ether vivifies my brain;
And I, made up of these, also am not these,
Exist in personal being.[9]

Again, the material world, life as it is or as it appears, is accepted as the only context available. The 'noblest' kind of mind, he tells us in the same poem, is the 'sane clear mind/ To see, and to imagine'. But the seeing comes before the imagining, and the comma after 'see' and its placing at the beginning of the line shows the kind of emphasis Allingham wants to place on it. He goes on:

> Through appearances
> Beheld with keen and sympathetic eyes
> Imaginative insight pierces deep
> To something secret, – not mechanical
> But spiritual.[10]

Again, seeing with the eyes precedes the imaginative vision. That, when it comes, must root itself in the substance of things.

Allingham, however, is famous for his poems and little verse dramas about fairies. If an author *is* so interested in being substantial how is it then that he takes for theme something so insubstantial as fairies and their ways? These fairies of Allingham's are basically very fanciful, a harmless indulgence in the 'elfin gold of phantasie'. But though they are fantastic they are nevertheless closely related to things, to the countryside, to flowers, to the twigs and stones of the forest. Most of the fairy poems are located in the hills and woods around Ballyshannon, and are seen as part of the invisible though definite atmosphere of the place:

> The Moon was bright, the Sea was still,
> The Fairies danced on Fairy Hill;
> The Town lay sleeping far below . . .
> A Boy within that Town did dwell
> Loved by the Fairy People well.[12]

In this poem, 'Fairy Hill, or The Poet's Wedding', the fairies draw the boy's attention to the delightfulness of the reality around him; they locate themselves in the details of nature, and are, in a sense, like presiding spirits of the natural:

> When the Child
> Grew older, then in flowers they smiled,
> Or shining clouds, or sparkling streams,
> Or forest shadows.

For all Allingham's optimistic materialism, for all his espousal of the actual as the only place available under the given aspect of things, for all his belief in man's potential for evolution and improvement, nevertheless, like Ruskin and many Victorians (including his friend Tennyson), there was a dark side to his character. It is not a side that is allowed much scope in Allingham's writing, but it is there.

In this dark mood reality loses its attraction. The surface of life, the appearance, becomes absurd, meaningless, lacking any reference to a centre. All is chance, inanity, and the imagination itself, because there is no law, becomes capricious, even malignant. Speaking in these terms we could be discussing Mangan but Allingham, unlike Mangan, kept that darkness under control. We get a hint of it in his much anthologised poem, 'The Fairies'. There are good and bad fairies, and while 'Fairy-Hill' was given over to the benign sort, this poem is given over to the more malignant. At first all is fanciful and pleasant; these fairies have strong connections with the actual:

> Down along the rocky shore
> Some make their home,
> They live on crispy pancakes
> Of yellow tide-foam.[13]

But their connection with the actual has also been cruel and heartless. They took 'little Bridget' with them for seven years, for no reason, then returned her again, capriciously. She finds all her human friends gone when she returns, and dies of grief. The fairies take her back with them:

> They have kept her ever since
> Deep within the lake,
> On a bed of flag-leaves,
> Watching till she wake.

In Allingham's writing (as in the early Yeats's), the fairies might be thought of as a metaphor for the imagination, in that they were, for him, the presiding spirits of the natural, the material, from which all vision must come. Here the fairies destroy, kill and torture for no reason. The poem is a minor version of a great Romantic theme, but the dark vision of life is held down, minimised, by the use of the fairies as a way of expressing it.

The darkness can also be seen intruding on the idyllic village pastoralism of the poem Allingham eventually called 'George; or the Schoolfellows'. The opening of this narrative is a brilliant piece of painterly evocation. The narrator stands looking out over his small garden on a summer evening. The garden and the house are his little fortress of sweetness:

> The noisy sparrows in our clematis
> Chatted of rain, a pensive summer dusk
> Shading the little lawn and garden-ground
> Between our threshold and the village street;
> With one pure star, a lonely altar-lamp
> In twilight's vast cathedral; for the clouds
> Were gravely gathering, and a fitful breeze
> Flurried the window-foliage that before
> Hung delicately painted on the sky,
> And wafted, showering from their golden boss,
> The white-rose petals.[14]

All is well. The narrator thinks fondly of his wife upstairs, as she puts the child to sleep, and hears her soft footfall. He thinks back to the time when he saw her for the first time since an inland childhood, against the 'downs and dells' above some seashore:

> I knew her the first glimpse,
> While yet the flexile curvature of hat
> Kept all her face in shadow to the chin.

His past life and his present seem blessed, full. He feels a part of all the life around him and glories in it, the moths that brush the dry grass of the garden, the 'tone of passing voices in the street', the train flying past, shaking the white rose with its vibrations. The train makes him think of the larger world outside, and of how this little village is linked to it by the railway, by ships, and by letters. It is something of a Whitmanesque vision of the goodness and blessedness of being human, of truly belonging to the life one finds oneself in.

His wife agrees to walk with him in the gathering dusk that smells of rain, and he waits for her downstairs, by the door, savouring the musky smell of the geranium leaves:

> Peace, as of Heaven itself, possess'd my heart,
> A footstep, not the light step of my wife,
> Disturb'd it.

The train that has just whistled past has brought George Levison, an old acquaintance of the narrator's schooldays, a youth who had been full of fire and promise. 'Saint George' they had called him at school. Now, it soon turns out, George is an alcoholic and a failure. As he drinks, his talk becomes wilder and wilder, until eventually he breaks down and begins to whine about those who have wronged him. The narrator feels powerless to do anything. How can he possibly even begin the salvage operation necessary to bring the old George back to life? He cannot even bear to think of him lodging in his house, the centre of his village idyll, sleeping in the room of his sister-in-law Emma. He takes him to a lodging house, carefully avoiding the pools of rain. The morning finds George gone.

It is quite obvious what George is. He is the darkness that must be kept out. He is failure, debauchery, anger, lack of control. In the end he is death:

> Through all the summer-time
> The touch of that unhappy visit lay,
> Like trace of frost on gardens, on our life.

He ruins the sense of belonging to life, because he is a negation of all structure. But the poem doesn't allow him to get too far. The narrator will not allow George to sleep in 'Emma's room'; the thought disgusts him. He spends the night in some lodging house well away from the fortress of sweetness that the house is.

'Bridegroom's Park' is another poem where the dark forces find an entry to trouble the sane and pleasing surface of life, save that here they succeed in overwhelming it. This is a highly accomplished poem, probably Allingham's best, and remarkable for its formal control. The poem is in four sections and each section deals with the central situation from a different angle.

The central situation is this: the young bridegroom (unnamed) has prepared the house and its extensive parkland for his young bride at great cost. The first section of the poem, 'From the Highway', is a monologue by a local spoken to a younger man who is going into exile to make his fortune. This monologue sets the scene by describing the park from the outside at a distance. There is, again, the sense of an enclosed, protected, and therefore somewhat fragile beauty in the glimpses of the 'terraces of emerald sward' the 'vases full of many blooms' that the local can get 'through beechen boughs'. Way below him the speaker sees a movement in a coppice. He thinks at first that it is a deer, but then he sees that it is a woman. He wonders what she can be up to, then dismisses it from his mind, and bids farewell to his companion who is going into exile.

The next section, 'By the Pond', is another monologue, this time spoken by the bridegroom to his young bride as they wander through the parkland he has made for her. He draws her attention to the details of nature about them, a nature he has subdued and made beautiful for her in this enclosed place:

> These walls of green, my guarded Queen!
> A labyrinth of shade and sheen,
> Bar out the world a thousand miles.[15]

Nature seems to have co-operated with his intent. All seems ordered within the park. When the lady loses her book he finds it again, without a smirch on it, her place still kept by a sprig of jasmin:

> I found it, free of spot or smirch,
> On a pillow of wood-sorrel sleeping
> Under the Fox's Cliff to-day.
> Not so much as your place is lost,
> Given to this delicate warden's keeping, –
> Jasmin that deserves to stay
> Enshrined there henceforth, never toss'd
> Like other dying blooms away.

But the walls the bridegroom has put up will not keep the world out, its darkness, its guilt and violence. The next section, 'Through the Wood', is another monologue, spoken this time by the girl the local observer in the first section saw moving through the coppice. She is demented, and does not quite know where she is at first:

> Stay, let me think,
> Is this the place where I knelt to drink,
> And all her hair broke loose and fell,
> And floated in the cold, clear well
> Hung with rock-weeds?

Through her broken, chaotic speech, it emerges that she has been deserted by the bridegroom of this place, and that his betrayal has driven her mad. She has come to the park through the 'torturing light' to claim her 'husband'. Through a clump of thick laurel she sees the bride and groom coming towards her. They stop and embrace, and she rushes out upon them.

In the next section, 'Mossgrown', seven years have gone by, the auditor of the first section has come back from exile, and the local narrator tells him what has happened. They can now walk through the park, as the grounds and house are deserted. The narrator tells the returned traveller how the girl who had been betrayed came and threw herself into the pond before the bride and bridegroom, how the bride fainted and after sickened, and how she eventually died the following winter in her mother's house. The master of the house has gone away and left the house and park to fall into disuse.

The order, arrangement and beauty of the park, the 'emerald sward', the pond where insects waltzed 'over the liquid glass' are all gone. The sweet texture of life, its ordered surface, has been obliterated by the dark forces of the past, by guilt, horror, madness:

> These half-obliterated walks,
> The tangling grass, the shrubberies choked
> With briars, the runnel which has soak'd
> Its lawn-foot to a marsh, between
> The treacherous tufts of brighter green,
> The garden, plann'd with costly care,
> Now wilder'd as a maniac's hair.

The place is haunted, the toad has got into the pre-Raphaelite garden, the Victorian bower of bliss:

> Here's a chair!
> Once a cool delightful seat,
> Now the warty toad's retreat,
> Cushion'd with fungus, sprouting rank,
> Smear'd with the lazy gluey dank.
> No doubt the ghost sits often there –
> A Female shadow with wide eyes
> And dripping garments.

In 'Bridegroom's Park' Allingham presents a situation where the texture of life, those dear 'appearances' through which one may proceed to 'something secret' are overwhelmed by the mad girl, an image of ruin, of lack of control, of guilt and of death. But the poem itself is not overwhelmed by these forces; it contains them powerfully. By showing the situation from four different angles, the poem keeps the central tension and misery at a distance. Furthermore, in the narrative, the misery and tension is contained within the walls of the park. The life outside that park is mercifully free from the darkness and dankness within. Outside these futile walls people come and go, life goes on. Bridegroom's Park is allowed to fall into ruin, but the village life remains unaffected.

Because Allingham doesn't attempt to get too close to the centre of tension, and to the inner lives of the central characters, he can rely on what he does best, the description of exteriors, to suggest the dark core within. Indeed at one point in the last section, 'Mossgrown', the local narrator reflects on the impossibility of conveying adequately what the inner life is really like:

> A man's true life and history
> Is like the bottom of the sea,
> Where mountains and huge valleys hide
> Below the wrinkles of the tide,
> Under the peaceful mirror, under
> Billowy foam and tempest-thunder.

Allingham's sense of the impossibility of saying anything adequate about the inner life of the self would seem to have driven him to value the objective world. The self was labyrinthine, unfathomable, whereas reality, the outward texture of things, was not. A desire to find an alternative to the kaleidoscope of subjectivity made him value paintings and made him something of a painter in verse, whereas it drove de Vere towards the consolations of Catholic dogma. The danger for Allingham was aestheticism, but he was too much of a humane moralist to fall into that trap.

III

Not only is a man's true life and history 'like the bottom of the sea', but, Allingham would have maintained, a nation's is also. The desire to set down and to analyse the fundamental forces operating on Irish life formed the basic motivation for the writing of *Laurence Bloomfield in Ireland*. In it Allingham consciously addressed himself to the contemporary Irish scene. It was to be a poem 'on every-day Irish affairs' and he recognized this to be 'a new and difficult, and for more than one reason a ticklish literary experiment'.[16] He does not neglect the forces of the past – in fact one of the main concerns of the poem is to show how the past operates on the present in Ireland, distorting it, simplifying it – but his preoccupation is with the pressure of the time,

with history as it is unfolding in the present. Allingham knows
the poem has its faults:

> As a work of art it has glaring faults and defects . . . there is
> too much detail, and the handling is often awkward; yet some
> indulgence may be possibly conceded to an attempt to cultivate
> English narrative poetry on entirely new ground; and he (the
> author) ventures to plead on its behalf, as a presentment of
> various characteristics of modern Ireland derived from close
> acquaintance with life there among all classes, that it has not
> one unmeaning line or phrase written at random.

Laurence Bloomfield was not a poem written in the objectivity
of exile; most of it was written amidst the sort of scenes and
tensions which it describes. In 1860 he wrote to Rossetti, telling
him he was at work on a long poem on Irish matters, but, he
asks, 'who will like it? Think of the Landlord and Tenant
Question in flat decasyllables!'[17] John Hewitt suggests that the
poem was a kind of watershed for Allingham, that in it, before
finally leaving Ballyshannon for a new life in England at the age
of thirty-nine, he 'concentrated the strongest feelings and most
telling experiences of his native country into a coherent statement, realising himself in the act'.[18]

The poem is set in a district in Ireland which could be anywhere. It has a town, Lisnamoy, with two churches, a psuedo-
Gothic Catholic one and a neat Protestant one, 'all prim and trim
in tidy ugliness'.[19] Near the town is Lisnamoy House, the mansion
of Sir Ulick Harvey. Under Croghan Mountain and near Lough
Braccan is Croghan Hall, Laurence Bloomfield's mansion. The
lands are under the care of the local agent, an efficient, ruthless,
but not unsympathetic man, Pigot. Allingham goes to some
length to create a fictional situation which will carry in it as much
as possible of the tensions and complexities of rural Irish life
as they existed in the late 1850s and the early 'sixties. He wants
to be entirely fair-minded and says, quite truly, that the poem
is 'neither of an orange nor a green complexion'. The poem
proposes a liberal, non-sectarian solution to the problems of Irish
life, and it is Bloomfield himself, the young landlord, who is the
agent of this solution in the story, at least as far as his own
tenants are concerned.

At the beginning of the poem, returning home from years

abroad spent in study and travel, during which time he has explored
the attractions of various ideologies, Bloomfield finds himself in
instinctive if somewhat inarticulate disagreement with the
received opinion among the local landlords and their agents
about how tenants should be treated. At a dinner at the home of
his uncle, Sir Ulick Harvey, he talks in favour of peasant land
ownership, at which suggestion 'sundry lips were curl'd'.[20] Bloomfield, however, goes on to develop the idea that if the peasant
could be encouraged with the prospect of eventual ownership this
would breed 'diligence, content, and loyalty'; the texture and
quality of life would be enhanced, not only for the poor, but for
the rich as well. The debate goes on around the table, all disagree-
ing (with varying degrees of intolerence) with Bloomfield's
idealism, until eventually Pigot, the agent, completely alters the
tone of the discussion by putting a letter from the local Ribbonmen (as the rural revolutionary organizations were called) on the
table. The letter threatens Pigot's life if he dares to evict the
people of Ballytullagh, a little village near Lisnamoy. Allingham
describes the letter as a 'dirty leaf' of the present; he sets the
sordid facts of Irish rural violence against Bloomfield's optimism:

> 'Take Notis, Big gut, if one claw you lay
> On Tullah, you'll for ever roo the day –
> So change your tune, and quickly, or by God
> This mornin is your last – we'll have your blud
> Sined, Captin Starlite'.

After this the talk turns to revolvers, informers and evictions.

Allingham has a deep hatred of violence, of abstract political
hatred and its sordid rhetoric, of entrenched positions, of com-
placency and what he sees as the pseudo-mysticism of the Catholic
church, because all of these, for him, conspire against the sane
relations of ordinary life, as people live it, day to day. They
conspire against that reality, because they simplify human
complexity into slogans and prejudice. They ruin the texture
of life.

One of the 'strongest feelings' (to use John Hewitt's phrase)
that runs through *Laurence Bloomfield* is Allingham's feeling for
the variety and richness of human life in Lisnamoy and environs.
The town itself, the different sorts of houses in the area, from
the well-kept cottage of the Doran family, honest industrious

peasants, to the showy tastelessness of Pigot's house, to the
dilapidated mansion of the Dysart family, all these are depicted
with a sureness of touch and an exactness of detail that remind
one of Maria Edgeworth. The mountains too, and Lough Braccan
with its old castle and round tower, all find their place. We are
shown the young girls going to the fair, changing into their
white stockings and blackened shoes just outside the town. We
see the tinkers and their donkeys, and the reckless way in which
they ride them through the crowd. It all reads like a collection
of Jack B. Yeats engravings and indeed Jack B. Yeats was to
find his inspiration in this kind of vigorous life much later. But
Lisnamoy and the surrounding district is for Allingham more
than just picturesque rural or semi-rural scenery; he wants to
make Lisnamoy an image of mid-nineteenth century Ireland,
containing all the national tensions, in the way that John
Montague has made Garvaghey an image of mid-twentieth
century Ireland in *The Rough Field*.

There is a good deal that is wrong with Lisnamoy: the greed
of the landlords and their distrust of the peasants, breed idleness,
squalor and eventually violence in their tenantry. The social
fabric is riven by hate, a hate intensified by historical simplicities.
Nothing is known clearly or seen simply. Life has become
so perverted from its natural order that the small 'snug'
cottage of the Dorans is something of an exception. The visitor
finds:

> Clean chairs and stools, a gaily-quilted bed,
> The weather-fast though grimy thatch o'erhead,
> The fishing rods and reels above the fire,
> Neal's books and comely Bridget's neat attire,
> Express'd a comfort which the rough neglect
> That reign'd outside forbade him to expect.[21]

The 'neglect' outside is in fact carefully cultivated, so as not to
give Paudheen Dhu the bailiff the idea that the Dorans are doing
a little too well, and so should pay a higher rent. If old Jack
Doran had his way, indeed, the inside would show 'less neat
array'. He knows full well that for the peasant, enjoyment of
the good things in life, the pleasures of order, comfort, civilization, mean trouble.

Allingham has an intense admiration for the way of life which the Dorans represent. For him the peasant way of life is the most authentic because it is rooted in real things. There is an order and naturalness about what the peasant does and when he does it; his life is attuned to the movements of the larger life outside him. He is part of its texture:

> He's friends with earth and cloud, plant, beast and birds,
> His glance, by oversubtleties unblurr'd,
> At human nature, flies not much astray;
> Afoot he journeys, but enjoys the way.
> Th' instinctive faith, perhaps, of such holds best
> To that ideal truth, the power and zest
> Of all appearance; limitation keeps
> Their souls compact; light cares they have, sound sleeps;
> Their day, within a settled course begun,
> Brings wholesome task, advancing with the sun.

Life and work in this vision (and it is a vision, though a secular one) are drawn into harmony. An 'instinctive faith' informs this harmony; the spirit of each individual is part of the greater spirit that lies, in Allingham's thought, under all appearance, giving its 'zest' to life.

The state of mind and life Allingham ascribes to the peasantry is not a state that he sees might be brought about if things could only be other than what they are; it is Allingham's conviction that this is the way things really are in rural Ireland, at root, under the turbulence and distraction of political violence and sectarian strife. The forces that pervert this reality, that turn the peasant into a fanatical incendiary or a cringing whelp, are the inter-related evils of rural agitation, vicious landlordism and historical simplification.

Neal, Jack Doran's son, falls victim to these forces, not because he is mindless and ignorant, but because he has a certain intellectual curiosity, and an emotional dissatisfaction with the unnatural limits imposed on him by the economies of peasant hardship:

> For rich and poor, contrasted lots at best
> Here plainly mean oppressors and oppressed.[22]

To compensate for his present lot (though he is a good deal

better off than most) Doran begins to imagine Ireland's past glories, his dreams fed by the storytellers round his father's fireside.

Allingham also acknowledges that the routine of everyday life can become tedious, peasant or not, that it is natural to feel the desire for change, for adventure:

> By fits, moreover, hide them as we may,
> It frets us all, this tedious every-day.

The 'gleam of bold romance', of Byronic restlessness, is in 'every bosom'. It is this that 'gives war/Its frenzied life', this 'unquiet, lawless, dangerous mood', to which the 'present' seems a prison-house. Because Neal Doran's life is so trammelled by economic pressure, because his fancy has been fed with images of Ireland wronged and shackled, a normal discontent with the constraints of actuality intensifies and he becomes a revolutionary, joining the Ribbonmen. In doing so he turns aside from the blessedness of the everyday, to 'feed his heart on fantasies', as Yeats was later to put it. He submits to the fantasy of historical simplification. England oppressed Ireland, was unjust, failed in its responsibility, therefore the landlords, the representatives of English power and privilege, are at the root of all injustice, all discontent. The fantasy is all the more potent for having truth in it. What happens is that the legitimate element of truth is enlarged, blown out of all proportion, until all contact with reality is lost. Allingham has his spokesman Bloomfield wittily analyse this lethal process towards the close of the poem:

> 'Common evils which to life belong
> Patricius will account a personal wrong;
> Suckled on grievances, his mind is bent
> To charge on others all his discontent;
> Half curses England when his tooth-ache stings,
> Half blames Th' Established Church for frosty springs
> And rainy summers; thinks it passing hard
> From any joy of life to live debarr'd,
> As though the English, French, or German poor
> Lead plenteous lives, with nothing to endure'.[23]

Allingham shows us the growth of the fantasy of historical

simplification and its eventual fanaticism in a wonderfully tele-
scoped account of Irish history in the section called 'Neal at the
Lough'. Neal Doran has gone fishing on Lough Braccan. It is
an autumn evening, against the 'yellow light that pours/On
half the lough and sloping fields' the two massive towers of a
shattered castle are silhouetted. Neal beaches his boat on Innisree,
the island where the castle stands. He climbs its winding stair and
looks out over the Lough.

Allingham then intrudes on the narrative with a compressed
account of Irish history, from the earliest times down to Castle-
reagh, finding striking images to bring each period before the
mind of the reader. Elizabeth I, the daughter of 'the bloated
king', is described as follows, for example:

> Entrench'd within the fortress of her frill
> His sour-faced daughter works her shrewish will.

Ireland is an 'island of bitter memories, thickly sown'. Little
is said about Doran's state of mind (in any case Allingham is not
very good at individual psychology) but the intention is clear
enough. Doran is the product of a violent and bitter history, his
revolutionary discontent is understandable, if odious.

After Allingham completes the survey of Irish history, a history
which Neal Doran has inherited, he returns to the actual. It is
getting dark, appropriately enough, when Neal descends the
winding stair, bends his head to pass through the low arch, and
is attacked. His assailant is Tim Nulty, local Ribbonman, and
contributor to the seditious national, *The Firebrand*. The attack
is a mistake, Nulty thinking Doran to have been spying on his
rendezvous with the county delegate from the Grand Ribbon
Lodge. Seizing his moment, making it more dramatic by pointing
to the mytserious 'delegate' in his cloak and hood, Nulty gets
Doran to take the revolutionary oath there and then. It is
absolutely right that Doran should meet Nulty at the bottom of
the winding stair, after Allingham's compressed meditation on
the bitterness of Irish history. The meeting with Nulty and all
that he embodies – racial hatred, fanaticism, secretiveness – is
inevitable for a young Irishman such as Doran, who is thoughtful
and passionate, and somewhat reckless. Thought and passion
combined with the unease of youth can easily betray an Irishman
into the terrible simplicities of violence. The Neal Dorans can

easily become the marionettes of men like Nulty who like conflict and friction, and the simplification of life's complexity that they bring.

Nulty embodies the dark force of historical violence, of political abstraction and inherited hate, that threatens to overwhelm the fabric of Irish life. It is the force against which Bloomfield pits himself, his weapons tolerance, goodwill, intelligence, and the courage to go his own way. He is fighting for life, for the 'zest' which should belong to appearances. If the dark forces of Irish history cannot be controlled then life will become impossible, no-one will be what he seems, there will be a schism between appearance and reality. The texture of life itself will be undermined; there will be no point in whitewashing the cottage, or planting flowers to grow up against the wall. All rooted things will be set at nought, made subject to the whim of unreason. It is the peasant life that will be most in danger, because the peasants are the first to suffer in any social upheaval. And peasant life is most precious to the whole fabric of society, as the sanity and order it has give a rootedness and authenticity to the social structure.

However, this authenticity is not only under threat from the revolutionary forces that gather strength among the peasants themselves; it is also threatened by the complementary disfigurement of Irish life, the greed and rapine of the landowners and their agents. One of the poem's main strengths is a moral one, its fairmindedness, and Allingham gives as much weight to the greed of the landlords as he does to the passion of the revolutionaries. The Ribbonmen are not the only villains.

The section following 'Neal at the Lough' is entitled 'Tenants at Will' and describes the destruction of Ballytullagh, the mountain village, and the eviction of its inhabitants at the hands of Pigot and his men. Old Oona, a kind of living embodiment of the place, is put out into the cold and rain, where the 'ranks of polished rifles wetly shine'.[24] A naked child runs out of a hovel, grim-faced men lean against the walls, while the hired wreckers from another parish tear the little cluster of dwellings to pieces with crow-bars. This account of an eviction, rendered with cold alert passion, acts as a counter to the preceding section in which Neal takes the oath of violence, and the following section, 'A Ribbon Lodge', where it is revealed that the Ribbonmen have decided to assassinate Pigot. The violence of the eviction begets the violence of the Lodge. Both to some extent owe their origin to man's innate tendency to evil, but both are also, to a greater extent, the product of prejudice, inherited hatred and historical simplification. The tenants are not to be trusted, say the landlords, so why consider them seriously as human beings? The landlords are not to be trusted, say the Ribbonmen, so why not terrify them into giving us what we want?

The issues of the poem are complex, and Allingham does not simplify that complexity: he even makes Pigot a not entirely unsympathetic figure, acting according to his best lights, trying to do his job. The poem, more than any other poem of the nineteenth century, is thoroughly sensitive to the complexities of Irish life, and we can hardly blame Allingham if his solution is not entirely convincing, seeing that the problems the poem sets forth have still not been resolved over a hundred years later.

Allingham's solution is Bloomfield himself, the liberal reformer, the idealist, the sympathetic well-intentioned man. Jack Doran is summoned to the bailiff's office to learn that he must give up his holding, his lease is not to be renewed. We have learned in the meantime that a list of the members of the Ribbon Lodge has come into Pigot's possession and that young Doran's name is on it, hence, we presume, his father's dismissal. Old Doran decides to speak to Bloomfield himself, and while he is waiting to see him news is brought that his son has been arrested on Lodge 'business'. Doran faints at the shock and Bloomfield comes to his assistance.

Bloomfield reverses Pigot's decision to dispossess the Dorans. Pigot resigns his agency at this and Bloomfield accepts the resignation. Not only that, he tears up the list of members of Ribbon Lodge 260, and promises, in a long speech of good intentions, to be a good landlord to his neglected tenantry. Pigot is shot on his way home; the old order must give way to the new.

For Allingham there was a relationship between a man's attitude of mind and the natural world around him. A room, a house, a district, a whole countryside (if the man were powerful enough) could take its moral and emotional atmosphere from the tenor of a man's mind. This is not just simply a subtler form of pathetic fallacy but a tradition that goes back to Horace, a tradition that has to do with the effect civilised men have on the life around them. In Bloomfield Allingham tries to create the kind of individual who has this civilizing effect. But we are

told nothing at all about Bloomfield's psychology. Allingham
prefixes the section 'Lord and Lady' (which describes Bloomfield's
estate seven years after he takes over from Pigot) with a discussion of the spiritual quality underlying the actions of a good man,
a quality which he calls 'soul', and which, we are to assume,
Bloomfield has in abundance. It is miraculous in its effects and
'simple as the imperial sun's broad light'.[25] Bloomfield has a sense
of the informing power of the spirit present in all life and in all
people, in the peasants, the town-dwellers, and even in the
landscape itself. His actions are authentic, things take his impress,
he feels

> the artist's joy, to find
> The rugged world take pressure from his mind.

It takes his pressure because his mind is in harmony with the
'something spiritual', the 'zest' that lies beneath appearances.

However, Allingham is no Wordsworth, and certainly not poet
enough to show the growth of these convictions in Bloomfield's
mind. But he is a masterly poet of exteriors, and in describing
the changes that have taken place in the quality of life around
Croghan Hall in the seven years Bloomfield has been there,
Allingham suggests much about the sort of mind that could effect
these changes:

> Look round from Croghan Lodge, and not in vain
> You seek the records of a seven years' reign;
> So long have Laurence and his Queen borne rule.
> The smoky hovel with its fetid pool
> Has disappear'd – poor Paddy's castle-moat,
> Which kept the foulness, let the use run out;
> White walls, gay rustic gardens meet your eyes,
> Trim gates and fences, haggarts, barns and styes;
> Down the wet slope a net of drainage spreads,
> The level marsh waves wide with osier-beds,
> Among the barren fields of windy hills,
> Round solitary boughs, by rock-strewn rills,
> And up to crags that crown the heathery steep,
> Larch, pine, and sycamore begin to creep.

Nature is being reclaimed from the wilderness, from chaos, and is being made both practical and beautiful. Order and civilisation are extending themselves through the benign, humane influence of Bloomfield. The trees that are beginning to creep up into the hitherto unredeemed wilderness are planted not just for Bloomfield's delectation, but for the benefit of all his tenants. Even his parklands lie open, 'no churlish prison wall defeats (the) eye'. He is not afraid to trust in humanity, in its potential for generosity and goodness. In Croghan Hall itself Bloomfield has been busy restoring and redecorating:

> Good sense, refinement, naïvety reconcile
> Man's work and nature's, and the genial smile
> Is brotherhood's, not condescension's, here;
> No bitterness flows in, but strength and cheer
> From every aspect; 'tis a kindly place,
> That does not seem to taunt you with its grace,
> But, somehow, makes you happy, stray or stay,
> And pleased to recollect it when away;
> For manners thus extend to horse and field,
> And subtle comfort or discomfort yield.

The interrelationship between Bloomfield's mind and the world outside him is summed up in the last couplet, a couplet that reminds us of the tradition of country house poems that includes Ben Jonson's 'To Penshurst', Marvell's 'Upon Nun Appleton House' and Yeats's Coole Park poems.

Bloomfield is the liberal humanist, optimistic, idealistic, believing in man's potential for civilized progress towards selflessness. In the poem he is the antithesis of the entrenched simplicities of the Ribbon Lodge, and of Nassau Blunderbore, who believes that 'Papists are but rebels in disguise'. Bloomfield is attentive to the particulars of life, to the individual case (he overlooks Doran's membership of the Lodge), and to the minutiae of daily life. He gives thought to the kind of fencing round his land that will leave the 'prospect' most 'free', and to the colours he should use in the different rooms of Croghan Hall.

But Bloomfield is not just a clever landscape gardener and interior decorator. He is no aesthete. Allingham's attention to his 'artistry' in these and other matters, is meant to imply a great deal about Bloomfield's attitudes. There is much about him that reminds us of the nineteenth century radicalism of Ruskin and Morris, but there is a strong streak of the eighteenth century enlightenment in him also, a streak that looks back to the writings of Maria Edgeworth, and to the benevolent landlordism of her father, Richard Lovell Edgeworth. George Eliot was on the right track when she compared *Laurence Bloomfield* to the poetry of George Crabbe. Not only does the poem share what Terence Brown calls Crabbe's 'sturdy realism', it also has the kind of moral overtones we often find associated with late eighteenth century realism. Maria Edgeworth (like Jane Austen) could make a description of a garden, the lay-out of a house, the arrangement of furniture in a room, resonate with moral overtones. Such exteriors, in this kind of writing can be made to suggest either an ordered, sane, reasonable and civilized life, or the frantic disproportions of misery and fraud. Maria Edgeworth's description of Mrs Rafferty's villa Tusculum in *The Absentee* suggests all sorts of things about the pretentiousness and wastefulness of the Raffertys themselves, and the kind of life they embody.

Bloomfield's life (unlike Mrs Rafferty's) is sane and clear, simple and well-ordered. His touch is always 'true', authentic and natural:

> His own true touch alive in every part
> Gave without cost the luxury of Art.

When he decorates a room, or fits it out, he inevitably finds the right colours for that room's atmosphere:

> Dim-splendid needlework of Hindostan,
> Grave solid furniture of useful plan;
> Here a soft blaze of flowers in full daylight,
> There, ivied casement, shadowing aright
> The mournful relics of the secret Past.

His hands find the right colours, the appropriate combination of light and shade because his life proceeds in harmony with a higher purpose than his own. Pigot's interior, on the other hand, is hopelessly brash and barren, discordant, recognizing no true law higher than the self:

> Harsh lights upon discordant colours fall,
> Large, costly, dull engravings deck the wall;
> Chair, ottoman, by some unlucky doom
> Door, window, fire, stand wrong in every room.[26]

The texture of life here is hopelessly wrong; there is no zest, no joy in the placement of anything because Pigot's hand lacks the 'true' touch that only comes from giving the self up to life, from surrendering it to the larger and truer reality that lies outside.

Bloomfield distrusts all vapoury fulminations, whether it be about the Irish past, or whether it be religious quasi-mysticism. They break the links with life, which is a living relationship with the present. Indeed the Irish past is domesticated in Croghan Hall; the square bell 'of thinnest gold' that St Patrick brought to Ireland is a show-piece in one of the ivied casements, along with other relics of ancient Irish life. Bloomfield studies these antiquities and sometimes gives a short, clear lecture on them to his neighbours. We may be sure he indulges in no fanciful theorizing, that the relics stay relics and do not become fetishes.

Religious enthusiasm disgusts him, because it shackles the spirit, blinding the eyes to the glory of everyday, that glory Allingham's friend Carlyle had celebrated in *Sartor Resartus*. In the last section of the poem, 'Midsummer', Laurence and some house guests are boating on Lough Braccan. On the shore they see a woman with a child making her way towards a holy well. A young pre-Raphaelite in the company admires the blue of her mantle against the green shrubs and grey rocks; a London girl claps her hands for joy, but Bloomfield reacts differently:

> It is indeed a woman, with a boy,
> A ten-year baby, pined in face and limb,
> Whose mother many a mile has carried him,
> And now bends low in pray'r, her sick one laid
> Gasping and white within the elder-shade.
> 'Lets go', says Bloomfield, and they turn away.[27]

As he says later, Bloomfield believes that Ireland tends, all too easily, to live 'amidst intangibilities'. This dissolves the strength needed to knit the mind to action and to the present.

At the end of the poem Bloomfield remembers Ferguson's translation, 'The Fair Hills of Holy Ireland':

' "A plenteous place of hospitable cheer
    Is Holy Ireland! " – often did I hear
    That song in Gaelic from my nurse. Poor land!
"There's honey where her misty vales expand".
Her sons and daughters love her; yet they fly
As from a city of the plague'.[28]

In Ferguson this was a Protestant vision of a plentiful future, which might be brought about if the Irish Catholics could learn greater industry, more independence of spirit. Here in Allingham the lustrous images of the translation indicate Ireland's potential for full, zestful, peaceful life. The reality, though, is emigration, brought about by the evils of a harsh economic system, the injustice of the landlords and the rancour of the peasantry. But the Irish also emigrate because of their tendency to live in the intangible hope of a rosy future in some other place. If they could be made to draw closer to the reality of life, to its texture as it unfolds moment by moment then Ferguson's translation might come true. In the end it is Bloomfield's conviction that it will:

'This Ireland should have been a noble place',

he says to his wife, who, replying for his better instincts, says:

'It will be'.

In time both races of Ireland will shake off their shackles to share more fully in each others' life.

Allingham is a realist, but an optimistic not a psychological one. Terence Brown makes the telling criticism of *Laurence Bloomfield* that it fails to convince because we are given no insight into Bloomfield's character, into the inner processes of thought and feeling that give rise to his actions. Such an insight, Brown claims, is necessary if we are to believe in what he does on his estate.[29] It is true that Allingham is a hopeless psychologist: that is not where his strength lies, as a poet. His strength lies in the suggestive depiction of exteriors. If the realism of exteriors be suggestive enough it can carry sufficient moral weight and overtone to compensate for the lack in psychological penetration. The descriptions of external life in *Laurence Bloomfield* do seem to have that quality of moral resonance, a quality that has more in common with Jane Austen and Maria Edgeworth than it has with the psychological realism of the Victorian novel.

IV

Allingham, then, is an optimistic materialist. Man will adjust his mind to the actual, to the living moment as it expands. He will dismiss the enticing but fatal allurements of unreason, of hatred, of violence, of quasi-mysticism, to put himself in touch with life itself, as it exists. Only then will he recover his true zest, his joy in all appearances, for under all things lies the ever-present spiritual reality. This is why Allingham is drawn to colour, outline, exterior. In them is to be found the blessedness of life, a blessedness he felt Chaucer had naturally.

He was not blind to the dark forces in life. He knew them to be especially potent in the Ireland of his day and tried to set them forth in *Laurence Bloomfield*. It is not a despairing analysis of Ireland that he gives us, though there is much to be depressed about. The poem eventually asserts, by the strong and tactful delineation of Bloomfield himself through what he does, Ireland's potential for civilization, for a life lived in joy, peace and plenty.

Yeats and Oisin

I

One of the most haunting passages in Mangan comes in a piece he published in the *Dublin Satirist* for 19 October 1833, called 'My Transformation: A Wonderful Tale'. The story is a pathetic account of the emotional consequences of his useless love affair with Margaret Stackpoole. The passage in question describes the view from the window of the room he lived in after the 'transformation' wrought upon him by the drastic love affair:

> The house I dwelt in was in an isolated and remote quarter of the city. Solitary, silent, and prison-like it was; nevertheless a dwelling I would not have forsaken for the most brilliant pleasure-dome under the Italian heaven. To the rear of the house extended a long and narrow courtyard, partly overgrown with grass and melancholy-looking wild flowers, but flagged at the extremity, and bounded by a colossal wall. Down the entire length of this wall, which was connected with a ruined old building, descended a metal rain-spout, and I derived a diseased gratification in listening in wet weather to the cold, bleak, heavy plash, plash, plash of the rain as it fell from this spout on the flags beneath.[1]

The dreariness of this powerfully suggests Mangan's nervous state; it is almost as if the objects he describes have a fascinating power over him, the same kind of power we saw in the description of the stranger seated opposite Mangan in the Shades tavern.[2] Mangan, we remember, had a fear of the natural, a troubled sense that the ordinary objects of everyday masked a yawning chaos of unnameable flux and absurdity. Reality was intractable, so remembering again the essay about the Shades tavern, the

205

only way to approach it, to deal with it, was to adopt some pose, some manner. Hence Mangan's 'mannerism', and his delight in translation, which for him was a kind of mask whereby he could flee the intractability of the self. But it was not just exterior reality that was unnameable and chaotic; internal reality, the self, was equally unfathomable. For all his posings, for all his miserable joking, for all his exoticism and passionate frenzies (all of them attempts at self-forgetting) Mangan was the most self-absorbed and self-conscious of the nineteenth century Irish poets. External things, the beauty of midsummer or the texture of leaves, either mocked the man's Faustean sadness or they seemed far removed from the intricacies of his personality, the 'intricacies of blind remorse' that Yeats knew so well.

As a poet and as a man Yeats was also very self-absorbed, and it is not surprising to find him drawn to Mangan early in his career. He found him of interest first because Mangan identified himself with Young Ireland: he 'sang to sweeten Ireland's wrong'.[3] He admired the passionate intensity of Mangan's Irish translations, which are fiercely nationalist in sentiment. But he admired Mangan mostly for his personal quality, for the way in which he brought his pained, wrecked psyche into his writing in poems like 'The Nameless One' and 'Twenty Golden Years Ago'. In one of his earliest prose pieces, published in the *Irish Fireside* for 12 March 1887, Yeats praised this 'scrivener's clerk' for bringing 'one thing into the world that was not there before, one new thing in letters – his misery – a misery peculiar in quality'.[4]

It is difficult, however, especially for Yeats, to praise a poet seriously for his misery, for his failure to gain some mastery of the self. By 1891 Yeats had changed his attitude and in an article published in that year in *United Ireland* for 22 August he says that he does not now bother much with the poetry of Mangan but with the 'making and marring' of the man.[5] He has become interested in Mangan as a poetic type, as an example of a supremely subjective man, like Yeats himself, who became swamped by that very subjectivity. Mangan lost himself in the labyrinth of the mind. His poses, his masks, allowed him a temporary release from the talons of self-consciousness, perhaps, but they eventually failed to bring him into contact with a fuller, more authentic life. Yeats describes Mangan's subjectivity in the 1891 essay as follows:

When the internal eye grows bright the outward gaze sometimes is bleared and uncertain, and we confuse the real and the unreal, and see men as trees walking. It was thus with Mangan.

Yeats then goes on to consider briefly the *Autobiography* Fr Meehan persuaded Mangan to write and shows its utter lack of fidelity to objective truth, to the texture of the real that Allingham prized so highly.

Yeats knew that temperamentally he had a lot in common with Mangan, that he was a subjective man, one of those who 'spin a web out of their own bowels'.[6] In other words, Yeats had to be careful not to lose himself, as Mangan did, in the labyrinth of his own being, and yet that labyrinth had to be explored if his work was to have substance, if it was to have a theme, even. Yeats's theme is most often himself, his making and re-making of himself. Mangan, on the other hand, failed to make himself and was 'marred'.

II

For Yeats, the exploration of the self's complexity in order to achieve self-realization was, as Mary Catherine Flannery has shown in *Yeats and Magic,* intimately connected with magic. She has shown that the methods of the Cabalists and particularly of MacGregor Mathers, in their use of symbols to evoke images and states of mind, opened up, for Yeats, a way into the labyrinth of the mind. The individual mind, in Yeats's thinking, was connected to the great mind, or the great memory, of history. In his essay, 'Magic', of 1901, Yeats set down the basic precepts of his magical belief, arrived at through the self-scrutinies of the 'nineties, his friendship with Mathers, his membership of the Order of the Golden Dawn, and his study of Irish mythology and folklore. These are:

(1) That the borders of our mind are ever shifting, and that many minds can flow into one another, as it were, and create or reveal a single mind, a single energy.

(2) That the borders of our memories are as shifting, and that our memories are a part of one great memory, the memory of Nature herself.

(3) That this great mind and memory can be evoked by symbols.[7]

The great mind, the great memory, is the *Anima Mundi,* source of images, storehouse of all human experience and knowledge, that Yeats still later described in *Per Amica Silentia Lunae* as a 'vast luminous sea':

> Our daily thought was certainly but the line of foam at the shallow edge of a vast luminous sea; Henry More's *Anima Mundi,* Wordsworth's 'immortal sea which brought us hither', and near whose edge the children sport, and in that sea there were some who swam or sailed, explorers who perhaps knew all its shores.[8]

Mangan was such an explorer, but one hopelessly lost, through lack of self-mastery, through lack of a proper direction, which Yeats felt could come from the proper use of magical symbols. For Yeats the labyrinth of one's own being could become the great sea of the *Anima Mundi,* sea of great richness, happiness and blessing. It could also become, though, the sea of loss, boredom and *ennui* that Mangan (like other Romantics) knew so well. It was a sea to be ventured on if one were to begin to be a poet. Its difficult, sometimes deceitful, sometimes blessed, waters had to be charted.

Yeats's 'The Wanderings of Oisin', first published in 1889, twelve years before he wrote the 'Magic' essay, is his first large scale venture onto this sea. Though he could hardly have been conscious of it, this long poem is a navigational chart for the deeps of the mind, those deeps which become the deeps of the 'one great memory, the memory of Nature itself'. Needless to say the poem is inconclusive; it is blurred, hesitant, repetitive, but it has a power and magnetism all its own. This comes from the very personal nature of the voyage Yeats sets Oisin on, the strange tensions, moods and atmospheres he goes through. Oisin is the explorer who survives, heroic rage intact, the voyage into the self where Mangan went astray.

III

Yeats chose to write on Irish themes in the 1880s mainly for nationalistic reasons. He wanted to create a literary movement in Ireland that would be recognisably different from contemporary English literature, a desire we have seen before in Moore, Callanan, Mangan and Ferguson. In all these cases cultural nationalism was also cultural separatism. Yeats, under John O'Leary's influence in the 1890s, inherited this tradition of separatism, a tradition strengthened by the political message of Parnell and the Home Rule movement.

The political nature of Yeats's concern with Irish literature at this time made him overpraise his predecessors in nineteenth century Irish poetic tradition. We have seen how in 1887 he valued Mangan for his emotional sincerity; around the same time he praised the poems of Callanan for their fidelity to Munster tradition; he admired Thomas Davis for his popular verse, and he praised the poets of the *Nation.* Moore he always found wanting; there was too much of the tear and the smile there for his taste. Obviously he did not look at the *Melodies* closely, and if he read Moore's Whig satires at all they would, almost certainly, have bored a man who later ranted against all that 'Whiggery' stood for.

Of all the nineteenth century poets the man he most admired was Samuel Ferguson. They were alike in many ways: Ferguson, like Yeats, was Protestant, yet Nationalist in imagination; his background, like Yeats's, had been slightly impoverished upper middle class Anglo-Irish. Ferguson, like Yeats, had been moved imaginatively by the great brooding figures of Gaelic mythology and had made them the centre of his poetry. His failed epic, *Congal,* had been haunted by these great figures. For this reason, when Yeats wrote about Ferguson in 1886, he praised him for his 'centrality': 'The author of these poems is the greatest poet Ireland has produced because the most central and most Celtic'.[9] Yeats thought that Ferguson's poems embodied most completely 'the Irish character'. Like Ferguson, Yeats was convinced of a national identity; in fact he took Ferguson's thought a step further and believed in a living national being of some kind.

Long before he formed the idea that it was possible for a
nation to achieve unity of culture, in the same way as it was
possible for a man to find unity of being, the seeds of this notion
are there in the Ferguson essays of 1886:

> We (the Irish) are often told that we are men of infirm will and
> lavish lips, planning one thing and doing another, seeking
> this and that tomorrow. But a wildly different story do these
> legends tell. The mind of the Celt loves to linger on images
> of persistence; implacable hate, implacable love . . . Of all the
> many things the poet bequeaths to the future, the greatest
> are legends; they are the mothers of nations.

Yeats then goes on to argue that the 'high companionship' of
these legends will save the devotee from the 'leprosy of the
modern – tepid emotions and many aims'. The legends carry the
integrity and energy of the ancient Celt, qualities that would fit
a modern man for 'heroic deeds'.

Ferguson, through his poetry, is the transmitter of these
qualities; he has kept the faith with the ancestral roots of race.
This gives him strength and simplicity, as against the 'personal
perplexities' of modern life. He is out of phase among the
'sybaritic singers of his day', and the professional classes of
Victorian Dublin, of which he was a member. He is, in his poetry,
'like some aged sea-king sitting among the inland wheat and
poppies – the savour of the sea about him, and its strength'.

It is not surprising, perhaps, that a poet reared in Sligo and the
surrounding area, should associate an authentic Irish imagination,
in touch with the deepest roots of the race, with the sea. We
have seen that the mature Yeats associated the sea with Henry
More's *Anima Mundi,* that seething reservoir of life and energy
where all images come from, where there is joy, energy and
exhilaration. The Yeats of the late 'eighties had not, of course,
discovered the idea of the *Anima Mundi,* but even then we find
him associating Ferguson's authentic Irish imagination with the
sea. Already the sea is an image for the complex emotions of
race, of those energies that lie under race and personality. The
Celts themselves, he writes in an essay entitled 'Bardic Ireland'
(published in 1889, the year of 'The Wanderings of Oisin'), are
'of the fellowship of the sea, ever changing, ever the same'.[10]
The way into that sea, the sea of the intrinsic Celtic nature, was

through legend, mythology; they provided a chart, a blurred and indefinite one, but a chart. Through mythology one could find a way back into the deepest energies of race, energies that were associated with the energy of personality itself. In other words the sea of Celtic imagination, for which the native legends were a navigational chart, was also the sea of the individual imagination. The deeps of racial consciousness were also the deeps of the individual psyche. As Yeats would have put it by the time he wrote his 1901 essay on 'Magic', the great memory and the individual memory were constantly shifting one into the other. The great memory, he wrote in 1901, could be evoked by symbols; in 1889 he knew, instinctively, that Celtic mythology was leading him into great sources of power and energy, racial and personal.

Mangan had become lost in the deeps of the individual psyche, perhaps because he did not have a mythology to guide him. Ferguson, on the other hand, had retained a fidelity to its 'barbarous truth': this made him like a 'sea-king among the inland wheat and poppies'. But Ferguson, in that striking phrase, is out of his element, though he has kept faith with the memory of the sea. In an essay written in 1896, called 'An Irish Patriot', Yeats sees Ferguson's imaginative life in contradistinction to the public life his duties as lawyer and as Deputy Keeper of the Public Records of Ireland compelled him to lead. Ferguson now becomes a watery oasis in the parched desert of Protestant, Anglo-Irish, urban Victorianism. This, for Yeats, was a society of 'dignitaries, professional condemners of the multitude, archbishops and bishops, deans and archdeacons, professors and members of learned societies, Lord Chancellors and leaders of the Bar'.[11] Dublin was comparable to 'that fabled stony city of Arabia', or 'that circle of outer space where Milton saw "cowls, hoods and habits with their wearers, tossed and fluttered into rags" '. It is a dead place, with a stifled frustrated life, in Yeats's simplification. Ferguson, though, was something of an antithesis to all this stony life; he had a vision of the sea of the imagination, which, for a time, kept him fertile. In time, though, he too succumbed to the deadness around him, the paralysis, as Joyce was later to call it, in another, equally necessary, simplification. Ferguson's imagined fate is described by Yeats as follows: 'as he wrote and talked, a hardness and a heaviness crept into his rhythm and his language, from the dead world about him'. He became the victim of comfortable Unionism. The sea of the Celtic imagination, which must also, in Yeats's early thought, be the imagination of an Irishman, if he is to keep faith with the sources of his energy, lay unvisited until he himself published *The Wanderings of Oisin* in 1889.

IV

At the end of *Congal,* the poet Ardan stayed outside the convent enclosure, into which Lafinda, Congal's beloved, had invited him for sanctuary. He chose to face the Christian forces of Domnal coming up the hill towards the convent. We saw how in the poem Domnal is associated with a new order, centralized, efficient, not lacking in its own nobility, but having very little sympathy with the imaginative life. We saw how Domnal could, in fact, in the context of the Ireland of the third quarter of the nineteenth century, be associated with the new mixed society that was on its way, a society of democracy and Catholicism, having little emotional attachment to the old loyalties, the old structures of society, that held landlord and peasant together. Ardan's defiance of the glittering army of Domnal as it climbs the hill where Manannan has revealed himself in benign and true aspect to the dying Congal, is a gesture, though a futile one, against the lifelessness and anonymity of the new Ireland that is on its way. Domnal may be efficient, his rule may be centralised, but he lacks the 'needful charge of life' that it is Ardan's function, as poet, to communicate to his king. Now that king is dead, taken into the convent of the new order. The poet is in isolation, left to his futile heroism.

Yeats is the inheritor of the spirit of Ardan, bearing witness to an energy and richness that has passed out of life. This, of course, is his major theme throughout his work, and in his maturity he took it out of the Irish context to apply it to the whole of Western culture. But even in 'The Wanderings of Oisin' the theme of tragic isolation is there, of Oisin being out of harmony with the life of the time, of that life having a death-like quality about it.

The Ireland of 'The Wanderings of Oisin' is a sad place, strewn with the dead and with images of the dead. The Fenians themselves no longer have a proper role; the king has turned against them, and when the poem opens they have recently been defeated at the battle of Gavra:

> We rode in sadness above Lough Laen,
> For our best were dead on Gavra's green.[12]

Oisin and the remaining Fenians are engaged in a miserable hunt, where the stag they pursue is not sadder than they. Oisin's own thoughts keep running on his dead son, Oscar, slain at the battle of Gavra, and on the 'pencilled urn' which holds his dust. The phrase is based on a line and a half from Ferguson's 'Aideen's Grave' ('A cup of bodkin-pencilled clay/ Holds Oscar') as A. N. Jeffares has pointed out in *W. B. Yeats: Man and Poet*. 'Aideen's Grave' is another poem about misery, sadness, and death-in-life, about a culture (and a past) failing in energy.

A beautiful woman named Niam breaks into this dismal pursuit, seated on a white steed, her eyes as soft 'as dewdrops hanging / Upon the grass-blades' bending tips'. She has come for Oisin, to take him to the Land of the Young, because she has heard of his strength and virility, and also of his ability with words;

> And drops of honey are his words
> And glorious as Asian birds
> At evening in their rainless lands.[13]

This is beautiful and exotic, but there is a richness of complexity here as well in that, 'glorious' as Oisin's words are, they are parched in a rainless land of the imagination. Ireland is this rainless land, the place is dry and dead from the grief time brings. She wants to take him out of time, out of Ireland with its memories of sadness, its images of the dead. She wants to take him into the sea of the imagination, which, in Yeats, is also the sea of the individual psyche and of racial memory. From Yeats's point of view, the journey on which Niam takes Oisin is a journey into the self, into the imagination, the racial memory. It is a journey out of circumstance, out of the pressures of everyday, out of the false Ireland of the late 'eighties, into a truer one of the mind. Knowing Yeats's tendency to qualify, to 'vacillate' (as he called it much later) it is not surprising that the journey turns out to be an unsuccessful one.

Oisin and Niam ride out together, away from the 'human ground' of Fenian grief, over the 'oily sea', as it is curiously described in the 1889 edition. They soon see an image of the futility of their escape, and they are to see it at each of the three stages of their flight throughout the poem. A hornless deer is chased by a phantom hound over the bright inhuman sea. After the hound a lady rides, in her turn pursued by a young man. Their pursuit is useless and eternal; the figures are astray on the sea, they will never get anywhere. Already the contrary motion of Yeats's vacillating imagination has begun: Niam persuades Oisin to leave Ireland to free himself from the futility of time and chance; here on the inhuman sea of the imagination the first thing they encounter is another kind of futility, the futility of eternal non-achievement.

However, Oisin obeys Niam's command not to fret these futile immortals with human speech, and they continue their journey until they come to the first of the three islands in the poem. As they arrive it is evening, and the sun is setting directly behind the island, suffusing the shore with its brightness. Sea and land merge; the trees grow out of the water along the shore; it is a place where things are intermingled. As they ride towards the island it is as if the trees were beating time upon the centre of the sun:

> Like fingers many, many a tree
> Rose ever from the sea's warm floor,
> And they were trembling ceaselessly
> As though they all were beating time
> Upon the centre of the sun.[14]

The inhabitants of the island rush to meet them, 'Youths and maidens hand in hand', singing together in perfect unison. It is a place of harmony, where birds, trees, flowers and people achieve an interrelationship. It is a place of interwoven identities, of dance. Oisin is asked to sing, but sings of 'human joy'. One of the dancers takes his harp and flings it into a 'dolorous pool' underneath the woven shade. Along with the dancers they go to Niam's father Aengus in a forest house of animal skin and antlers, where he awakens from his Druid swoon to give them the *mantra* for this place, the verbal formulation that all chant in unison: 'joy is God and God is joy'. It is a protective incantation against 'sorrow with her osprey claw', which had been the theme of Oisin's mortal song.

Oisin's and Niam's identities now dissolve and merge with those of the dancers; with them they wind through the 'windless' pathways of the island, the 'ever summered solitudes'. Oisin remains content with participation in this dance for a hundred years, until one day, standing on the shore, he finds a staff of wood worn smooth by the sea:

> I turned it in my hands; the stains
> Of war were on it, and I wept,
> Remembering how along the plains,
> Equal to good or evil chance
> In war, the noble Fenians stept.[15]

The island he is on now is not a place 'equal to good or evil chance'; it is insulated, there being no conflict there, no tension, nothing to oppose the will, so the individual dissolves into a plurality of dance. There can be no heroism here, only passivity, acceptance. Using the definitions Mary Catherine Flannery has employed in *Yeats and Magic*, this is a place of Vedantic renunciation of the will and its energy, the ideal state that George Russell, following Mohini Chatterjee, sought to attain.[16] It has its attractions, but it leaves Oisin's (and Yeats's) will unsatisfied. That desires conflict, opposition, and it must have it regardless of the attractions of renunciation. He leaves the island of dancing, of calm joyousness, to find the intriguing darknesses of the Island of Victories.

Oisin, then, in the first part of his voyage on the sea of the imagination, which is also the sea of his mind (or a labyrinth of consciousness, to exchange one Shelleyan metaphor for another) finds within a quiet, passive, peace, a joy that has a relationship with the Druid swoon of the island god Aengus, who gives the protective *mantra* to the newcomer. It is the passive quiet within of certain meditative states, and involves the suspension of the active will. Oisin (like Yeats), being a Celt of the western shores, and not a disciple of the Vedas, cannot suspend his will forever; it desires the conflict wherein it can test itself and so define personality.

Being reminded of human actuality and conflict by the staff of wood, Oisin seeks the dark antagonisms of the Island of Victories, or the Isle of Many Fears as Yeats also called it. Once again we see the contrary motion of Yeats's vacillating imagination swinging into action. The Island of Victories is the opposite to the Island of the Living, with its dancers. Opposed to calm joyousness we find the loneliness and the essentially unnameable fears of the stone stairways and dark recesses of the second island.

A castle rises out of the sea, a white surge of foam springs from a gateway with 'black / Basaltic pillars marred with hew and hack'. On both sides of the gateway there are 'huge forms of stone', one of them an emblem of self-scrutiny and fearful self-absorption. This figure

> Stretched his long arm to where, a misty smother
> The stream churned, and churned. His lips were rolled apart,
> As though unto his never slumbering heart
> He told of every froth-drop hissing, flying.[17]

Passing by this statue Niam and Oisin climb a difficult stairway to find a 'maiden' chained to two aged half-blind eagles, with scarcely a feather left on their wings. A demon keeps this girl prisoner whose 'passions cold /Long while are whips of steel'.

Oisin offers to oppose this demon, even though warned by the girl that he cannot win. His 'hands burn /For battle'. He breaks the sea-rotted chains that bind her to the eagles and all three climb to a huge hall with a basalt floor covered in 'greenish and slippery' slime. There they can see 'netted marks of crawling scales sea-sprung'. The girl gives Oisin a sword with a 'wizard shine', deeply graven with ogham letters spelling 'Mananan', the sea-god, who originally built this hall and stairway.

Next morning, after a night of terrors, Oisin finds a tiny door in the great wall,

> The least of doors; beyond the door a plain,
> Dusty and herbless, where a bubbling strain
> Rose from a little runnel on whose edge
> A dusk demon, dry as a withered sedge,
> Swayed, crooning to himself an unknown tongue.
> In a sad revelry he sang and swung,
> Bacchant and mournful, passing to and fro
> His hand along the runnel's side, as though
> The flowers still grew there.[18]

This sad demon sees Oisin, and his slow deliberate turn towards him has all the exactness of nightmare:

> Turned he slow –
> A demon's leisure. Eyes first white as snow
> Kingfisher colour grew with rage. He rose
> Barking.[19]

Changeableness is this demon's nature. Oisin engages with him, but in the fight the demon alters at the sight of Mananan's sword, growing to many forms, a 'fir tree roaring in its leafless top', the 'sunken shape' of a drowned corpse. Eventually Oisin lunges at the demon, driving the sword through his heart and spine, and throws the 'loose bulk' into the tide.

Niam and the maiden return, they bring food and wine with them, and they feast the hero. This feasting goes on for three days, but on the fourth day the demon appears on the stair again, slimy, 'dull and unsubduable'. The same pattern repeats itself for another hundred years until Oisin finds another remembrance of actuality in the sea-foam, this time a beech bough. This evokes images of peace and content, out of the predictability and repetitiveness of the Gothic strife he is stuck in now. He thinks of the beech trees at Eman, how with Fin, Oscar and others he had stood under them, watching the hares leap in the long grass. Once again he longs to be out of the predictable pattern he has found, the pattern of struggle and conquest, of the same difficulty endlessly overcome.

What does all this mean? It is difficult to say, and it may well be that Yeats himself was unsure of the exact meaning of the powerful images he created. Powerful they are; they have a haunting, impressive quality, a sense that they resonate with the poet's central preoccupations. In writing to Katharine Tynan Yeats was guarded and defensive about this section of the poem:

The second part is much more coherent than I had hoped. You did not hear the second part. It is the most inspired but the least artistic of the three . . . It was the greatest effort of all my things. When I had finished it I brought it round to read to my Uncle George Pollexfen and could hardly read, so collapsed I was. My voice quite broken. It really was a kind of vision . . . It is not inspiration that exhausts one, but art.

The first parts I felt. I saw the second. Yet there too, perhaps,
only shadows have got themselves onto paper . . . In the second
part of 'Oisin' under disguise of symbolism I have said several
things to which I only have the key. The romance is for my
readers. They must not even know there is a symbol anywhere.
They will not find out. If they did it would spoil the art, yet
the whole poem is full of symbols – if it be full of aught but
clouds.[20]

The reader knows, of course, that there are symbols everywhere.
How clear he can be about them is another matter. Certain things
do detach themselves, however, and can be set down.

This dark castle where the maiden is enchained is Mananan's
creation, the same god who haunts the action of Ferguson's
Congal, and who reveals himself in benign aspect at the close.
The neglected magnificence of the place, with its essential sadness,
with its great pillars hacked and hewn in countless battles, its
huge hall with a basalt floor covered in phosphorescent slime, is
an image for Ireland's oppression. Ireland herself is bodied forth
in the image of the girl enchained by the miserable eagles. She is
long-suffering Éire, Róisín Dubh, Caitlín ní h-Uallacháin, or what
you will. She is to make her next appearance in Yeats's work as
the Countess Cathleen, in the play which was the 'counter-truth'
(as he described it in 'The Circus Animals' Desertion') to this
poem: 'counter-truth' because the play sees the spirit of Ireland
in heroic aspect, not condemned forever to the Gothic chamber
of history's sadness as she is in 'The Wanderings of Oisin'.

Though Oisin frees her from the aged eagles of imperialism
he cannot defeat the demon, whose guardians they are. The
demon keeps on resurrecting himself, always presenting himself
on the stairway to be struggled with again. He is, on the most
obvious level, England, holding the white girl in terrified subjection. He could also be seen as the forces of industrialization,
(connected with England, anyway), which denude the Irish landscape, withering the green and making the fresh water dull and
heavy. He is, too, an image of Yeats's sexual tension, seemingly
ungovernable despite constant struggle.[20A]

This second section derives much of its power from this inter-
play of meanings; the political intertwines with the personal,
making the symbols more resonant. Oisin's voyage is not just
a venture on to a Celtic sea, it is also a journey into the interior

of the psyche, into the sea of consciousness itself. In this section Yeats discovered images of struggle, of discontent, which the will craved after the lassitude of the Island of Dancing. But these images of struggle, deeply personal though they are, are shadowed with political and racial overtones. The imagery of personal discontent becomes also the imagery of political circumstance, as we saw happening in one of the most characteristic pieces of nineteenth century Irish verse, Mangan's 'Siberia'. Mangan's poem and this section of 'The Wanderings' both deal with failure; the personae of both poems – nameless in Mangan, Oisin in Yeats – cannot overcome the obstacles they find. Mangan cannot alter the contemporary horror of the 1840s, so he builds a poem out of the inability to articulate, the 'cloven tongue'; Yeats is oppressed by the strength and variableness of the demon of Irish subjection and British domination, and he makes a poem out of Oisin's heroism in the constantly renewed struggle. For Mangan, the most satisfying image is dumbness, for Yeats Oisin's heroic failure.

We may even go further, to indicate how closely the racial and the personal are bound up in this section of the poem. The girl is Ireland, Cathleen herself, that delicacy of temperament Moore felt present in Irish music, to which his words in the *Melodies* paid homage. She is held in subjection in a miserable place by a sad, tired, English demon. Oisin's heroic attempt to free her fails, because in the end she cannot be freed. He is drawn into a potentially endless round of pointless victory (victory which is defeat), when a beech bough brings him remembrances of actuality, and he leaves, 'doom-eager' once again, eager for fate and chance.[21] The sad racial iconographies of lady, demon and Mananan's hall are attractive in their curious misery. The girl is beautiful, the demon fascinating, but the place is sterile. It is a place of endlessly renewed pointless conflict, conflict with the sad Gothic terrors of Irish history. It is a trap, a 'net', (Joyce's word in *A Portrait of the Artist as a Young Man*) which Irish history throws about the soul, seeking to imprison it. Allegiance to the frail maiden means a struggle with a demon that cannot be overcome. But for the adventitious beech bough Oisin would be locked into a combat he could never win. No one man can take on Ireland's woe and redeem it.

The demon is not just England, he is also Irish recollections of English violence and misrule. When we first meet him in the poem he is self-absorbed, brooding, crooning to himself 'in an unknown tongue'. He is lost in sterile reproachful reverie.

But one could go on and on. The images of this section are rich and vague at once, and thus easily lend themselves to ceaseless interpretation. Here Yeats has found images for personal discontent, for imaginative difficulty and sterility, which also have strong political and racial overtones. Racial and individual mix, their borders overlap, in this voyage of Oisin's, a voyage based on the charts of Irish Ossianic legend.

Part III of the poem is an antithesis to Part II, itself an antithesis to Part I. In Part III Niam and Oisin find the Island of Forgetfulness because as Niam herself says neither the Island of Dancing nor the Island of Victories have 'power'. After the 'vain battle' (as it is described in 'The Circus Animals' Desertion') of Part II they go to a place of dream, of anaesthesia, where the will, so active in the antagonisms and fears of Part II, is once more suspended. Once again we become conscious of Yeats's delight in opposing states of mind and being: the calm, joyous anonymity of Part I contrasts with the activity and energy of II, but it also contrasts with the dreamy stupors of Part III. The poem is a sequence of vacillating states, looking forward to the structure of such mature poems as 'Meditations in Time of Civil War', and of course 'Vacillation' itself.

Despite the beech bough that came at the end of Part II to remind Oisin of his days with the Fianna, the journey in Part III is not back to actuality, but to an island of dream. There they find a 'monstrous slumbering folk/ Their mighty and naked bodies heaped loose where they lay', in the long grass under the dripping oaks and hazels. Strewn around them the voyagers see implements of war, but the bodies, 'long-warless', have 'grown whiter than curds'. Oisin tries to rouse the king of these giant sleepers (who are half men, half birds,) by reminding him of those things he must have loved in life, the names of his fathers, the works of his hands. But though the king tries to make answer, so sunken is he into his trance-like sleep that he can scarcely move his lips. Oisin can hear no sound from him, but then the king shakes the bell-branch ('sleep's forbear') and the sound of it, 'softer than snowflakes in April' pierces the marrow, 'like flame'. All sadness drops from Oisin, and a 'softness' from the starlight fills him with sweetness. He and Niam sink into the sleep of these Titans of dream, into their forgetfulness:

a century there I forgot;
That the spearshaft is made out of ashwood, the shield out of
    osier and hide;
How the hammers spring on the anvil, on the spearhead's
    burning spot;
How the slow blue-eyed oxen of Fin low sadly at evening
    tide.[22]

In his sleep he dreams of Irish legendary figures, and of the
'Fenians' themselves, of Grania sewing with her 'needle of bone'.
His companions have become creatures of dream in this place,
which seems, of the three islands he has visited, the one furthest
from the actual, the 'common things that crave'.[23] It is the most
aesthetic of the islands; indeed it is an epitome of certain
dominant moods of aesthetic indulgence Yeats was to find in
himself and in the Rhymers of the 'nineties, moods that Yeats
never really surrendered himself to, even here, in this narrative
poem written in his early twenties, before the 'nineties began.

Oisin becomes dissatisfied with this luxurious sleep, richly
tapestried with scenes from the Gaelic past and from his own
past life. Where the state of mind or being in Part I is reminiscent
of certain meditative trances, the mood here is one of narcoticized
sleep, such as opium might bring. Once again Yeats is exploring
the labyrinth of self, discovering its varying moods, its different
conditions.

However, in the midst of this thickly woven landscape of dream
a starling comes from the actuality of 'common things', and
Oisin awakes. Once again he finds within 'the ancient sadness of
man', which had been narcoticized by sleep, and he is once more
eager for fate and chance, for actuality, where things always
come to challenge the dream's authority. This time he wants to
go back to Ireland.

Niam weeps at his going, but does not accompany him. She
knows he needs the sting of the real, of opposition, of conflict;
that he cannot be satisfied with one state of being for long. He
finds an image for himself in his present state of inactive
lassitude, and appropriately enough the image is one of a boat,
but one out of use, languishing in dock:

No more to crawl on the seas with long oars mile after mile,
But to be 'mid the shooting of flies and the flowering of
    rushes and flags.[24]

Niam begs him to return, but warns him not to touch the land of Ireland, not even with his foot, but to stay on the magical horse.

Once again the contrary motion of Yeats's imagination swings into action; after the communal dream of aestheticism on the Island of Forgetfulness comes the lone heroic journey of the voyager returning to his native shore. Then at last he gets the smell of new-mown hay coming over the sea, and, heart-smitten with emotion his tears fall 'like berries' from his eyes. Exultant, he comes ashore singing, the hooves of his magical horse thundering in the mast of tiny shells. Eagerly he rides into the country, but, to his astonishment, he sees churches everywhere, and no one guards the 'sacred cairn and rath'. The populace have become smaller, more stooped, and they toil with 'mattock and spade'.

Three hundred years have passed. The Fenians are all dead, and St Patrick has come with his Christianity. Even the Celtic gods themselves have died, he is told; a new one has taken their place. He turns to leave this Ireland that is so different to his memory of it. He wants to head out to sea again, to go once more among the magical (and the reader knows, unsatisfactory) islands. On the shore of the western sea he comes upon two men trying to carry a sack of sand. In contempt Oisin leans down and throws it five yards. But the saddle girth breaks, Oisin falls to the ground, and all the three hundred years come upon him. The two men bring him to Patrick's church, where the saint tries to Christianize him, and bring him into the new order of things. St Patrick is the interlocutor in the poem; its form is a dialogue between the saint and the old heathen. To Patrick Niam was an 'amorous demon' and Oisin was trapped by her. According to Patrick the Fenians of Oisin's fond memory are now in hell:

> Where the flesh of the footstool clingeth on the burning
>   stones is their place;
> Where the demons whip them with wires on the burning
>   stones of wide hell.[25]

Oisin, however, will have none of Patrick's system. He longs to be with his old friends even if they are in hell. He imagines them tearing the demons to pieces, ripping the stones of hell from the floor and battering the brass gateway of heaven until they force entry and take over the place.

Now that he is bowed down with years, now that the Ireland
he has come to after all his voyaging is lacking in vitality and
energy, Oisin finds solace in being a 'wild old wicked man', in
imagined energy, imagined violence, opposed to the feebleness of
his everyday actual life among the miserable Christians. He thinks
the new Ireland very different to the one he knew, but we
remember that was not a very cheerful place either. It was
darkened with images of death; the Fenians on their dismal hunt
had begun to be useless. Saddened by the death of his son,
Oscar, Oisin had gone on the voyage with Niam. Now that he
has come back, he finds an Ireland that is even sadder, less
energetic, so he takes another journey, in despite of 'bodily
decrepitude' (the word, 'decrepitude' is Yeats's, who had it out
of Mangan's 'Lament for the Princes'), but this is a journey
of the imagination, solely. It is a journey to hell, to the Fenians,
where they will root out the stones and batter the gateway of
brass. As Yeats was to write later in 'Sailing to Byzantium',
another poem about a voyage across the sea of being:

> An aged man is but a paltry thing,
> A tattered coat upon a stick, unless
> Soul clap its hands and sing, and louder sing
> For every tatter in its mortal dress.[26]

In 'The Wanderings of Oisin' and in 'Sailing to Byzantium',
Ireland is 'no country for old men'. The Ireland Oisin discovers
when he returns is early Christian Ireland, from the point of
view of the narrative, but it is also the Ireland of the late nineteenth century, with its enfeebled discouraged populace, its
priests who would dry up the old life-giving mythology of the
race, its many cheap Catholic churches disfiguring the landscape.
The clergy would have the peasantry bend to their miserable tasks
and forget all the magical grandeur of the past. The Fenians that
Patrick disapproves of are not just the Fenians of legend; they
are also the revolutionary Fenians of the nineteenth century.
John O'Leary, the old Fenian Yeats met in 1885, seemed like a
figure of Ossianic legend, in his dignity and Roman sense of
integrity outfacing what Yeats saw as the craven Ireland of his
time. The poem itself, which was an oblique act of homage to
him, appeared with O'Leary's assistance. Oisin's rant against
Patrick and his Christianity is a kind of victory over the pressure

of circumstance, the victory of what Yeats would later call the subjective man, who in imagination re-creates 'all that exterior fate snatches away'.[27] Oisin is a man whom exterior fate has stripped, yet he retains his passion, his loyalty to his dead friends, his conviction that the life he once knew was a true one. His fidelity to that life means a passionate rejection of the modern Christian one, the one that surrounds him.

V

'The Wanderings of Oisin' rounds off the poetic tradition of nineteenth century Ireland. It is Yeats's first major poem, and in it we come full circle from Macpherson. We are back with the Ossianic tradition, save that in Yeats's rehandling of it that tradition achieves a new and subtle resonance.

In his story of Oisin's voyage Yeats has drawn personal and racial concerns together. Oisin's voyage is a journey into the labyrinth of consciousness, the sea of being and becoming. It is an exploration of the recesses of the self, of its varying moods and longings, of its depths. These depths fascinated Yeats, as they did Mangan, the difference being that in Mangan, the fascination easily became terror. For him the deeps of the psyche were such that it was best to distract attention from them by whimsy, or by the impersonations of translation. Mangan's mask was simply a business of pretending to be somebody else, whereas Yeats's mask was the discovery of the opposite, the embodiment of all that was unavailable in daily life, of all that that life snatched away. It was, in a phrase that Yeats used time and again in *Autobiographies,* the finding of an image for that state of mind, 'which is, of all states of mind not impossible, the most difficult. . . . Only the greatest obstacle that can be contemplated without despair rouses the will to full intensity'.[28]

Oisin, a poet, does not find his true mask, his opposite, as Dante, another poet, does in a poem of 1912, 'Ego Dominus Tuus'.[29] In 1889 Yeats has not worked out his theory of opposites, of the self and its mask. Nevertheless Oisin's quest is a quest for constancy, firmness, indomitability, all that he has, in the words of 'Ego Dominus Tuus', 'handled least, least looked upon' in the Ossianic Ireland of the beginning of the poem, a place full of troubles, of grief, of sadness.

Yeats wrote that myths and legends were the mothers of nations, implying, not just that they once begot them, but that Irish mythology, forcefully deployed, might yet beget a new Ireland, a more vigorous one. For this reason he took to native mythology, thinking that it had in it energies which careful handling could re-direct, and that a poetry which took advantage of these ancient reservoirs of power might become a more effective stimulus to Ireland's spirit than the wranglings of party politics. Such was Yeats's nationalism, a combination of racial pride and belief in the occult force of hallowed symbol. In using Ossianic lore, based on a translation of an eighteenth century Gaelic re-telling of the story of Niam and Oisin, Yeats was using material that had been hallowed by continual contact with the Gaelic imagination for over a thousand years. This gave him a racial authenticity, a 'centrality', (the word he used to praise Ferguson's versions of the sagas) upon which English Victorian poets could lay no claim. Yeats was bent on turning Ireland's cultural handicap, the fact that it had little poetic tradition to speak of in English, into an advantage. Being isolated from the mainstream of nineteenth century English poetry gave Irish poets a positive advantage, in that, not only could they remain, if they wished, free of the taints of modern mixed society, – they also, by virtue of their isolation, had access to sources of power and energy long denied English writers. They had Gaelic mythology, which they could re-cast, and in doing so help recreate a quality of simplicity and heroism in life itself. In Yeats's view there was an intrinsic power in the old stories themselves, a power which had its source in the racial memory. The sensitive and respectful handling of the figures of mythology would make them into what they once were, crystallizations of the racial power, forceful icons for the new Ireland. This, basically, was the occult theology of MacGregor Mathers's Order of the Golden Dawn, which Yeats joined in 1890, and which believed in the evocation of the great memory by symbols.

But we must remember that Yeats was no simple-minded occultist, wishing to use Irish legendary material to spell out his theosophy. 'The Wanderings of Oisin', while it reveals much about Yeats's racial pride, also reveals much about the ambiguity of his feelings for the Ireland of his own time.

Oisin is a surrogate for Yeats, and the Ireland he leaves is a miserable, saddened one, darkened by death and ingratitude. The

Ireland Oisin goes into voluntary exile from has no time for him
or his kind. Niam comes to him not only through love, but also
through pity. Then, when he does venture onto the sea of
becoming, where he may find his true image – as the later Yeats
would say – he is seen to be continuously deluded, falling into
different kinds of meaningless repetition. The sea of consciousness, of which the Ossianic mythology is a chart, may be a sea
of Homeric delusions. The mythology itself, potent as it is, may
lead the poet into different kinds of frantic gesture.

'The Wanderings of Oisin' is a poem where Yeats has his cake
and eats it. He uses Gaelic mythology, thus satisfying the
nationalist side of his nature, that, in his youth, was given to
emotional simplicities about Irishness. But he also enters an
imaginative caveat, by making each successive stage of the myth,
as it unfolds in the narrative, quite obviously delusive and unsatisfactory. It is a poem full of qualification, of vacillation,
steadied, at the close, by the energy of Oisin's heroism, his
enraged defiance against the closed system of Patrick's Christianity. The ending of 'The Wanderings of Oisin' reminds one of
the ending of the poem 'Vacillation' itself, where Yeats, now
speaking in his own voice, again chooses pagan heroism rather
than Christian consolation:

> I – though heart might find relief
> Did I become a Christian man and choose for my belief
> What seems most welcome in the tomb – play a predestined
>   part.
> Homer is my example and his unchristened heart.
> The lion and the honeycomb, what has Scripture said?
> So get you gone, Von Hügel, though with blessings on your
>   head.[30]

The impression 'The Wanderings of Oisin' finally leaves us with
is one of imaginative complexity and flexibility. The flexibility is
there in the way Yeats has made his vacillating tendency, his
tendency to undermine his own imaginative structures, an
essential part of the poem's narrative. Each movement is a
counter-movement to the preceding, and in this we have the
characteristic mode of Yeats's mind already clearly in evidence.
This imaginative hesitancy, which could, in another poet, so
easily have become a disabling lack of certainty, enabled Yeats

to keep his distance from the crippling simplicities of nineteenth century Irish culture, simplicities imaged forth in the Isle of Many Fears with its demon, who is, appropriately, both 'bacchant' and 'mournful'. We meet him again as Joyce's Cyclops, the Citizen, in *Ulysses*.

Notes

Chapter One

1 *Memoirs, Journals and Correspondence of Thomas Moore*, I, xxxvi.
2 By 1808, when Theophilus O'Flanagan, a Gaelic speaker from Co. Clare, came to edit the *Transactions of the Gaelic Society*, he could speak of the faked Macpherson originals of 1807 as 'a new-fangled post-original translation' (*Transactions*, pp. 142-3). O'Flanagan had been one of Charlotte Brooke's advisors, as had Bishop Percy of Dromore, collector of *Reliques of Ancient Poetry*, 1765.
3 *Memoirs, Journals and Correspondence of Thomas Moore*, I, 58.
4 *The Poetical Works of Thomas Moore*, edited by David Herbert, p. 135. The Herbert edition is the one referred to throughout, except where otherwise indicated. Herbert's chronological ordering of the poems is most useful.
5 *The Letters of Thomas Moore*, I, 143.
6 *The Poetical Works of Thomas Moore*, collected by himself, IV, p. vii.
7 *Reliques of Irish Poetry*, p. cxxxiv.
8 *The Poetical Works*, p. 436.
9 It is frequently thought (indeed Bunting himself thought so) that Moore was guiltless of interfering with the airs as they were in Bunting, and that the culprit was Sir John Stevenson. In his diary for 15 to 17 July, 1840, however, commenting on the recently published third volume of Bunting's collection, Moore says that he himself frequently 'ventured in these very allowable liberties', and that 'poor Sir John was entirely innocent of them'. *Memoirs, Journals and Correspondence*, II, 278.
10 *Memoirs, Journals and Correspondence*, I, 17 and 60.
11 L. A. G. Strong, *The Minstrel Boy*, p. 126.
12 *The Poetical Works*, p. 434.
13 *The Poetical Works of Thomas Moore*, collected by himself, p. xxx.
14 *The Poetical Works*, p. 426.
15 See, for contrast, Leopold Bloom's remembrance of Emmet at the end of the 'Sirens' episode in *Ulysses*.
16 *The Poetical Works*, p. 431.
17 Moore tells us that Fox wrote a letter of sympathy to Lord Henry Fitzgerald, Lord Edward's brother, on the latter's capture and arrest in '98. See *The Life and Death of Lord Edward Fitzgerald*, II, 130-1.
18 H. M. Jones, *The Harp that Once*, p. 112.

19 *A View of the Present State of Ireland*, p. 75.
20 *The Poetical Works*, p. 436.
21 *The Poetical Works*, p. 438.
22 Moore, *The Life and Death of Lord Edward Fitzgerald*, I, 301-2.
23 The version in *The Poetical Works*, edited by Herbert, pp. 438-9, is somewhat different to the one quoted. I quote from Moore's own collected edition, III, p. 281.
24 See Howard O. Brogan, 'Thomas Moore, Irish Satirist and Keeper of the English Conscience', *Philological Quarterly*, 24 (1945), pp. 255-76.
25 The Regent had been the dedicatee of the *Anacreon* and the friend of Fox and Sheridan. On assuming the Regency, however, he ditched his Whig friends, to the disgust of Holland House, where Moore became a frequent visitor. Moore's 'Parody of a Celebrated Letter' ridicules the Prince's letter of 12 February 1812 to the Duke of York explaining that his 'sense of duty' to his father George III (now mad) had decided him to keep the Tories in. See H. M. Jones, *The Harp that Once*, p. 138.
26 Terence de Vere White, *Tom Moore*, p. 133.
27 Seán Lucy, *Irish Poets in English*, pp. 21-4.
28 *The Poetical Works*, p. 444.
29 *The Poetical Works*, p. 452.
30 *Memoirs, Journals and Correspondences*, VII, 35-9; and VI, 183.
31 *The Letters of Thomas Moore*, II, 758-9.

Chapter Two

1 See the account of a ramble through the Keimaneigh area of West Cork in *Bolster's Quarterly Magazine*, 2 (1827), 341-42, by John Windele. While his friends think of Homeric parallels to the landscape in their excursion, Windele (a close friend of Callanan's) thinks of 'creaghadóirí' (raiders) and 'gallowglasses'.
2 T. Crofton Croker, *Researches in the South of Ireland*, p. 203.
3 James S. Donnelly Jr., *The Land and People of Nineteenth Century Cork*, p. 46.
4 *Poetry and Legendary Ballads of the South of Ireland*, p. 259.
5 Breandán Ó Buachalla, *I mBéil Feirste Cois Cuain*.
6 John Windele, 'Dr. Mac Slatt in the West', *Bolster's Quarterly Magazine*, 3 (1829), 209-33.
7 For an account of 'The Anchorites' see *Bolster's Quarterly Magazine*, 3 (1829), 298-312.
8 See Michael Curren, 'The Poetry of Jeremiah J. Callanan 1795-1829' (unpublished minor dissertation for the M.A. Mode II, U.C.D., 1952) for an account of the contents of the Windele MS. I am indebted to Mr. Pádraig Ó Maidín, the Cork County Librarian, and to his assistant, Miss Anna O'Sullivan, for drawing my attention to this source.
9 T. Crofton Croker, *Researches in the South of Ireland*, pp. vi, vii.
10 John Windele, 'Memoir of the Late Mr. Callanan', *Bolster's Quarterly Magazine*, 3 (1829), 290. Michael Curren, 'The Poetry of Jeremiah J. Callanan', pp. 75-6 has convincingly shown this 'Memoir' to be Windele's.

11   John Windele, 'Memoir of the Late Mr. Callanan', *Bolster's Quarterly Magazine*, 3 (1829), 292.
12   It should be said, however, that Curren (p. 4) disagrees with this tradition and makes a convincing case.
13   Royal Irish Academy MS 12.1.13. *Literary Remains of Jeremiah J. Callanan*, pp. 343-5. Hereafter R.I.A. MS 12.1.13. It appears from the letter that Callanan delivered an ultimatum to Alicia Fisher, that she either convert to Catholicism or that they part.
14   R.I.A. MS 12.1.13, p. 49.
15   *The Poems of J. J. Callanan* (Cork, 1861), p. 1.
16   *The Poems*, p. 65.
17   R.I.A. MS 12.1.13, pp. 355-7.
18   R.I.A. MS 12.1.13, p. 209.
19   T. Crofton Croker, *Researches in the South of Ireland*, pp. 178-9.
20   R.I.A. MS 12.1.13, pp. 480-2.
21   R.I.A. MS 12.1.13, p. 86.
22   R.I.A. MS 12.1.13, p. 17.
23   J. J. Callanan, 'Irish Popular Songs', *Blackwood's Edinburgh Magazine*, 13 (1823), p. 209.
24   *The Poems*, p. 115.
25   Edward Walsh, *Irish Popular Songs*, pp. 74-5.
26   *The Poems*, p. 108.
27   See *Caoineadh Airt Uí Laoghaire*, edited by Seán Ó Tuama, for a full discussion of this and other aspects of the *caoineadh*.
28   *The Poems*, pp. 105-6.
29   'The Poetry of Jeremiah J. Callanan', p. 7.
30   As quoted in B. G. MacCarthy, 'Jeremiah J. Callanan, II: His Poetry', *Studies*, 35 (1946), pp. 392-4.
31   *The Poems of J. J. Callanan*, p. 112.
32   David Jones, *Epoch and Artist*, (1959), pp. 236-9.

Chapter Three

1   D. J. O'Donoghue, *The Life and Writings of James Clarence Mangan*, p. 226.
2   *The Autobiography of James Clarence Mangan*, edited by James Kilroy, (1968), p. 19.
3   *Life and Writings*, p. 19.
4   Samuel Ferguson, 'The *Dublin Penny Journal*', *Dublin University Magazine* (1840), p. 116.
5   Jacques Chuto, 'James Clarence Mangan: In Exile at Home', *Etudes Irlandaises*, I-Nouvelle Serie (1976), p. 37.
6   *Autobiography*, p. 28.
7   *The Poems of Samuel Taylor Coleridge*, edited by A. T. Quiller-Couch, p. 208.
8   *Autobiography*, p. 33.
9   *The Poems of Coleridge*, p. 290.
10   *Autobiography*, p. 26.

11 *The Prose Writings of James Clarence Mangan*, edited by D. J. O'Donoghue, p. 295.

12 Chuto, 'Mangan as Translator from the German' (unpublished paper submitted to the second triennial conference of IASAIL, Cork, 1973), p. 21.

13 *The Poems of John Dryden*, edited by James Kinsley, I, 182.

14 Chuto, 'Mangan as Translator from the German', p. 22.

15 Mangan, 'Anthologia Germanica. — No. 1', *Dublin University Magazine*, 5 (1835), p. 42.

16 R. P. Holzapfel, 'Mangan's Poetry in the *Dublin University Magazine*: A Bibliography', p. 45.

17 Alan Menhennet, *Order and Freedom: Literature and Society in Germany from 1790-1805*, p. 57.

18 Friedrich Schiller, 'On Simple and Sentimental Poetry', *Essays Aesthetical and Philosophical*, p. 325.

19 *Poems of James Clarence Mangan*, edited by D. J. O'Donoghue, p. 142.

20 Mangan, 'Anthologia Germanica — No. IV', *Dublin University Magazine*, 6 (1835), p. 405.

21 Mangan, 'Anthologia Germanica - No. VII', *Dublin University Magazine*, 8 (1836), p. 148.

22 'Anthologia Germanica - No. VII', p. 160.

23 *The Prose Writings of James Clarence Mangan*, p. 260.

24 *Poems*, p. 329.

25 *Poems*, p. 138.

26 *Poems*, p. 259.

27 Chuto, 'James Clarence Mangan: In Exile at Home', *Etudes Irlandaises*, I – Nouvelle Serie (1976), p. 38.

28 *Poems*, p. 180.

29 Mangan, 'Literae Orientales. Persian and Turkish Poetry – First Article', *Dublin University Magazine*, 10 (1837), p. 275.

30 Chuto. 'James Clarence Mangan: In Exile at Home', *Etudes Irlandaises*, I – Nouvelle Serie (1976), p. 39.

31 *Poems*, p. 187.

32 *Poems*, p. 13.

33 Chuto, 'Mangan, Petrie, O'Donovan, and a Few Others: The Poet and the Scholars', *Irish University Review*, 6 (1976), p. 179.

34 *Poems*, p. 17.

35 *The Poets and Poetry of Munster*, edited by C. P. Meehan, p. xi, n.

36 Chuto, 'Mangan, Petrie, O'Donovan and a Few Others', p. 180.

37 See A. Norman Jeffares, 'Mangan', *Envoy*, 4 (1951), p. 30; see also Chuto, 'A Further Glance at Mangan and the Library', *Long Room*, 5 (1970), pp. 9-10.

38 *Poems*, p. 303.

39 *Poems*, p. 151.

40 *Poems*, p. 94.

41 Gearóid Ó Tuathaigh, *Ireland Before the Famine, 1798-1848*, p. 221.

42 *Poems*, p. 83.

43 *Poems*, p. 5.

44 *Poems*, p. 8.

45 *Poems*, p. 122.

Chapter Four

1 M. C. Ferguson, *Sir Samuel Ferguson in the Ireland of his Day*, 1, 42-5.
2 Samuel Ferguson, 'Hardiman's *Irish Minstrelsy* – No. I', *Dublin University Magazine*, 3 (1834), 457.
3 Samuel Ferguson, 'The *Dublin Penny Journal*', *Dublin University Magazine*, 15 (1840), 121.
4 Samuel Ferguson, 'A Dialogue Between the Head and the Heart of an Irish Protestant', *Dublin University Magazine*, 2 (1833), 588.
5 M. C. Ferguson, *Sir Samuel Ferguson in the Ireland of his Day*, II, 361.
6 *Sir Samuel Ferguson in the Ireland of his Day*, I, 4.
7 A. P. Graves, ed. *Poems of Sir Samuel Ferguson*, p. 66.
8 Séamus Ó Casaide, *The Irish Language in Belfast and County Down*, pp. 45-50.
9 Samuel Ferguson, 'Hardiman's *Irish Minstrelsy* – No. III', *Dublin University Magazine*, 4 (1834), 447.
10 Samuel Ferguson, 'Hardiman's *Irish Minstrelsy* – No. IV'. *Dublin University Magazine*, 4 (1834), 516.
11 Samuel Ferguson, 'Hardiman's *Irish Minstrelsy* – No. 1V', 4 (1834), 523.
12 Samuel Ferguson, 'Hardiman's *Irish Minstrelsy* – No. II', *Dublin University Magazine*, 4 (1834), 153.
13 Samuel Ferguson, 'Hardiman's *Irish Minstrelsy*' – No. III', *Dublin University Magazine*, 4 (1834), 155.
14 Samuel Ferguson, 'Hardiman's *Irish Minstrelsy* – No. II', *Dublin University Magazine*, 4 (1834), 154.
13 Samuel Ferguson, 'Hardiman's *Irish Minstrelsy*' – No. III', *Dublin University Magazine*, 4 (1834), 448.
16 Samuel Ferguson, 'The *Dublin Penny Journal*', *Dublin University Magazine*, 15 (1840), 115-6.
17 Samuel Ferguson, 'Thomas Davis', *Dublin University Magazine* 29 (1847), 196.
18 *Sir Samuel Ferguson in the Ireland of his Day*, I, 226.
19 Gearóid Ó Tuathaigh, *Ireland Before the Famine*, p. 216.
20 *Sir Samuel Ferguson in the Ireland of his Day*, I, 250.
21 F. S. L. Lyons, *Ireland Since the Famine*, p. 128.
22 Terence Brown. *Northern Voices*, (1975), p. 34.
23 *Northern Voices*, p. 32.
24 A. P. Graves, ed. *Poems of Sir Samuel Ferguson*, p. 31.
24A *Poems of Sir Samuel Ferguson*, p. 206.
25 *Poems of Sir Samuel Ferguson*, pp. 9-10.
26 *Sir Samuel Ferguson in the Ireland of his Day*, II, 184.
27 Samuel Ferguson, 'Robert Burns', *Dublin University Magazine*, 25 (1845), 156.
28 *Sir Samuel Ferguson in the Ireland of his Day*, I, 36.
29 *Northern Voices*, pp. 28-41.
30 *Congal*, p. 23.
31 *Congal*, p. 63.
32 *Congal*, p. 94.
33 *Congal*, pp. 170 – I.

34 *Sir Samuel Ferguson in the Ireland of his Day*, II, 272 – 3.
35 *Congal*, p. 7.

Chapter Five

1 Aubrey de Vere, *Recollections*, pp. 252-3.
2 *Recollections*, p. 256.
3 Wilfrid Ward, *Aubrey de Vere: A Memoir*, p. 29.
4 *Aubrey de Vere: A Memoir*, p. 49.
5 *Aubrey de Vere: A Memoir*, p. 52.
6 *Aubrey de Vere: A Memoir*, p. 59.
7 *Aubrey de Vere: A Memoir*, p. 184.
8 *Recollections*, p. 354.
9 Aubrey de Vere, *Inisfail*, p. xx.
10 *Aubrey de Vere: A Memoir*, p. 151.
11 *The Poems of Gerard Manley Hopkins*, edited by W. H. Gardner and N. H. MacKenzie, p. 66.
12 *Aubrey de Vere: A Memoir*, p. 246.
13 *May Carols or Ancilla Domini*, p. 53.
14 *Aubrey de Vere: A Memoir*, p. 261.
15 *May Carols*, p. xix.
16 *May Carols*, p. xxxiv.
17 *May Carols*, p. 60.
18 *Recollections*, p. 356.
19 *The Legends of St. Patrick*, p. 72.
20 *Aubrey de Vere: A Memoir*, p. 393.
21 *The Legends of St. Patrick*, p. 105.
22 *Inisfail*, pp. xxxi-ii.
23 *Inisfail*, p. 11.
24 *Inisfail*, p. 25.
25 *Inisfail*, p. 38.
26 *Inisfail*, pp. 64-5.
27 *Recollections*, p. 250.
28 *Inisfail*, p. 84.
29 *Inisfail*, p. 100.
30 *Inisfail*, p. 152.
31 *Inisfail*, p. 168.
32 *Recollections*, pp. 372-3.
33 *Uncollected Prose by W. B. Yeats*, I, edited by J. P. Frayne, (1970), p. 216.
34 *Uncollected Prose*, p. 381.

Chapter Six

1 *William Allingham, A Diary*, p. 12.
2 *Laurence Bloomfield in Ireland*, p. 97.
3 *A Diary*, p. 161.
4 *Irish Songs and Poems*, p. 54.

5　*The Poems of William Allingham,* edited by John Hewitt, p. 11.
6　*Irish Songs and Poems,* p. 114.
7　*The Poems of Allingham,* p. 17.
8　*A Diary,* p. 326.
9　*Thought and Word,* pp. 36-7.
10　*Thought and Word,* p. 27.
11　*Irish Songs and Poems,* p. 121.
12　*Irish Songs and Poems,* p. 118.
13　*Irish Songs and Poems,* p. 129.
14　*Life and Phantasy,* p. 27.
15　*Life and Phantasy,* p. 84.
16　*Laurence Bloomfield,* p. xi.
17　Alan Warner, *William Allingham,* p. 20.
18　*The Poems of Allingham,* p. 12.
19　*Laurence Bloomfield,* p. 182.
20　*Laurence Bloomfield,* p. 45.
21　*Laurence Bloomfield,* pp. 74-5.
22　*Laurence Bloomfield,* p. 118.
23　*Laurence Bloomfield,* p. 272.
24　*Laurence Bloomfield* p. 141.
25　*Laurence Bloomfield,* p. 225.
26　*Laurence Bloomfield,* p. 214.
27　*Laurence Bloomfield,* p. 263.
28　*Laurence Bloomfield,* p. 287.
29　*Northern Voices,* p. 51.

Chapter Seven

1　D. J. O'Donoghue, *The Life and Writings of James Clarence Mangan,* p. 62.
2　See chapter three, section I.
3　*Collected Poems,* p. 56.
4　*Uncollected Prose by W. B. Yeats I,* p. 118.
5　*Uncollected Prose,* p. 194.
6　*Autobiographies,* p. 189.
7　*Essays and Introductions,* p. 28. Quoted too in *Yeats and Magic.*
8　*Mythologies,* p. 346.
9　*Uncollected Prose,* p. 103.
10　*Uncollected Prose,* p. 166.
11　*Uncollected Prose,* p. 404.
12　*The Variorum Edition of the Poems of W. B. Yeats,* p. 2.
13　*The Variorum Edition of the Poems of W. B. Yeats,* p. 7.
14　*The Variorum Edition of the Poems of W. B Yeats,* p. 13.
15　*The Variorum Edition of the Poems of W. B. Yeats,* p. 14.
16　*Yeats and Magic,* pp. 22-3.
17　*Variorum Poems,* p. 35.
18　*Variorum Poems,* p. 39.
19　*Variorum Poems,* p. 40.
20　*The Letters of W. B. Yeats,* edited by Allan Wade, pp. 87-88.

20A See Brenda S. Webster's obsessively Freudian interpretation of these images in her *Yeats*, pp. 22-6.

21 *Mythologies*, p. 336: 'In an Anglo-Saxon poem a certain man is called, as though to call him something that summed up all heroism, "Doom eager" '.

22 *Variorum Poems*, p. 52.

23 *Collected Poems*, p. 35.

24 *Variorum Poems*, p. 55.

25 *Variorum Poems*, p. 61.

26 *Collected Poems*, p. 217.

27 *Autobiographies*, p. 189.

28 *Autobiographies*, p. 195.

29 *Yeats and Magic*, p. 128.

30 *Collected Poems*, pp. 285-6.

List of Works Cited

Dates given are those of editions used by the author.

A. Books, theses, and manuscripts

Allingham, Helen, and D. Radford, ed. *William Allingham, A Diary* (London, 1904).

Allingham, William, *Laurence Bloomfield in Ireland,* new edition (London, 1869).

—————————, *Irish Songs and Poems,* uniform edition (London, 1890).

—————————, *Life and Phantasy,* uniform edition (London, 1889).

—————————, *Thought and Word,* uniform edition (London, 1890).

Allt, Peter, and Russell K. Alspach, ed. *The Variorum Edition of the Poems of W. B. Yeats* (New York, 1957).

Brooke, Charlotte, *Reliques of Irish Poetry,* second edition (Dublin, 1816).

Brown, Terence, *Northern Voices* (Dublin, 1975).

Callanan, J. J., *The Poems,* new edition (Cork, 1861).

Croker, T. Crofton, *Researches in the South of Ireland* (London, 1824; reprinted Shannon, 1969).

Curren, Michael, 'The Poetry of Jeremiah J. Callanan 1795–1829' (unpublished minor dissertation for the M.A. Mode II, University College, Dublin, 1952).

de Vere, Aubrey, *English Misrule and Irish Misdeeds* (London, 1848).

—————————, *Inisfail – a Lyrical Chronicle of Ireland* (London, 1897).

—————————, *May Carols or Ancilla Domini, Legends of the Saxon Saints* (London, 1897).

—————————, *Recollections* (New York and London, 1897).

——————, *The Legends of St Patrick,* Cassell's National Library edition (London, 1889).

de Vere White, Terence, *Tom Moore* (London, 1977).

Donnelly, James S. Jr., *The Land and People of Nineteenth Century Cork* (London and Boston, 1975).

Dowden, Wilfrid S., ed. *The Letters of Thomas Moore* (Oxford, 1964).

Edgeworth, Maria, *Castle Rackrent and The Absentee,* Everyman edition (London, 1972).

Ferguson, M. C., *Sir Samuel Ferguson in the Ireland of his Day* (Edinburgh and London, 1896).

Ferguson, Samuel, *Congal,* third edition (Dublin and London, 1907).

Flannery, Mary Catherine, *Yeats and Magic* (Gerrards Cross, 1977).

Frayne, John P. ed. *Uncollected Prose by W. B. Yeats,* I (London, 1970).

Gardner, W. H., and N. H. Mac Kenzie, *The Poems of Gerard Manley Hopkins,* fourth edition (Oxford, 1970).

Graves, A. P., ed. *Poems of Sir Samuel Ferguson* (Dublin and London, 1918).

Herbert, David, ed. *The Poetical Works of Thomas Moore* (Edinburgh, 1872).

Hewitt, John, ed. *The Poems of William Allingham* (Dublin, 1967).

Jeffares, A. N., *W. B. Yeats: Man and Poet,* second edition (London, 1966).

Jones, David, *Epoch and Artist* (London, 1973).

Jones, David, *In Parenthesis* (London, 1969).

Jones, Howard Mumford, *The Harp that Once* (New York, 1937).

Joyce, James, *A Portrait of the Artist as a Young Man,* Penguin edition (Harmondsworth, 1963).

——————, *Ulysses,* Odyssey Press edition (Hamburg, Paris, Bologna, 1933).

Kilroy, James, ed. *The Autobiography of James Clarence Mangan* (Dublin, 1968).

Kinsley, James, ed. *The Poems of John Dryden* (Oxford, 1958).

Lucy, Seán, ed. *Irish Poets in English* (Cork, 1973).

Lyons, F. S. L., *Ireland Since the Famine,* second edition (London, 1975).

MacDonagh, Thomas, *Literature in Ireland* (Dublin, 1916).

Meehen, C. P. ed. *The Poets and Poetry of Munster,* first series (Dublin, n.d.).

Menhennet, Alan, *Order and Freedom: Literature and Society in Germany from 1720–1805* (London, 1973).

Montague, John, *The Rough Field* (Dublin, 1972).

Montgomery, H. R. ed. *Specimens of the Early Native Poetry of Ireland* (Dublin, 1846).

Moore, Thomas, *Memoirs of Captain Rock* (London, 1824).

Moore, Thomas, *The Life and Death of Lord Edward Fitzgerald* (London, 1831).

Moore, Thomas, *The Poetical Works,* collected by himself (London, 1853–54).

Ó Buachalla, Brendán, *I mBéil Feirste Cois Cuain* (Dublin, 1968).

Ó Casaide, *The Irish Language in Belfast and County Down* (Dublin, 1930).

O'Donoghue, D. J., ed. *Poems of James Clarence Mangan* (Dublin and London, 1903).

——————, ed. *The Prose Writings of James Clarence Mangan* (Dublin and London, 1904).

——————, *The Life and Writings of James Clarence Mangan* (Edinburgh, 1897).

O'Flanagan, Theophilus, *Transactions of the Gaelic Society* (Dublin, 1808).

Ó Laoghaire, Peadar, *Mo Scéal Féin,* schools edition (Dublin n.d.).

Ó Tuama, Seán, ed. *Caoineadh Airt Uí Laoghaire* (Dublin, 1965).

Ó Tuathaigh, Gearóid, *Ireland Before the Famine 1798–1848* (Dublin, 1972).

Quiller-Couch, A. T., ed. *The Poems of Samuel Taylor Coleridge* (Oxford, 1907).

Renwick, W. L., ed. Edmund Spenser: *A View of the Present State of Ireland* (London, 1934).

Royal Irish Academy MS 12.I.13. *Literary Remains of Jeremiah J. Callanan Collected and Compiled by John Fitzpatrick Fitzthos Windele of Blair's Castle Cork 1847.*

Russell. Lord John, ed. *Memoirs Journals and Correspondence of Thomas Moore* (London, 1853–56).

Schiller, Friedrich, *Essays Aesthetical and Philosophical,* newly translated (London, 1875).

Strong, L. A. G., *The Minstrel Boy* (London, 1937).

Various Hands, *Poetry and Legendary Ballads of the South of Ireland* (Cork, 1894).
Wade, Allan, ed., *The Letters of W. B. Yeats* (London, 1954).
Walsh, Edward, *Irish Popular Songs* (Dublin, 1847).
Ward, Wilfrid, *Aubrey de Vere: A Memoir* (London, 1904).
Warner, Alan, *William Allingham: an Introduction* (Dublin, 1971).
Webster, Brenda, S., *Yeats, Psychoanalytic Study* (London, 1974).
Yeats, W. B., *Autobiographies* (London, 1970).
─────────, *A Vision* (London, 1937).
─────────, *Collected Poems* (London, 1958).
─────────, *Essays and Introductions* (London, 1969).
─────────, *Mythologies* (London, 1977).
See also Allt *and* Alspach, above.

B.   Articles and papers

Brogan, Howard O. 'Thomas Moore, Irish Satirist and Keeper of the English Conscience', *Philological Quarterly,* 24 (1945).
Callanan, Jeremiah J., 'Irish Popular Songs', *Blackwood's Edinburgh Magazine,* 13 (1823).
Chuto, Jacques, 'A Further Glance at Mangan and the Library', *Long Room,* 5 (1972).
─────────, 'James Clarence Mangan: In Exile at Home', *Etudes Irlandaises,* I – Nouvelle Serie (1976).
─────────, 'Mangan as Translator from the German' (unpublished paper submitted to the second triennial conference of the International Association for the Study of Anglo-Irish Literature, Cork, 1973).
─────────, 'Mangan, Petrie, O'Donovan, and a Few Others: The Poet and the Scholars', *Irish University Review,* 6 (1976).
Ferguson, Samuel, 'A Dialogue Between the Head and the Heart of an Irish Protestant', *Dublin University Magazine,* 2 (1833).
─────────, 'Hardiman's *Irish Minstrelsy.* – No. I', *Dublin University Magazine,* 3 (1834).
─────────, 'Hardiman's *Irish Minstrelsy.* – No. II', *Dublin University Magazine,* 4 (1834).
─────────, 'Hardiman's *Irish Minstrelsy,* – No. III', *Dublin University Magazine,* 4 (1834).

——————, 'Hardiman's *Irish Minstrelsy.* – No. IV', *Dublin University Magazine,* 4 (1834).

——————, 'Robert Burns', first and second article, *Dublin University Magazine,* 25 (1845).

——————, 'Thomas Davis', *Dublin University Magazine,* 29 (1847).

——————, 'The *Dublin Penny Journal*', *Dublin University Magazine,* 15 (1840).

Holzapfel, R. P., 'Mangan's Poetry in the *Dublin University Magazine*: A Bibliography', *Hermathena,* 105 (1967).

Jeffares, A. Norman, 'Mangan', *Envoy,* 4 (1951).

MacCarthy, B. G., 'Jeremiah J. Callanan II: His Poetry', *Studies,* 35 (1946).

MacCarthy, M. F., 'The Anchorites', *Bolster's Quarterly Magazine,* 3 (1829).

Mangan, James Clarence, 'Anthologia Germanica. – No. I', *Dublin University Magazine,* 5 (1835).

——————, 'Anthologia Germanica – No. IV', *Dublin University Magazine,* 6 (1835).

——————, 'Anthologia Germanica, – No. VII', *Dublin University Magazine,* 8 (1836).

——————, 'Literae Orientales. Persian and Turkish Poetry. – First Article', *Dublin University Magazine,* 10 (1837).

Windele, John, 'Gougane Barra', *Bolster's Quarterly Magazine,* 2 (1827).

——————, 'Dr MacSlatt in the West', *Bolster's Quarterly Magazine,* 3 (1829).

——————, 'Memoir of the late Mr Callanan', *Bolster's Quarterly Magazine,* 3 (1829).

Index

243